ReFocus: The Films of Delmer Daves

ReFocus: The American Directors Series

Series Editors: Robert Singer and Gary D. Rhodes

Editorial Board: Kelly Basilio, Donna Campbell, Claire Perkins, Christopher Sharrett, and Yannis Tzioumakis

ReFocus is a series of contemporary methodological and theoretical approaches to the interdisciplinary analyses and interpretations of neglected American directors, from the once-famous to the ignored, in direct relationship to American culture—its myths, values, and historical precepts. The series ignores no director who created a historical space—either in or out of the studio system—beginning from the origins of American cinema and up to the present. These directors produced film titles that appear in university film history and genre courses across international boundaries, and their work is often seen on television or available to download or purchase, but each suffers from a form of "canon envy"; directors such as these, among other important figures in the general history of American cinema, are underrepresented in the critical dialogue, yet each has created American narratives, works of film art, that warrant attention. *ReFocus* brings these American film directors to a new audience of scholars and general readers of both American and Film Studies.

Titles in the series include:

ReFocus: The Films of Preston Sturges
Edited by Jeff Jaeckle and Sarah Kozloff

ReFocus: The Films of Delmer Daves
Edited by Matthew Carter and Andrew Patrick Nelson

ReFocus: The Films of Amy Heckerling
Edited by Frances Smith and Timothy Shary

ReFocus: The Films of Kelly Reichardt
Dawn Hall

edinburghuniversitypress.com/series/refoc

ReFocus:
The Films of Delmer Daves

Edited by Matthew Carter and Andrew Patrick Nelson

EDINBURGH
University Press

Edinburgh University Press is one of the leading university presses in the UK. We publish academic books and journals in our selected subject areas across the humanities and social sciences, combining cutting-edge scholarship with high editorial and production values to produce academic works of lasting importance. For more information visit our website: www.edinburghuniversitypress.com

© editorial matter and organization Matthew Carter and Andrew Patrick Nelson, 2016
© the chapters their several authors, 2016

Edinburgh University Press Ltd
The Tun—Holyrood Road
12 (2f) Jackson's Entry
Edinburgh EH8 8PJ

Typeset in 11/13 Monotype Ehrhardt by
Servis Filmsetting Ltd, Stockport, Cheshire

A CIP record for this book is available from the British Library

ISBN 978 1 4744 0301 6 (hardback)
ISBN 978 1 4744 0302 3 (webready PDF)
ISBN 978 1 4744 1370 1 (epub)

The right of the contributors to be identified as authors of this work has been asserted in accordance with the Copyright, Designs and Patents Act 1988 and the Copyright and Related Rights Regulations 2003 (SI No. 2498).

Contents

List of Figures	vii
Notes on Contributors	viii
Acknowledgments	xi
Introduction: "No One Would Know It Was Mine": Delmer Daves, Modest Auteur *Matthew Carter and Andrew Patrick Nelson*	1
1 Don't Be Too Quick to Dismiss Them: Authorship and the Westerns of Delmer Daves *Andrew Patrick Nelson*	48
2 Trying to Ameliorate the System from Within: Delmer Daves' Westerns from the 1950s *John White*	63
3 Bent, or Lifted Out by Its Roots: Daves' *Broken Arrow* and *Drum Beat* as Narratives of Conditional Sympathy *Józef Jaskulski*	80
4 This Room is My Castle of Quiet: The Collaborations of Delmer Daves and Glenn Ford *Adrian Danks*	102
5 Delmer Daves, Authenticity, and Auteur Elements: Celebrating the Ordinary in *Cowboy* *Sue Matheson*	118

6 Home and the Range: *Spencer's Mountain* as Revisionist Family
   Melodrama   135
   Joseph Pomp

7 Delmer Daves' *3:10 to Yuma*: Aesthetics, Reception, and Cultural
   Significance   149
   Fran Pheasant-Kelly

8 Changing Societies: *The Red House, The Hanging Tree, Spencer's
   Mountain,* and Post-war America   166
   Fernando Gabriel Pagnoni Berns

9 Partial Rehabilitation: *Task Force* and the Case of Billy Mitchell   184
   Andrew Howe

10 "This Is Where He Brought Me: 10,000 Acres of Nothing!": The
   Femme Fatale and other Film Noir Tropes in Delmer Daves' *Jubal*   199
   Matthew Carter

Index   222

Figures

I.1	Johnny and Molly in *A Summer Place*	4
I.2	Pages from Daves' illustrated, annotated shooting script of *3:10 to Yuma*	6
I.3	Subjective camera in *Dark Passage*	35
1.1	Cochise breaks the arrow in *Broken Arrow*	51
2.1	Jeffords and Soonseeahray embrace in *Broken Arrow*	70
2.2	Anita rallies the Mexicans against the rich businessmen in *The Badlanders*	72
3.1	Johnny and Captain Jack converse prior to Jack's execution	90
4.1	Ben Wade in *3:10 to Yuma*	108
5.1	"Fill 'er up": the cowhand's funeral	123
5.2	Homosocial bonding in *Cowboy*	126
6.1	On location in Jackson Hole, Wyoming	138
6.2	In a sea of Jackson, Wyoming locals	145
7.1	Opening of *3:10 to Yuma*	153
7.2	Inside the Contention Hotel in *3:10 to Yuma*	156
8.1	Nath dines with the "mysterious Morgans" in *The Red House*	169
8.2	Frail is saved from hanging by Elizabeth and Rune in *The Hanging Tree*	176
9.1	Advertisement for *Task Force* (*Daily Variety*, 28 September 1949, p. 14)	186
10.1	The "ideologically safe" woman: Jubal opens up to Naomi	208
10.2	The "female gaze": Mae's display of desire and agency	213
10.3	Pinky assaults Mae in the livery: woman as "victim of male power"	216

Notes on Contributors

THE EDITORS

Matthew Carter is Senior Lecturer in Film, Television, and Cultural Studies at Manchester Metropolitan University. He is author of *Myth of the Western: New Perspectives on Hollywood's Frontier Narrative* (2014). He has contributed chapters to two edited volumes: *Contemporary Westerns: Film and Television since 1990* (edited by Andrew Patrick Nelson, 2013) and *The Post-2000 Film Western: Contexts, Transnationality, Hybridity* (edited by Marek Paryz and John R. Leo, 2015). His work has appeared in the *European Journal of American Studies*, the *IUP Journal of American Literature*, and *Alphaville: Journal of Film and Screen Media*.

Andrew Patrick Nelson is Assistant Professor of Film History and Critical Studies in the School of Film and Photography at Montana State University, Bozeman. He is author of *Still in the Saddle: The Hollywood Western, 1969–1980* (2015) and editor of *Contemporary Westerns: Film and Television since 1990* (2013).

THE CONTRIBUTORS

Fernando Gabriel Pagnoni Berns currently works at Universidad de Buenos Aires (UBA)—Facultad de Filosofia y Letras (Argentina). He teaches seminars on American Horror Cinema and Euro Horror. He is director of the research group on horror cinema "Grite" and has published articles in the books *Horrors of War: The Undead in the Battlefield*, edited by Cynthia Miller;

To See the Saw Movies: Essays on Torture Porn and Post 9/11 Horror, edited by John Wallis; and *James Bond and Popular Culture: Essays*, edited by Michele Brittany, among others.

Adrian Danks is Director of Higher Degree Research in the School of Media and Communication, RMIT University. He is also co-curator of the Melbourne Cinémathèque and was an editor of *Senses of Cinema* from 2000 to 2014. He is the author of *A Companion to Robert Altman* (2015) and is currently writing several books including a monograph devoted to the history, aesthetics, and practice of 3-D cinema, a co-edited collection on the complex relationships between Australian and US cinema, and a volume examining "international" feature film production in Australia during the post-war era (*Australian International Pictures*, with Con Verevis, to be published by Edinburgh University Press).

Andrew Howe is an Associate Professor of History at La Sierra University, where he teaches courses in American history, popular culture, and film studies. Recent publications include book chapters on the depiction of Latino characters in *Breaking Bad*; the suspicion of governance structures in *Firefly*; and the transformation of the Mohican myth in *Avatar*.

Józef Jaskulski is a Ph.D. student at the Institute of English Studies, University of Warsaw, Poland. In his dissertation, he investigates the narrative tropes of the Western in American television commercials after 9/11. His research interests also include Native American fiction and the Western.

Sue Matheson is an Associate Professor of English Literature at the University College of the North in Manitoba, Canada. She teaches in the areas of American film and popular culture, Canadian literature, children's literature, and Aboriginal literature. Her research interests in film, culture, and literature are reflected in more than forty essays published in a wide range of books and scholarly journals. She is the editor of *Love in Western Film and Television: Lonely Hearts and Happy Trails* (2013) and the founder and co-editor of *the quint: an interdisciplinary quarterly from the north*. Currently, she is the Book Review Editor for the *Journal of Popular Film and Culture*.

Fran Pheasant-Kelly is M.A. Course Leader and Reader in Film and Television Studies at the University of Wolverhampton, UK. She is the author of numerous publications including two monographs—*Abject Spaces in American Cinema: Institutions, Identity and Psychoanalysis in Film* (2013), and *Fantasy Film Post-9/11* (2013)—and the co-editor of *Spaces of the Cinematic Home: Behind the Screen Door* (2015).

Joseph Pomp is a Ph.D. student in the Department of Comparative Literature at Harvard University, with a secondary field in Critical Media Practice. He has contributed to *Film Quarterly*, *Film & History*, and the Media History Digital Library (the recipient of the Society for Cinema and Media Studies' Anne Friedberg Award for Innovative Scholarship in 2014), and also frequently writes for online film journals such as *Senses of Cinema*. Current research interests include postcolonial French and Francophone literature, figurations of space in Korean cinema, and writers-cum-filmmakers of the African diaspora.

John White teaches film and writing at Anglia Ruskin University in Cambridge. He is co-author of textbooks for both AS Film Studies and A2 Film Studies, and before his current career worked as a journalist. He is co-editor of *Fifty Key British Films* (2008), *Fifty Key American Films* (2009), and *The Routledge Encyclopedia of Films* (2015). John has written chapters for books on Budd Boetticher, Fred Zinnemann, and Delmer Daves, in the Edinburgh University Press *ReFocus* series, and is the author of *Westerns* (2011). He is currently working on an introductory book to European Art Cinema.

Acknowledgments

We would like to extend our gratitude to ReFocus series editors Gary D. Rhodes and Robert Singer for their support, patience, and enthusiasm, and to our contributors for their dedication and painstaking scholarship. At Edinburgh University Press, thanks are due to Rebecca Mackenzie, Richard Strachan, Eddie Clark, and freelance copyeditor Camilla Rockwood.

Matthew Carter dedicates his contributions to the book to Caja Dan, as always. He also thanks Artie, his pet cat, for being a loyal writer's companion.

Andrew Patrick Nelson thanks Kathy Zonana and the Bill Lane Center for the American West at Stanford University for hosting him in the summer of 2014; Tim Noakes and the intrepid staff of the Stanford Libraries' Special Collections and University Archive, who helped make his stay both productive and enjoyable; and, above all, Leah and Jacob for their love and support (and perennial forbearance).

Introduction: "No One Would Know It Was Mine": Delmer Daves, Modest Auteur

Matthew Carter and Andrew Patrick Nelson

> I much prefer the audience not to know that there's a director. That's my general thesis in regard to directing.
>
> Delmer Daves[1]

> Delmer Daves is the property of those who can enjoy stylistic conviction in an intellectual vacuum. The movies of Delmer Daves are fun of a very special kind. Call it Camp or call it Corn. The director does not so much transcend his material as mingle with it.
>
> Andrew Sarris, *The American Cinema*[2]

> American critics have never taken Delmer Daves seriously, and the way things look, they probably never will.
>
> Jean-Pierre Coursodon, *American Directors*[3]

It is tempting, in introducing a book of this nature, to declare at the outset something like, "Delmer Daves is the best filmmaker you've never heard of!" Alas, we cannot resort to such rhetoric—not because Delmer Daves is not a great, critically overlooked filmmaker, but because you likely *have* heard of him. Daves is remembered principally as a maker of Westerns, and of two Westerns in particular: *Broken Arrow* (1950) and *3:10 to Yuma* (1957). The former, about an Army scout who brokers a peace treaty between the American government and the Chiricahua Apache, offered viewers a comparatively nuanced, sympathetic depiction of Native American culture, and in so doing helped to transform how American Indians are represented in cinema. The latter, a stylish, psychological frontier drama about a poor farmer who agrees to help escort a dangerous outlaw to the train that will take him to prison, is frequently considered among the best Westerns of the 1950s, and was even subject to a high-profile remake in 2007. As these synopses suggest, however, *Broken Arrow* and *3:10 to Yuma* are quite different films, and are remembered for different reasons: the former for its sociocultural significance, the latter for its style. This perceived difference, it turns out, matters a great deal.

Making the jump from discussing individual films to discussing *filmmakers* normally requires us to detect consistency, not difference. Identifying recurring features of style or theme across multiple films implies the underlying presence of an impelling, organizing personality: an artist who imbues his work with his own vision of the world. It is on such a basis that the Westerns of several of Daves' contemporaries, like John Ford and Anthony Mann, have been examined, reexamined and, ultimately, to a certain extent, become synonymous with the genre in the 1950s. By contrast, what criticism there is of Daves' Westerns is apt to acknowledge their diversity of themes and subject matter (and to note how this is an impediment to discussing his Westerns collectively). This diversity, in turn, is emblematic of the wide range of material produced by Daves throughout his lengthy Hollywood career.

THE MAN WHO GETS AROUND

> AND THE MAN WHO GETS AROUND . . . Delmer Daves, who directs, writes and produces, is a veteran Hollywood craftsman. A native of San Francisco, he is a graduate of Stanford University, with his earlier schooling taking place in Los Angeles. His first studio work was as a property man with James Cruze. He became an actor in "The Duke Steps Out" with William Haines and Joan Crawford because the director thought he looked more like a college man than the film's prop boy. He started writing scripts. In 1942, for Warners, he directed his first picture, "Destination Tokyo," from his own script. It was for the Burbank studio that he has made some of his best films, including the recent "Parrish," "Susan Slade" and "Rome Adventure."
>
> Warner Brothers production notes for *Spencer's Mountain*[4]

Delmer Daves did, indeed, "get around"—in *nearly* every sense. (A desirable Hollywood bachelor in his twenties and early thirties, Daves wed actress Mary Lawrence in 1938 and the couple remained together until his death in 1977). Born in San Francisco on 24 July 1904, Daves was evacuated with his parents from the city after the great earthquake of 1906, and they soon settled in Los Angeles. Despite demonstrating talents for both art and drama as a youth, Daves elected to study law at Stanford University. There he supported himself with what he later described as "a bewildering variety of activities":

> [P]ainting posters, designing Christmas cards and bookplates, acting as a draftsman for the city of Palo Alto, teaching engineering lettering and drawing, managing the Glee Club, acting as art director of the *Quad* for two years, while simultaneously acting as dramatic manager for the same length of time—which meant managing as many as ten productions a year, not to mention acting in or directing many of them, as well as being president of my class.[5]

After graduating from Stanford with a law degree in 1927, Daves decided to follow his passion for drama and moved south to Hollywood, where he worked continuously from the late 1920s until the mid-1960s.

Daves wore many hats over the course of his career: actor, writer, director, producer. He worked in multiple genres: college comedies and musicals in the 1930s, war films and *films noir* in the 1940s, Westerns in the 1950s, and teen and family melodramas in the 1960s, always with a smattering of other subjects thrown in. And he was for most of his career a freelance writer and director, accepting assignments at different studios. Of the eight Westerns Daves directed in the 1950s, for example, three were made for Columbia, two for 20th Century Fox, two for Warner Brothers, and one for MGM. From his directorial debut *Destination Tokyo* (1943), which studio boss Jack Warner insisted he direct because only he could comprehend the intricacies of his meticulously researched screenplay about a naval submarine on a reconnaissance mission in the Pacific; through his series of intelligent, critical Westerns of the 1950s; to his hit, teen-oriented melodramas of the late 1950s and 1960s like *A Summer Place* (1959) and *Parrish* (1961), few filmmakers created as distinctive a body of work in Hollywood. Why, then, has Daves' work been heretofore neglected in histories of American cinema?

Filmmaker and critic Bertrand Tavernier poses this question at the start of a 2003 essay on Daves in *Film Comment*.[6] The first reason Tavernier lists for Daves' neglect, which he insists has "little to do with his true stature as a filmmaker," is that Daves was "unlucky enough to end his career with a string of Warners sudsers that seemed sorely lacking in ambition."[7]

In overviews of Daves' career, his final seven features, from *A Summer Place* in 1959 to *The Battle of the Villa Fiorita* in 1965, are little more than an afterthought. Daves' entry in the encyclopedic *World Film Directors Volume 1: 1890–1945* devotes only two sentences to these films: "None of Daves' later pictures was of much merit. Most of them were rather turgid romances that he wrote and produced as well as directed."[8] In *American Directors*, Jean-Pierre Coursodon is more expansive, writing that Daves' "sudden and

Figure I.1 Johnny and Molly (Troy Donahue and Sandra Dee) in *A Summer Place*.

incomprehensible steadfast dedication to adapting mediocre popular bestsellers featuring such Warners juveniles as Troy Donohue, Connie Stevens, and Suzanne Pleshette looked dangerously close to artistic suicide."[9] Though Coursodon concedes that Daves no doubt elevated the source material, and that the visual and stylistic touches of the better films like *Parrish* "vouch for Daves's taste and care" (even as they "underscore the vapidity of the plot and characterization"), the director's turn from Westerns to melodrama ultimately remains for him a puzzle.[10]

In a 2007 interview, Daves' son Michael explained this transition as one necessitated by health considerations. His father had a heart attack in 1958, and was advised by his physicians to take it easy. Studio-based domestic melodramas were thus preferable to shooting action films on location in the high desert of Arizona.[11] Yet if Daves' concern for his own wellbeing prompted, or at least contributed to, his decision to make melodramas, it certainly didn't diminish his productivity. Daves' final seven films, each of which he wrote, directed, *and* produced, were released within the span of six years. While these pictures did require more extensive studio work than his Westerns, Daves was far from confined to the backlots of Burbank. These seven films were shot on locations across the United States, from the California coast to the Grand Teton Mountains of Wyoming to New York City to the Connecticut River Valley, as well as in England and Italy. During this period he also did extensive work, including completed screenplays, on two projects that never came to fruition: *Mothers and Daughters*, adapted from the novel by Evan Hunter, to be made at Columbia, and *Seventeenth Summer*, from the novel by Maureen Daly, at Warner Brothers.[12] The general subject matter of these unrealized projects—both are youth-oriented family melodramas in the mode of *A Summer Place* and *Susan Slade* (1961)—indicate that Daves had found a new niche and was clearly regarded by studio executives, especially at Warner Brothers, as a reliable shepherd for these types of films, and for the studio's stable of young talent.

The reaction of the critics to these films was lukewarm at best. The typical review of any of Daves' final movies praises the visuals (and the memorable music of Max Steiner), but little else. Not that it mattered because, in the end, these films made money. Part of this was obviously down to the appeal of stars like Troy Donahue and Connie Stevens, but we should not overlook Daves' demonstrated facility for melodrama, in evidence in his screenplays for Frank Borzage in the 1930s; his script for Leo McCarey's *Love Affair* (1939), remade in 1957 as *An Affair to Remember*; and, perhaps most clearly, in his second directorial effort *The Red House* (1947), with its emphasis on intergenerational conflict and teenage sexuality. There is also the not-so-small matter of Daves' economy as a filmmaker, an important asset at what was a time of profound change and uncertainty in Hollywood, as the last vestiges of the studio era began to give way to the age of conglomeration. Said Daves in 1963, "Jack Warner tells me I'm the only director in Hollywood who's never lost money on a picture."[13]

By the mid-1950s, Daves had refined a number of pre-production strategies and procedures that translated to time and money saved during filming. For every page of screenplay Daves completed, he wrote two or even three times that number about the history of the events surrounding the story, or about the motivations of the various characters. He drew detailed maps of his locations, from expansive plots of the area surrounding Sedona, Arizona—a favored location for making Westerns—to the intimate interior sets of films like *Dark Passage* (1947) and *A Summer Place*. In his shooting scripts we find not only copious annotations, but detailed storyboards: illustrations, hand-drawn by Daves, of how he wanted particular shots to look, complete with notes about staging, camera lenses, and camera movement. Some of these storyboards are even in watercolor.

For his adaptations of popular novels, which included his final "sudsers," Daves cut and glued publisher's galley proofs onto yellow notepaper. The original text is always heavily annotated with notes about what could be excised or condensed from the source narrative, with additional comments jotted in the right-hand margin of the notepaper. Each annotated novel is then followed by Daves' typewritten comments, thoughts and ideas about scenes, which are also marked up with additional handwritten notes.

The financial success of Daves' forays into melodrama in the early 1960s can be thus attributed to the filmmaker's talents. This success came with a price, however, and these pictures also did far more than has been previously

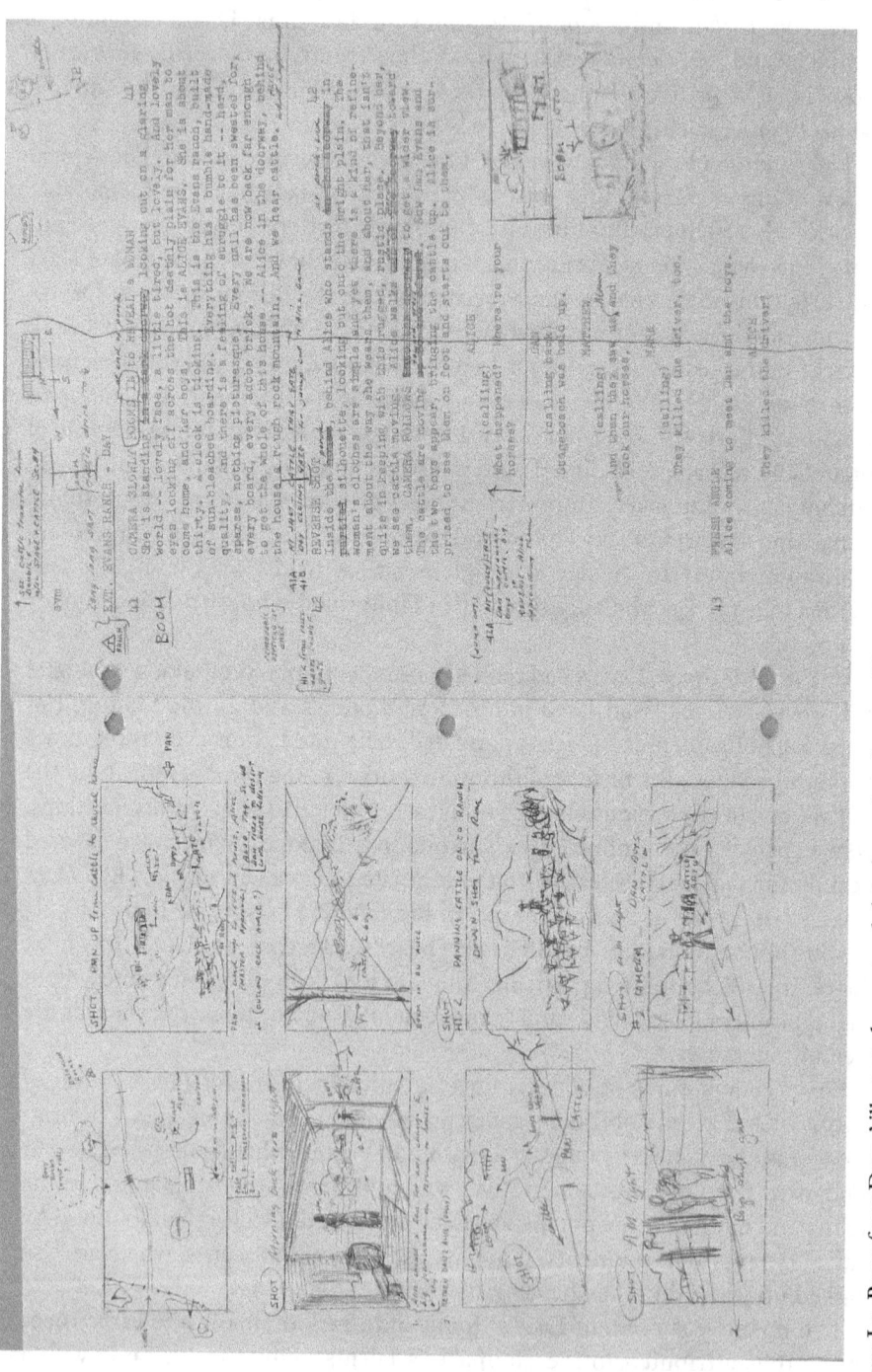

Figure I.2 Pages from Daves' illustrated, annotated shooting script of *3:10 to Yuma*. Delmer Daves Papers, box 44, folder 15. Courtesy of the Department of Special Collections and Archives, Stanford University Libraries

acknowledged to shape Daves' reputation. For evidence of this we can look to film critic Andrew Sarris's evaluation of Daves in his 1968 book *The American Cinema*, quoted at the start of this chapter, in which he calls Daves' films "fun of a special kind," "Camp," and "Corn." Clearly, the films Sarris has in mind are neither Daves' morally complex war films like *Destination Tokyo* or *Pride of the Marines* (1945), nor his unorthodox noirs like *The Red House* or *Dark Passage*, nor his progressive, stylish Westerns. He is referring to his later melodramas, which were described in the popular press of the time in the same terms that Sarris uses. Camp (with a capital C) was much in vogue in the mid-1960s following the 1964 publication of Susan Sontag's "Notes on 'Camp,'" in which she defined Camp as a "sensibility" that celebrates artifice, exaggeration, and irony over content.[14] A 1965 article in the *New York Times* titled "Not Good Taste, Not Bad Taste—It's 'Camp'" offers, as a means of defining Camp, a list of "a dozen random examples of movies, people and things that are generally agreed to be Pure Camp." *Parrish* "with Troy Donahue" is number three on the list, below *Gold Diggers of 1933* (Mervyn LeRoy, 1933) and Andy Warhol's *Sleep* (1964) and above Marlene Dietrich, Barbara Stanwyck, and feather boas.[15] Later in the article, Daves' *Youngblood Hawke* (1964) is named along with Kenneth Anger's *Scorpio Rising* (1963) as a "Camp favorite" of the East Village underground film movement.[16] Elsewhere, a review of *Youngblood Hawke* in *Vogue* urged readers to see the picture, but for its ironic pleasures: "Just go. In the wrong spirit."[17] Meanwhile, corn (lowercase c, contra Sarris) is a pejorative found frequently in reviews of Daves' melodramas. *New York Times* reviewer Bosley Crowther takes the corn crown, as it were, for managing to call *Susan Slade* "corny and cliché-ridden" no less than four times in the course of a 450-word review. An excerpt:

> If you want to see what the words corny and cliché-ridden mean when prudently put to a motion picture, you might muster your mental fortitude, grit your teeth, don a pair of dark glasses and take a fast look at "Susan Slade." Of course it will have to be a long look if you try to sit through the whole thing ... For it runs just four minutes shy of two hours, a characteristic length for one of these soap-sudsy dramas that has practically nothing to say. You don't really have to stick with it that long to get the message and the pitch. You can see pretty well how things are going and what corny and cliché-ridden mean, if you just stay until the teen-age heroine has given birth to her illegitimate child.[18]

But, like camp, corn could have some halfway-positive connotations. In a 1963 feature on *Spencer's Mountain* in the *Chicago Tribune*, entertainer Arthur Godfrey, who was making movies at Warner Brothers at the time and was enlisted to help promote the film, admitted to liking the picture for the scenery rather than the story. "The story was corny, but what story wasn't? 'After all, it's corn that makes money. How do you think I've stayed in business all these years?' he chuckled."[19] Daves himself used the term when describing his approach to scripting *A Summer Place*, telling the *New York Times*, "I have two kids who are just about the same age of these two in *A Summer Place* and I know how difficult communication between generations can be. And while this may sound corny, it can be assisted by love and understanding."[20] It is apparent that Sarris's appraisal of Daves' work is less original insight than a restatement of a critical consensus arrived at largely, if not solely, on the basis of the director's most recent films. This is a problem, however, because this consensus emerged at a time when film criticism was solidifying its canons of great films and pantheons of great filmmakers, both of which have proved to be exceptionally durable.

In many ways, cinema's status as art depends upon the premise that films, or at least some films, are the product of an individual artist. The idea that directors are "auteurs"—the authors, creators, or originators of their films—is both appealing and, indeed, persuasive, but it is also controversial. While the focus of our collection makes it implicit that Daves be regarded as an auteur, this implication comes with caveats attached. These relate both to the specifics of the medium itself, and to more general debates about cinematic authorship: in particular, those associated with structuralist and post-structuralist theories.

As many have noted, it is easy to claim too much for the film auteur, and critics have argued that auteurist critics tend to minimize the fact that cinema is a collaborative and highly technologically mediated form. Most obviously, film production involves the coordination of a very large number of creative and technical personnel whose influence is always felt (to varying degrees) in the final product. Consider, as an example, *Citizen Kane* (1941), a film for which first-time director Orson Welles is frequently pronounced the auteur. Chief among the film's many lauded features is its unconventional narrative structure. We might note, however, as some already have, that it was co-writer Herman J. Mankiewicz, rather than Welles, who is said to have originally devised the film's innovative use of flashbacks.[21] Maybe so, maybe not. Additionally, *Citizen Kane* is often noted for its use of deep focus cinematography, something for which the cinematographer Gregg Toland could be more suitably credited. And Welles was so appreciative of Toland's efforts that he famously shared equal billing with him on the film's final credit card. So, if *Citizen Kane*'s most innovative features were contributions from members of the crew other than Welles, should we consider Welles the film's author? Because so many individuals usually contribute to the filmmaking process, we may reasonably have reservations about assigning credit to a single authorial vision, especially in studio-produced work. At the same time, the fact that Welles's next major production, *The Magnificent Ambersons* (1942), employed deep focus techniques to very great effect, and this was down to a different cinematographer, Stanley Cortez, might turn our attention back to Welles as a unifying force in *Citizen Kane*. Again, maybe so, maybe not.

Economic determinants must also always be borne in mind. After all, cinema is a commercial product, requiring substantial capital investment and depending for its survival on the ability to attract a mass audience. This is a fact that Welles, to his detriment, failed to take into account. When costs began to spiral out of control during the shooting of *The Magnificent Ambersons*, RKO boss George Schaefer increasingly exercised the studio's prerogative and Welles's control over the project became weaker. Cuts by the film's editor, Robert Wise, plus further substantial cuts by RKO meant that the final product was far from Welles's original vision. Some of this can be attributed to Welles himself, in particular his long absences during the editing process, but it is also plausible that the studio really did not understand his original vision. The result proved a financial disaster for RKO, with Schaeffer losing his job and Welles subsequently denied the financial freedom he had enjoyed in his first two features. *The Magnificent Ambersons*, however, has since earned high critical acclaim as being extremely innovative, and few would argue that its innovations reflect the vision of anyone other than Orson Welles.[22]

In the end, a director's influence on the final product may be as much a function of his or her strength of personality—or degree of financial independence—as of artistic talent, although neither is any more of a guarantee of conferral of auteur status. At the end of his career Daves exercised the kind of control that Welles longed to reclaim: writing, directing, and producing his films—even dictating how they be marketed. Yet, somewhat paradoxically, Daves is considered anything but the auteur of the films he produced under these conditions, because his decision to make them was apparently motivated by practicality and professionalism rather than principle.

Like any other art form, film is also a product of culture, and filmmakers cannot but be influenced by history, politics, social environment and experience. Moreover, some even argue—and many did in the case of Welles—that they might not be fully cognizant of the various social forces within which they operate and which, in many ways, both structure who they are—their subjectivity—and ultimately shape "their" personal vision. As much as film scholarship has analyzed production and post-production processes, and taken pains to explain the important roles played by the dozens of individual crew members (without whom no film would be possible), they (we) also—either implicitly or explicitly—maintain a belief that the director is a central creative force in the whole process.

The person of the director also remains a source of meaning for film audiences and in many cases may well influence someone's experience of a film, or even their decision whether or not to see it in the first place. In spite of all arguments to the contrary, the notion of the director-as-auteur has become an accepted part of film scholarship, inextricably linked to the process of evaluation. Therefore, the emergence of auteur-based approaches as a means of interpreting cinema, their historical impact and development, strengths and weaknesses—together with the intense critical debates that they sparked—requires some elaboration.

AUTHORSHIP AND CINEMA

On 30 March 1948, the clandestine left-wing journal *L'Écran français* published what proved to be a highly influential essay by a young film critic called Alexandre Astruc.[23] In "Du stylo à la caméra et de la caméra au stylo," Astruc called for a new method of understanding film. "I would like to call this new age of cinema the age of *caméra-stylo*," he wrote. "The cinema will gradually break free from the tyranny of what is visual, from the image for its own sake, from the immediate and concrete demands of the narrative, to become a means of writing just as flexible and subtle as written language."[24] What Astruc was suggesting was "a form in which and by which an artist can express his thoughts, however abstract they may be, or translate his obsessions exactly as he does in the contemporary essay or novel."[25] Astruc's notion of film as a language of personal expression reflected traditional Romantic notions of the agency of the centered self. His Romanticism found a loving home in the context of late 1940s France where, ever since the end of the Second World War, cinema had been enjoying an intense vogue. This was especially so among the young intellectuals and aspiring filmmakers whose appetites for self-expression had been frustrated under the German occupation of 1940–4.

In Paris, Henri Langlois' *Cinémathèque français* stayed open twenty-four hours a day, devoted to screening a five-year backlog of previously *verboten* Hollywood films. Consistently among the audience and enthusiastically taking notes were François Truffaut, Jean-Luc Godard, Claude Chabrol, Jacques Rivette, and Eric Rohmer—young left-wing cinephiles who would become filmmakers themselves, finding international fame by pioneering *la nouvelle vague* in the late 1950s. During marathon screenings at the *Cinémathèque*, Truffaut et al. began to recognize recurring themes and stylistic consistencies in certain films. Seeking explanations for these patterns, they found that such groupings of films had, in many cases, a common factor in the person of the director. Through analysis of *mise-en-scène*, the cinephiles claimed to be able to identify a director's artistic "signature"—an expression of a personal vision.

These ideas were published in *Cahiers du cinéma*, a radical new film journal associated with the *Cinémathèque* and co-founded by the respected film critic and theorist, André Bazin. Under Bazin's editorship, the *Cahiers* group sought to re-evaluate the traditions of the dominant discourses in both French and international filmmaking practices. Developed over several years during the 1950s and 60s, this re-evaluation came to be known as the *politique des auteurs*—a "policy" or doctrine of singling out for praise certain directors whose distinct visual styles made their films immediately identifiable. These included French filmmakers like Jean Renoir and Jean Cocteau, as well as Hollywood directors such as Alfred Hitchcock, Fritz Lang, Howard Hawks, and John Ford. In order to assert the merits of Hollywood as something worthy of intellectual consideration on a par with other "serious" art forms, the *Cahiers* group wrote essay after essay enthusiastically extolling the notion of the director as auteur.

In 1954, Truffaut articulated the *politique*'s agenda most forcefully in his polemical essay "Une certaine tendence du cinéma français."[26] Here Truffaut foregrounded the concept of the director-as-artist with, as Susan Hayward relates it, "the intention of putting into practice the theories and styles advocated by the *Cahiers* group during the 1950s."[27] Truffaut's essay was a direct, emotive response to the formulaic and manufactured studio products of the post-war French film industry. This so-called *tradition de la qualité* was, as Pam Cook informs us, "a cinema of classical virtues, literary scripts, smooth photography and elegant décor," which Truffaut belittlingly referred to as *le cinema du papa*.[28] For adherents of the *politique*, film was not "a neutral form through which something else (literature or "reality") could be transmitted, but ... a specific aesthetic system, a language in itself."[29]

In his composite essay, "L'évolution de la langue du cinéma," Bazin also asserted the intellectual validity of popular film as an art form deserving the same respect as literature, painting, and the other arts.[30] Like Astruc, Bazin argued that film was a language that should reflect a director's personal vision. "Today we can say that at last the director writes in film," he declares. "The film-maker is no longer the competitor of the painter and the playwright, he is, at last, the equal of the novelist."[31] It is important to note, however, that Bazin was somewhat critical of the *politique*, in particular the emphasis on the director as a film's "organizing source of meaning" through a focus on *mise-en-scène*. Bazin was a passionate advocate for realism and, according to Cook, felt that "the film-maker should act as a passive recorder of the real world rather than a manipulator of it."[32] He did believe that a film should reflect a director's personal vision, but that this vision should be contained within "objective reality." In this sense, "a film's *mise-en-scène* should efface individual style to allow the inner meaning to shine through naturally so that the spectator could come to his or her own conclusions without being manipulated."[33]

Disagreements aside, the tripartite influence of Astruc, Langlois, and Bazin on the *politique des auteurs* was clear. As James Monaco summarizes it: "Astruc sounded the call; Langlois provided the material; Bazin supplied the basic architectonics. In the pages of *Cahiers du cinéma* in the 1950s, Truffaut,

Godard, Chabrol, Rohmer and Rivette argued out a new theory of film."[34] Through this "new theory" the *Cahiers* group embedded their notion of the cinema as art and of the director as auteur within film criticism. In so doing, they were largely responsible for the subsequent acceptance of film, not only as an art form in and of itself, but also as a subject meriting serious study. This led in part to the entry of film studies into the academy in the 1960s. Throughout Europe during this period, art cinema was in its ascendance, with such figures as Ingmar Bergman and Michelangelo Antonioni seen to be fitting the definition of auteur—autonomous writer-directors who were intimately engaged with the production process throughout, wielding the *caméra-stylo* as Leonardo da Vinci wielded his brush, or Honoré de Balzac his pen. However, in retroactively applying their concept of authorship to directors working in the Hollywood studio system, the *Cahiers* group's idea of such conscious, consistent, and *individual* creative artistry seemed far less appropriate.

From the 1920s until the 1950s, Hollywood studios relied heavily upon rationalized production methods. In order to produce a consistent product, studios were divided into departments, each specializing in one aspect of the production process. Rather than needing to assemble an entire team for the production of a single film, a project would often move from department to department during the production process. Essentially, writers would develop a script in line with a commercially recognized genre. The script would be assigned to a director but other crucial aspects of the film like sets, costumes, props, lighting, and casting would be assigned to different departments. On set, the director would coordinate most of the activity, and be responsible for actually filming the picture—following a schedule set by a producer. The completed footage would then be delivered to a series of departments responsible for post-production: editing, sound mixing, and so forth. A director seldom had any input into how a film would be edited. In each case, after personnel had completed their assigned task on one project, they would simply move on to the next one.

In such a context, it would seem extremely difficult for a director to establish much of an artistic signature. As we have seen in the case of Welles, even when more freedom was awarded a director and his team, the results were not always a success. Far from being dissuaded, however, the auteurists felt that Hollywood's system of collaborative mass production provided precisely the right environment in which individual talent, where it existed, could flourish. As outlined by Robert Lapsley and Michael Westlake, the *Cahiers* group "pointed out that there were undeniably directors working within Hollywood whose films displayed a discernible consistency and identity of style."[35] They reasoned that "given that they often had to contend with a variety of scriptwriters, studios, actors and genres, the only possible source of this unity was the director himself."[36] As far as they saw it, working within the codes of established genre formats actually empowered the director, with the auteur managing to rise above the greater mass of filmmakers who displayed technical competence but who lacked a strong streak of individual vision—what *Cahiers* described as a *metteur-en-scène*. Genre itself was also perceived to be a significant enabler for auteur filmmakers. As Lapsley and Westlake summarize the reasoning behind the *Cahiers* group: "Because any system of rules brings with it the possibility of transgression, genre can be seen as a field for variation and elaboration of meaning; hence genre is not something that imprisons a director but precisely allows him his freedom."[37] Ergo, their focus on *mise-en-scène* "as the characteristic domain of directorial choice: lighting, camera, sets, acting and so on," those formal aspects of a film that could not be tampered with after filming was completed.[38]

This reasoning did not convince everybody. Ed Buscombe for one criticized the transcendentalism inherent in the *politique*'s "[r]omantic conception of the director as the 'only begetter' of a film."[39] He felt that the focus on the director fueled the misassumption that "because there was meaning in a work someone must have put it there, and that someone must be the *auteur*."[40] In all fairness, Buscombe does acknowledge that the *politique*'s attitudes were not always so dogmatic, and mentions their many contributions to the study of film form and the film industry through essays on genres and "the technology of the cinema."[41] Nevertheless, there remained in the early days the "tendency in *Cahiers* to make a totem of the *auteur* [which] went to such extremes that every now and again the editors felt the need to redress the balance."[42] In this regard, Buscombe refers to Bazin's 1957 essay "La politique des auteurs."[43] "The evolution of Western art toward greater personalization should definitely be considered a step forward," Bazin declared, "but only so long (sic) as this individualization . . . does not claim to *define* culture."[44] Bazin's crucial point was that it must always be borne in mind that the individual is situated within society. Whilst he does not deny the *Cahiers*' belief that, in some cases, the "individual transcends society," he reminds them, and us, that "society is also and above all *within* him."[45] Therefore, "there can be no definitive criticism of genius or talent which does not first take into consideration the social determinism, the historical combination of circumstances, and the technical background which to a large extent determines it."[46]

According to Buscombe, the development of auteur theory into a "cult of personality" that hierarchizes filmmakers gathered strength with the emergence of the aforementioned Andrew Sarris who, during the 1960s, adopted and broadened the ideas of the *Cahiers* group.[47] "It is Sarris," Buscombe claims, "who pushes to extremes arguments which in *Cahiers* were often only implicit."[48] In his essay "Notes on the Auteur Theory in 1962," Sarris suggested, quite straightforwardly, that auteur criticism identifies three elements as being of significance to the director who "deserves" auteur status. These are "technique," "style," and "interior meaning."[49] Sarris claimed that these were uniquely identifiable in the work of an auteur.

Like the *Cahiers* group, Sarris's work depends on a deep cinephilia and an almost exhaustive knowledge of films—major and minor—released throughout the previous four decades. This comes across in "Toward a Theory of Film History," the introductory chapter to Sarris's 1968 book *The American Cinema*.[50] Sarris divides his introduction into two sections. The first is "The Forest and the Trees," which is a rejoinder to the tendency in film criticism to dismiss individual American films (the trees) because of suspicion of or distaste for the broader institution of American cinema (the forest). The second section, an elaboration of ideas he had been advocating in the preceding eight years, is "The Auteur Theory." This constitutes a defense of the value and utility of evaluating the films of an individual filmmaker within the wider context of his entire body of work in order to determine the ways in which that film is the expression of the director's personal vision. By looking closely at single films, Sarris sought to develop a means by which he could assess those films so as ultimately to be ranked. Ranking is, in fact, Sarris's principal activity in *The American Cinema*, the majority of which consists of a series of evaluative lists compiled and consolidated from his earlier criticism. Leading off is Sarris's "pantheon" of great filmmakers, which includes Hawks, Welles, Ford, and Alfred Hitchcock. At the same time as he elevates some directors, he deflates the reputation of others, including Academy Award winners such as William Wyler and John Huston, categorizing them under a chapter rather condescendingly entitled, "Less than Meets the Eye."[51] Delmer Daves is placed in a similarly patronizing grouping, "Lightly Likable," in the company of Busby Berkeley, Michael Curtiz, Henry Hathaway, and sixteen other directors. Sarris describes these directors as "talented but uneven . . . with the saving grace of unpretentiousness."[52]

The film history that Sarris envisages is both comprehensive and evaluative. It should also be noted that Sarris was critical of certain variants of auteur criticism practiced at *Cahiers*, in particular Bazin's penchant for appreciative criticism, whereby reviews of particular films were assigned to the critic most familiar, or enamored, with its filmmaker, and therefore most likely to produce a favorable review.[53] Such a procedure not only limited the number of films taken up by criticism, but also, however unintentionally, fostered the sense that a great filmmaker was incapable of making a bad film.[54]

Yet critics of auteur theory quickly raised the question of who gets to decide on this vague "evaluative criterion." On what basis was "greatness" achieved, or perceived? Buscombe for one felt that a distinction of directors as being either worthy or not worthy of the accolade auteur "led inevitably to a kind of apartheid," whereby only "great" directors could assert themselves over and against the constraints of the Hollywood studio system.[55] Buscombe suggests Sarris erred in "reject[ing] Bazin's attempt to combine the auteur approach with an acknowledgment of the forces conditioning the individual artist . . . If Sarris is not saying that genius is independent of time and place, then he comes dangerously close to it."[56] Helen Stoddart also cautions us against Sarris's "construction of a critical 'pantheon' of great auteurs within which directors were ranked hierarchically on a sliding scale of the more or less great."[57] As Stoddart has it, "the criteria for entry on top . . . remained entirely personal to Sarris."[58] Far from a critical methodology that sees the auteur as a part of a broader collaborative system conditioned by socio-economic and historical forces, Sarris's understanding of auteurism was "one which reinforced the Romantic cult of the individual as one who transcends the demands of the market place and effaces those very cultural and economic conditions which mark popular film production."[59] Therefore, in opening up to serious study the directors working in Hollywood, and therefore working to act against a broader culture of elitism in the arts, the auteur theory produced its own kind of elitism—canonizing some filmmakers based largely on personal preference whilst in the process condemning others to footnotes in cinematic history. In this hierarchy of Hollywood talent, it appeared that in the final analysis the judgment of the critic prevailed.

In addition to this, the rendering of the *politique* as the auteur theory was deemed somewhat misleading. Buscombe suggests the term was largely due to Sarris's apparently willful mistranslation of the *politique*.[60] As he explains, "the original *politique* of *Cahiers* [was] only loosely based upon a theoretical approach to the cinema that was never to be made fully explicit. The *politique* . . . was polemical in intent and was meant to define an attitude to the cinema."[61] Even as late as 1964, apparently, "questions of what an auteur is" and why "the cinema should be discussed largely in terms of individual artists" were answered in *Cahiers* only by "implication."[62] Any "theory" that was revealed, insists Buscombe, "appeared incidentally and at times incoherently."[63] Indeed, as Lapsley and Westlake note, "whatever else it may have been, auteurism was never a theory."[64] What Sarris did, they argue, was impute to the *politique* "a consistency and rigor rarely apparent in any of its manifestations, least of all his own."[65]

What is inarguable is that Astruc, Bazin, the *Cahiers* group, and Sarris all believed that cinema was a language, a medium of personal expression. Despite the appeal of this notion, it is not difficult to see that the film director is in a far more complex position than, say, the novelist in relation to their respective art forms. As Buscombe et al. (via Bazin) have convincingly argued, however one regards the relation between "author" and "text," the notion that a film is the product of a *single* creator is unsustainable. As Stoddart puts it,

> by forcing the contradictions immanent in the application of a Romantic, literary theory of authorship on to an industrial, mass art like film, [the

auteurists] pressed film theory into opening itself up to "new criticisms" which moved beyond this unsustainable Romanticism.[66]

These "new criticisms" had their roots in a complex theoretical method anterior to film studies, known as structuralism. Richard and Fernande DeGeorge rightly observe that structuralism "cuts across many disciplines—linguistics, anthropology, literary criticism, psychology, philosophy."[67] For some it was a "unifying force," putting "the social sciences, literature, and art ... on a scientific footing."[68] Conversely, many insisted that it was "an ideology; for others, its inherent antihumanisitic (or a-humanistic) tendencies [made] it less a value-free approach to human sciences than a value-drenched assumption about them."[69] Overall, however, there was a shared "conviction that surface events and phenomena are to be explained by structures, data, and phenomena below the surface."[70] In short:

> The explicit and obvious is to be explained by and is determined—in some sense of the term—by what is implicit and not obvious. The attempt to uncover deep structures, unconscious motivations, and underlying causes which account for human actions at a more basic and profound level than do individual conscious decisions, and which shape, influence, and structure these decisions, is an enterprise which unites ... modern structuralists.[71]

As an approach to linguistics and anthropology, structuralism's chief aim, as such, was to provide an understanding of cultural traditions—folklore, myths, etc.—in which "creative source" was replaced by "collective cultural phenomenon." In other words, it looked for common structures rather than originality. As Claude Lévi-Strauss famously put it: "not how men think in myths, but how myths operate ... in men's minds without their being aware of the fact."[72] In his extensive studies of kinship systems and tribal myths around the world, Lévi-Strauss observed consistencies or "deep structures" across apparently diverse cultural groups. According to Lapsley and Westlake, he took this "as strong evidence for supposing that there is a ... universal structure within the human mind, functioning irrespective of time and place."[73] This led him to conclude that, like language, "all human culture ... is governed by a system of mental constraints operating according to binary oppositional features."[74] From this, Lévi-Strauss proposed nothing short of a structural unconscious that governed human characteristics everywhere, from the primitive, "savage" mind, to its modern, "civilized" equivalent. In this structure, the individual does not *think*, rather he or she is *thought* by structures that shape and govern language and social groups.

Despite its inherent anti-humanism, proponents of auteurism adopted aspects of structuralism in order to re-consider the director as one among many determining structures that produce meaning in a film. The development of "auteur-structuralism" was an attempt to provide authorship studies with theoretical "legitimacy" in the face of its critics, and it certainly proved helpful in ameliorating the crude Romanticism surrounding some of its original suppositions. "Instead of the personal vision of the creative artist," as Lapsley and Westlake relate it, this "new methodology would reveal in any given oeuvre an objective structure that generated its characteristic meanings, patterns and intensities."[75] The British film theorist Peter Wollen crystallized this approach in his influential 1969 study *Signs and Meaning in the Cinema*.[76] In a chapter entitled "The Auteur Theory," Wollen extended Lévi-Strauss's notion of myths as a universal system, combined them with Vladimir Propp's formalist analyses of the plot functions of Russian fairy tales, and applied them to contemporary cinema.[77] Like Lévi-Strauss's attempt to account for the repetition of certain patterns of behavior across different cultures and historical moments, he looked for common "deep structures" operating within a director's oeuvre and identified and defined "a core of repeated motifs" or "structuring oppositions" organized around a so-called "master antinomy." Through this could be identified their "stylistic expressiveness."[78] Via this method, Wollen suggested that a film's characters "can be dissolved into bundles of differential elements, pairs of opposites," and the narrative structures likewise.[79] However, Wollen impressed that the identification of repetitions of themes and structuring oppositions alone was not enough, for this threatened (as Lévi-Strauss had apparently pointed out) to reduce "all the texts which are studied (whether Russian fairy-tales or American movies) . . . to one, abstract and impoverished."[80] What keeps myths and folklore relevant, Wollen insists, is their "synthesis" of the "system of differences and oppositions."[81] This is to say, myths become valuable not simply through their "universality," but through their "singularity (what differentiates them from each other)."[82] In terms of film, Wollen suggested that "the test of a structural analysis lies not in the orthodox canon of a director's work, where resemblances are clustered, but in films which at first sight may seem eccentricities."[83]

For example, in John Ford's films Wollen states that the "master antinomy . . . is that between the wilderness and the garden."[84] This master antinomy—a reference to the work of Henry Nash Smith—precedes Ford and exists as part of the "deep structure" of American culture. "The contrast between the image of America as a desert and as a garden," Wollen writes, "is one which has dominated American thought and literature, recurring in countless novels, tracts, political speeches, and magazine stories."[85] Under this "master antinomy," a further series of binary oppositions play out in a sequence of successive differences changing from film to film. For example, a common binary—not just in Ford, but also in the Western genre more generally—is that of civilization versus savagery.[86] This could then be placed under the master antinomy, with "savage" equating to "wilderness" and "civilization" equating to "garden". Then we might incorporate the binary opposition "European" versus "Indian", with "savage" equating to "Indian" and "civilization" equating to "European". However, as Lapsley and Westlake point out, in accordance with Wollen's insistence on singularity, "the elements within each opposition do not possess a fixed value but are determined relationally in every case."[87] For example, in *Stagecoach* (1939) the Apache assume the role of the savages, whereas the Euro-American occupants of the stagecoach represent civilization. However, Wollen observes that there takes place a "shift from an identity between civilized versus savagery and European versus Indian to their separation and final reversal, so that in *Cheyenne Autumn* [1964] it is the Europeans who are savage, the victims who are heroes."[88] Thus, as Stoddart summarizes, "it is the moments of variation, then, which lend the repetitions their significance."[89] It follows then that these structuring oppositions can reveal an interesting esotericism. So, for example, in *The Searchers* (1956), we might argue that Indian savagery is employed to draw attention to the savagery implicit in Euro-American civilization, which is crystallized through the agency of the hero Ethan Edwards (John Wayne), who embodies both civilization and savagery. As Wollen suggests, "the antinomies invade the personality of the protagonist himself. The oppositions tear Edwards in two; he is a tragic hero."[90]

Wollen argues, "the great directors must be defined in terms of shifting relations, in their singularity as well as their uniformity."[91] The "principle of variation," he writes,

> the esoteric structure . . . can only manifest itself or "seep to the surface," in Lévi-Strauss's phrase, "through the repetition process" [whereby] there will be a kind of torsion within permutation groups . . . a kind of exploration of certain possibilities, in which some antinomies are foregrounded, discarded, or even inverted, whereas others remain stable and constant.[92]

Of course, such a reading is not confined to genre boundaries, say, Ford's Westerns, but also extends to his other films, with each one helping to elucidate the structural meaning of the others. What is significant for Wollen is that "it is only the analysis of the whole *corpus* which permits the moment of synthesis when the critic returns to the individual film."[93]

Wollen clearly saw his analysis as a work in progress, concluding that "*auteur* theory leaves us, as every theory does, with possibilities and questions" and that "the task which the critics of *Cahiers du cinéma* embarked on is still far from completed."[94] He suggests that the auteur theory needs to consider many things: literary sources as "catalysts" for the auteur's vision, to compare "author with author," to "value [the] performances" of actors, to reconsider the *metteur-en-scène* in terms of also being potentially "great," and, finally, to draw "comparisons with authors in the other arts: Ford with [James] Fenimore Cooper, for example."[95] These are all valid appeals to avenues for future study, and subsequent film scholarship has certainly explored them. However, we might point out that Wollen's brand of auteur-structuralism raises a number of questions of its own that are not so easily answered. Primarily, his very referencing of Nash Smith acknowledges that the "master antinomy" of garden and wilderness was not "created" by Ford at all. It was, as Wollen admitted and as Stoddart reiterates, "a marker of American cultural opposition which predated Ford and which is simply confirmed through its restatement and reworking."[96] This alone is fine, but it begs the question of how this preexisting structural binary relates to an individual auteur. Wollen's explanation on this is somewhat confused. In insisting upon a synthesis between auteurism and structuralism, he suggests that "auteur theory" is imposed on the film by the critic—"which is the critic's task to construct"—as something extraneous rather than implicit and "in the filmmaker's mind" before its creation.[97] This forces the question of the creative autonomy of the individual auteur, and not just because of Hollywood's collaborative system of mass production, not just, as Wollen puts it, "because of 'noise' from the producer, the cameraman, or even the actors."[98] Wollen was also clearly troubled by the evaluative agenda inherent in auteur theory, and yet it is apparent that he discusses films from an evaluative point of view. He suggests, for example, that "Ford's work is much richer than that of Hawks and that this is revealed by a structural analysis; it is the richness of the shifting relations between antinomies that makes him a great artist."[99]

Wollen was evidently aware of such issues and in 1972, in order to clarify his position, he wrote a reflective supplement to the third edition of *Signs and Meaning*. In it, he sought to distance himself from those numerous branches of auteur theory that had promoted the Romantic cult of personality of the director. "What the *auteur* theory argues," he writes, "is that any film, certainly a Hollywood film, is a network of different statements, crossing and contradicting each other, elaborated into a final 'coherent' version."[100] Using the terminology of psychoanalysis, Wollen suggests that "the film the spectator sees is, so to speak, the 'film façade,' the end-product of 'secondary revision,' which hides and masks the process which remains latent in the film's 'unconscious'."[101] Through a comparison with other films by the same auteur (their "*corpus*"), he suggests that it is possible to see beyond the "disparate elements," beyond "the characters, the dialogue, the plot, and so on."[102] From this, the auteur analysis "disengages from a film . . . not a coherent message or world-view, but a structure which underlines the film and shapes it, gives it a certain pattern of energy cathexis."[103] The structure of a film could thus be "associated with a single director, an individual."[104] This was not "because he has played the role of artist, expressing himself or his own vision in the film."[105] Rather, through "the force of his preoccupations," an "unconscious, unintended meaning [could] be decoded in the film, usually to the surprise of the individual involved."[106] Thus, Wollen writes:

> The film is not a communication, but an artifact which is unconsciously structured in a certain way. *Auteur* analysis does not consist of retracing a film to its origins, to its creative source. It consists of tracing a structure (not a message) within the work, which can then *post factum* be assigned to an individual, the director, on empirical grounds. It is wrong, in the name of a denial of the traditional idea of creative subjectivity, to deny any status to individuals at all. But [Samuel] Fuller, or Hawks, or Hitchcock, the directors, are quite separate from "Fuller" or "Hawks" or "Hitchcock," the structures named after them, and should not be methodologically confused.[107]

We could consider Wollen's idea of a *post factum* assignation of a structure to an individual director a complex advancement—if not exactly clarification—of his attempt to reconcile structuralism with auteurism. That is to say, "to speak of a film *auteur* as an unconscious catalyst."[108] In spite of this (or perhaps because of it), criticism began to mount. One of the most vociferous was Brian Henderson, who doubted the suitability of Lévi-Strauss as a theoretical basis, pointing out that, as far as the anthropologist was concerned, "myths have no origins, no centers, no subjects, and no authors."[109] Whereas "bodies of films organized by auteur signature are obviously defined by their origin, which is a subject and an author as well as a definitive center."[110] Henderson charges Wollen with rhetorical sleight of hand. He argues that the "fundamental questions—whether films are like myths, whether modes of myth study are applicable to film study, and whether auteur theory is compatible with Lévi-Straussian structuralism—are avoided by Wollen, elided by a skillful rhetoric which seems to answer them" but does not.[111]

Even in light of Wollen's supplement, Henderson saw only more "twists and turns" and "vocabularic concessions to recent theoretical work"—namely, psychoanalysis—and, crucially, a failure to "escape the criticisms he is aware of because he retains the subject as producer of unique or distinctive meaning."[112] For him, Wollen has failed to explain the "foundational problems of auteur-structuralism," because he does not account for how "individual subjects produce unique or distinctive meanings (structures), which moreover have the integrity and constancy of mythic meanings."[113] After all, Lévi-Strauss's "work is founded upon the interchangeability of subjects in the production of meaning," therefore a theory of individual authorship "cannot be grounded in Lévi-Strauss."[114] For if, as Henderson argues and as the writings of Lévi-Strauss seem to suggest, conscious agency is itself a myth, then how can one attribute meaning to a single author? Indeed, as Lévi-Strauss stated: "It would perhaps be better to . . . [disregard] the thinking subject completely [and] proceed as if the thinking process were taking place in the myths, in their reflection upon themselves and their interrelation."[115]

Above all, Henderson argues, Wollen only nominally posits "auteur-structure" as "one code among man" but as he "continues to identify structure with auteur-meaning and therefore meaning with auteur-structure," he retains the "privileged position" of the director.[116] As Stoddart also asks, if the director as imagined by Wollen is a "neutral agent (rather than agency), through which wider social meanings are simply refracted," why does he describe a director, such as Ford, as if he were "a very specific, individualizing component"?[117] Buscombe points out that "earlier versions of the *auteur* theory made the assumption that because there was meaning in a work someone must have deliberately put it there, and that someone must be the *auteur*."[118] Whilst he acknowledges that Wollen rightly resists this notion, he, like Henderson, raises the issue of an application of "techniques which were developed for the analysis of forms of communications which are entirely unconscious such as dreams, myths and language itself."[119] He asks: "what is the exact relation between the structure called 'Hitchcock' and the film director called Hitchcock, who actually makes decisions about the story, the acting, the sets, the camera placing?"[120]

These are all valid criticisms and questions. After all, we might query why—or how—a film could coalesce into a "coherent version" but not contain a director's "coherent message." If such messages are "unconscious" and "latent" in a text, and if we are not seeing an auteur's "world-view" but, instead, a "structure which underlines it," then how can it be "associated with a single director, an individual"? Conscious or unconscious, individual or structure, as Stoddart reasons, it remains "clear that structuralism never really questioned why it should be that the director remains the chosen catalyst figure at the center of the text."[121] Under such scrutiny, auteur-structuralism appeared to have reached a theoretical impasse.

Nonetheless, operating on the truism that the "test of a theory is whether it produces new knowledge," Buscombe for one did concede that "structural analysis of *auteurs* has produced important results, not least in Wollen's own book."[122] His reservations remained, but as he offhandedly asked, "need we throw out the baby with the bath-water?"[123] "The conscious will and talent of the artist (for want of a better word) may still be allowed some part, surely," he writes, "but of course, that conscious will and talent are also in turn the product of those forces that act upon the artist."[124] Buscombe suggests that "*auteur* theory produced much, but of a very partial kind, and much it left totally unknown," and what was needed was "a theory of the cinema that locates directors in a total situation, rather than one which assumes that their development has only an internal dynamic."[125] By this he meant to reconsider the director, not in terms of a total theory, but in terms of cinema's social effects and, in turn, the effects of society on cinema—"in other words, the operation of ideology, economics, technology, etc."—and, also, the effects of films on other films. This last, he argues, "would especially involve questions of genre."[126] For him, traditional auteur theory did not deal with history, the notion that "all films are affected by the previous history of the cinema."[127] Having "identified the code of the auteur," Buscombe concludes, auteur theory "was silent on those codes intrinsic to the cinema, as well as to those originating outside it."[128]

Lapsley and Westlake also cautiously defend Wollen's brand of auteur-structuralism. They suggest that the confusion (or, for some, consternation) following Wollen's 1972 supplement—of the author as "unconscious producer of meaning" and "catalyst in the production of meaning"—may or may not be the same thing, but might actually be read more productively. "Not as a resolution of the problem of synthesing [sic] auteurism and structuralism," they write, "but as a transitional text from a pre-structuralist concept of the author as creator of meaning to a post-structuralist concept of the author as a construct of the reader."[129] In other words, "distinguishing the empirical author [John Ford] from the author ['John Ford'] constructed by (because desired by) the reader."[130] Indeed, what appeared to be missing in all this was the person of the reader—in film studies terms, the viewer/spectator—and Stoddart rightly called this a "blind spot for structuralism."[131] Indeed, as film scholars were struggling with the function of the auteur in relation to structuralism, literary theorists were developing the new approach of post-structuralism to call into question the traditional notion of the author by considering the function of the recipient of a text's "message."

Prominent among these literary theorists was the semiotician Roland Barthes. In a now-famous 1967 essay entitled "La mort de l'auteur," Barthes thought that the artist's conscious intention and biography should be set aside in favor of an analysis of the formal qualities of the work itself.[132] Arguing that "the image of literature to be found in ordinary culture is tyrannically centered on the author," he claims that "the explanation of a work is always sought in the man or woman who produced it, as if it were always in the end . . . the voice of a single person, the author 'confiding' in us."[133] In outlining the popular Romantic vision of the author as the symbolic font of his work, Barthes turned his attention to the critic. "Such a conception suits criticism very well," he writes. "[T]he latter then allotting itself the important task of discovering the Author . . . when the Author has been found, the text is 'explained'—victory to the Critic . . . Hence there is no surprise in the fact that, historically, the reign of the Author has also been that of the Critic."[134]

The image of what Barthes termed the "Author-God" gives way to a more complex and fractured assemblage. He describes the text as "a multi-dimensional space in which a variety of writings, none of them original, blend and clash."[135] The crucial term here is intertextuality, and Barthes brings its implications to bear on the text. "The text is a tissue of quotations drawn from the innumerable centers of culture," he writes, and "the writer can only imitate a gesture that is always anterior, never original."[136] In other words, the author merely copies things from the past—there may be changes, there may be alterations, but the notion of originality is a myth and the text becomes open. "In the multiplicity of writing, everything is to be disentangled, nothing deciphered . . . writing ceaselessly posits meaning ceaselessly to evaporate it, carrying out a systematic exemption of meaning."[137] And thus for Barthes "is revealed the total existence of writing: a text is made of multiple writings, drawn from many cultures and entering into mutual relations of dialogue, parody, contestation, but there is one place where this multiplicity is focused and that place is the *reader*, not, as was hitherto said, the author."[138] Barthes argued that focus should be on the reader who is, accordingly, free to make their own connections and to interpret texts as they wish. Not only does the reader bring their own meaning to the text, but meanings within a text change over time and within different cultures. "The reader is the space on which all the quotations that make up a writing are inscribed without any of them being lost," he writes. "[A] text's unity lies not in its origin but in its destination."[139] For, though "the sway of the Author remains powerful . . . it is language that speaks, not the author."[140] For Barthes it becomes necessary to debunk the myth of tyrannical author-centricity and open up the potential for reading a text's multiplicity. Hence his famous proclamation: "the birth of the reader must be at the cost of the death of the Author."[141]

Barthes' insistence that language is not a neutral medium through which meaning is generated by a singular agent (author) and sent to a recipient (reader) is informed by a much older theory, the structural linguistics model of Ferdinand de Saussure. At the start of the twentieth century, Saussure—often regarded as the progenitor of structuralism, and an inspiration to Lévi-Strauss—argued that the meaning of any utterance (*parole*) is produced only in relation to a pre-existing system of linguistic rules (*langue*) that precede the individual speaker. Language operates within broader systems of signification based upon culturally inscribed differences between a signifier and a signified which, when combined, produce linguistic meaning. The crucial point being made here is that the relationship between signifier and signified is arbitrary—not natural but cultural. Once applied to literary theory, the implications of Saussure's theories for the traditional conception of authorship are profound.

As language is productive—rather than expressive—of meaning, the author is no longer understood to be the source of a text's meaning and, in turn, meaning is also no longer fixed and changes when applied to different contexts within a language system.[142]

When applied to film studies, the shift in critical focus from the author/director to the reader/spectator as a producer of meaning rather than merely the recipient of it opened up analysis to erstwhile neglected, overdetermining factors. These include the relationship between film and society (cultural ideologies, socio-political determinants, the unconscious), historical contexts, institutional structures (including socio-economics), and the intertextual relationship films share with other films (all considerations, we might remind ourselves, that Buscombe had called for).[143] Embedded in this approach was the concept of the author as a "discursive subject," part of a system of meaning generating signifiers which, according to Cook, "did not reside in a single point of view or authorial position: it was produced in the interaction of discourses, and itself contributed to the production of meaning."[144] Furthermore, the "idea of the author as discursive subject, produced by the film text defined as a network of discourses, offered a more flexible account of the relationship between text and reader in which the latter, while clearly now seen as equally responsible with the author (if not more so) for constructing meaning, was also caught in history and society."[145] Essentially, it was reasoned that different historically and culturally contingent readings would produce their own historically and culturally contingent meanings. The text was thus always transitional, "it was transformed by, and accumulated meanings in, the historical process of reading. The reader's codes intersected the codes in the text, of which the authorial code was one, to produce meaning."[146]

To force the issue of how all these factors interplay to produce meaning undoubtedly provided a step toward resolving the auteur-structuralist debates raging at the time. In particular, to impress that "authorship is something that is historically variable," and to understand him or her as a "function" produced within "discourse" and whose name was associated with "relations of power."[147] In this respect, as Lapsley and Westlake suggest, "produced within discourse, organizing and regulating other discourses, the author-function has its effectivity."[148] However, the end-logic demonstrated by Barthes' notion of "Death of the Author" is extreme and led in some film theorists toward a virulent strand of anti-humanism. For instance, Lapsley and Westlake discuss the work of Stephen Heath in the 1970s. They point out that Heath was "a principal proponent of this view within film theory"[149], and as one of many whose thinking owed much to Barthes, he used such arguments "to attack any attempts to improve traditional auteurism."[150] Instead, Heath argued that "the notion of authorship was an ideological construction that blocked thinking about film's political functioning."[151]

These new pronouncements of the author's demise—as embodied in Heath's anti-humanist stance, together with Barthes' proclaiming the death of the author—by no means found universal appeal within film scholarship. For some, the idea of the author as a structural effect of the text, which was the position adopted by those who took up and developed Barthes' position *in extremis*, as well as those of other of his contemporaries, namely Michel Foucault, was indicative of some of the worst excesses of post-structuralism. In his 1992 work *Gunfighter Nation*,[152] Richard Slotkin delivers a reasoned critique of the subject of "linguistic autonomy' in post-structuralist theories. "At their best," he writes, "these approaches . . . highlight the crucial role of the reader in determining the actual or effective meaning of texts in any given social or historical setting, by asserting that textual meaning can never be determinate but is always 'in play.'"[153] Slotkin admits that such approaches are essential in serving "to expose the rhetorical conventions and mythic structures" that inform national ideologies; and additionally, that the help they provide in developing an understanding of cultural production as historically contingent through "the idea that texts have more than one 'author,' [that] successive generations possess both the power and the legitimate authority to rewrite, revise, or re-author their culture . . . is crucial to the depiction of human 'agency' in history."[154] However, and with the writings of Barthes, Foucault, and others (such as Jacques Derrida) evidently in mind, he cautions that the more extreme form of the post-structuralist position "is one that substitutes for the materialist or idealist determinisms it deconstructs a form of 'linguistic determinism,' in which 'Language has come to speak man,' and histories 'write us.'"[155] For Slotkin, the "notion of self-generating texts" is "implausible, and the concomitant idea of a linguistic 'prisonhouse' both excessively deterministic and inaccurate as a description of the historical activities of cultural production."[156]

Much is attractive in Slotkin's balanced attitude regarding the strengths and limitations of the post-structuralist position on authorship. Given his overriding concern with the cultural impact of frontier mythology on American society, however, *Gunfighter Nation* can hardly be considered an auteur study, or even an auteur-critique. Rather, the attempt to preserve a place for the auteur—in some semblance—was to be found in the continuously developing field of film genre studies. For some, genre provided the necessary code—the structure—within which the individual could "speak."

Arguably the key work in terms of influencing subsequent auteur scholarship on the Western genre was Jim Kitses' 1969 publication, *Horizons West*.[157] Here, Kitses famously contends that a "philosophical dialectic" is central to the Western and, in terms similar to Wollen, forwards the notion of a "structuralist grid"—a shifting play of antinomies organized beneath two overarching oppositions, "wilderness and civilization." As Kitses suggests, and as

Wollen has already pointed out, this dialectic is significant to American culture because, historically speaking, modern America was originally carved out of a wilderness. "What we are dealing with here," he insists, "is no less than a national world-view: underlying the whole complex is the grave problem of identity that has special meaning for Americans."[158]

Kitses' original monograph was a study of three filmmakers: Anthony Mann, Budd Boetticher, and Sam Peckinpah. A substantially revised version of the book published in 2004 added chapters on Ford, Sergio Leone, and Clint Eastwood. Throughout, Kitses envisioned a reciprocal relationship between his chosen "privileged" directors and the Western genre within which they primarily worked. According to Kitses, in the 1960s "genre—and most prominently the Western—offered a persuasive vehicle for combating dismissals of the popular . . . *Horizons West* was partly reacting to the challenge posed by auteurism at this embryonic stage of film studies."[159] He has held the belief that the pre-existing structures of the genre provided the terms by which directors could develop their own personal styles. In this fashion, the Western itself was an "active creative agent," and, as he wrote in 1969, "rather than an empty vessel breathed into by the filmmaker, the genre is a vital structure through which flow a myriad of themes and concepts. As such the form can provide a director with a range of possible connections and the space in which to experiment, to shape and refine the kind of effects and meanings he is working toward."[160] Furthermore, "The model we must hold before us is of a varied and flexible structure, a thematically fertile and ambiguous world of historical material shot through with archetypal elements which are themselves ever in flux."[161]

In 2004, and in light of subsequent critical-theoretical debates surrounding cinematic authorship, Kitses still held to his "model" and maintained a role for the director in shaping and influencing meaning production in a "varied and flexible structure" grounded in American history. "My basic premise," he writes, "is that at its core the Western marries historical and archetypal elements in a fruitful mix that allows different film-makers a wide latitude of creative play."[162] Kitses accepts the previous criticisms leveled at auteur theory—"for ignoring the ideology and industrial conditions that militate against personal expression in the mainstream cinema"—yet, as he has it, "in surveying the work of [his chosen] film-makers, it is difficult to escape the conclusion that each found in the genre a canvas . . . within which they could create a unique world and, yes, a personal vision."[163] In his view this did not mean subscribing "uncritically to a pure theory of great directors [as] none of these film-makers stands alone," and crucially, his use of the Western genre as "the structure of codes, conventions, characters, and settings," was precisely to "contest the notion of the unified and transcendent author."[164] In terms that appear to address at least some of the concerns and reservations held by many,

Kitses contends that "despite the misleading popular notion of auteur cinema as supremely a director's art, the evidence of creative collaborations, of shared or multiple authorship, of apprenticeships, mentorships and partnerships is everywhere in the American cinema."[165]

In considering the chronology of how "the structural analysis of authors has come in for its share of criticism over the years," Kitses makes reference to Wollen—specifically, his addressing "the problem of attribution of authorship to a unified originating source" by his aforementioned arguing of the need to distinguish between the actual Ford and "Ford," that cluster of "themes and stylistic properties . . . that the critic constructs in reading the films."[166] Kitses reasons that "underlying the distinction was an awareness of the critique flowing from the theoretical work of Roland Barthes and Michel Foucault suggesting variously that the author is dead, a fiction, a creature of the text rather than a creator of the text."[167] He then reiterates Wollen's proposal of a "half way point" whereby "the author is both determining and determined, a creative agent consciously developing themes and formal strategies, and simultaneously an effect or product of pre-existing linguistic forces in and surrounding the text—as in genre and narrative conventions, industrial practices and social contexts."[168] Kitses argues that "a structural analysis centered on the formal and internal character of the film within the framework of genre begins to address this issue by exploring the meaning-laden conventions available to the film-maker."[169]

One could no doubt raise objections to Kitses' methodology, and he himself concedes that more focus on social and industrial contexts is needed for the study of film and filmmakers. In terms reminiscent of the sorts of criticisms leveled at Sarris's "pantheon," he freely admits that his own study stands "guilty" in places of "critical preference and evaluative bias."[170] At the same time, he concurs with elements of the post-structural insistence that "films do not have fixed meanings, and [that] much depends on the context, ideology and objectives of the viewer."[171] Since we have already been through the strengths and limitations of the various major positions taken over the issue of auteur theory, it would not be fruitful to go into them once more. In any case, the questions that auteurism has raised, and will no doubt continue to raise, will probably never be satisfactorily answered by any single approach. Maybe, in the end, it does not really matter. For, as Richard Maltby states:

> Debates about authorship evaporated in the 1970s, more because post-structuralist criticism bypassed them than because the idea of directorial authorship was recognized as being a historically inaccurate account of Hollywood production. Criticism however continues to need an authority for the text, a figure with whom the critic can engage and argue and whom they can reassess. If the auteur theory is surely dead, so are

the debates over "the death of author" initiated by Roland Barthes and Michel Foucault at the outset of post-structuralism.[172]

Although pointing out that "hardly any academic would now call himself or herself an auteurist," Maltby rightly suggests that film studies has not abandoned the image of the author entirely, in that "the great majority of film criticism continues to be written as if the director could be named the author of the text."[173] We still use the image of the auteur in film theory, but in light of the structuralist and post-structuralist revelations surrounding politics, ideology, the unconscious, language, and intertextuality, their conception is undoubtedly changed. The function of the author is, to our mind, still valid, but as Terry Eagleton points out, a "text does not have a single 'correct' meaning [and, crucially] a writer's texts do not necessarily form a consistent whole."[174] Theoretical structures certainly assist our interpretations of film texts, but they cannot be said to define them. Additionally, the recipient of the text—the reader—"has some active role" in the process of meaning but, as Eagleton also points out, "no reader is innocent or without presuppositions."[175] Instead, much like the author, and very much like the critic, they come to the text imbued with their own "previous social and literary entanglements."[176] Aside from all this, because of the collaborative, industrial imperatives of commercial cinema production, perhaps we have always assumed to a certain degree (some evidently more so than others) that the director is only partially responsible for "his" or "her" films. We have always had the image of the ensemble and perhaps this is all the better for "democratizing" the study of Hollywood films, so to speak.

In this last regard, what we would like to highlight at this stage is that structuralist analyses in the form of genre studies actually offered a means of bringing critical attention to films that did not have the benefit of an "auteur" director. Yet, such was auteur theory's insistence on extolling the work of an elite "pantheon" or select few—presumably in a misguided attempt to "justify" popular cinema's value as art—that this never came to pass. As much as the nature of cinematic authorship has been debated over time, from the writings of the *Cahiers* critics, to Sarris, to Wollen, the particular directors who have served as evidence for authorship—Ford, Hawks, Hitchcock, etc.—have remained unchanged even as approaches and methodologies have been challenged and contested. Indeed, one of the perhaps unintended (and enduring) consequences of Kitses' genre-focused auteur-structuralism, one more specific to our purposes here, is one which he tacitly acknowledges in both editions of *Horizons West*: the creation of an authorial-defined canon of "great Westerns" that scholarship returns to time and again—rather than using the approach to examine the work of *other* filmmakers. It is to the work of one of these other filmmakers that we now return our attention.

RE-FOCUS ON DELMER DAVES

As part of the new ReFocus series on neglected American filmmakers, this collection offers readers a comprehensive introduction to and examination of the films of Delmer Daves. As the first such detailed examination, this book serves as both an introduction to his work and as a critical intervention into histories of classical and post-war American cinema that continue to venerate a limited group of auteur filmmakers.

As opposed to the "celebrity" status of a John Ford or a Howard Hawks, Daves is often regarded as an example of the self-effacing craftsmanship of classical and post-war Hollywood, a competent but conventional studio man who handled assignments professionally, but whose films lacked the kind of distinct perspectives and predilections detected by critics and scholars in the work of contemporaries like John Ford and Howard Hawks. One of the principal aims of this book is to dispel this notion of Daves-as-craftsman, and reveal the filmmaker for who he truly was: a talented artist with a distinct worldview, whose films offered viewers a progressive portrait of human relations and repeatedly avowed the importance of cooperation and community for the advancement of society. As Daves wrote—by hand—on his extensive "character notes" for his 1956 Western *Jubal*, "Each of us must have a REASON FOR LIFE, and no man can free himself of a sense of failure . . . while he refuses to see or create in himself a REASON for life."[177]

In addition to offering reassessments of Daves' role in the development of the Western in the 1950s, the essays that make up this volume address his role as screenwriter of many of his films, as well as his work across multiple genres. Adopting a range of approaches, from aesthetic and theoretical analyses to considerations of industrial context and how film mediates representations of history, the collected essays of this anthology offer a sustained, nuanced case for the importance of Daves in the history of American cinema.

In the first chapter of this collection, Andrew Patrick Nelson offers a re-evaluation of *Broken Arrow*, which is often credited with helping to inaugurate a cycle of "pro-Indian" Westerns featuring more sympathetic and even heroic portrayals of aboriginal characters. As a counterpoint to reflectionist readings of the pro-Indian cycle, Nelson explores an alternative explanation for the character of the famous Chiricahua leader, Cochise. He argues that Cochise is, in fact, a common character in Daves' Westerns: the stoic secondary hero who steadies, strengthens, and defers to the mildly neurotic leading man who, rather than being a natural agent, proceeds based on reason. Re-conceiving Cochise as a "Davesian" character is a small step toward reclaiming Daves' pivotal role of the development of the Western in the 1950s.

John Anthony White discusses a number of Daves' 1950s Westerns, from *Broken Arrow, 3:10 to Yuma,* and *Cowboy* to films he not only directed but for which he also wrote the screenplay: *Drum Beat*, *The Last Wagon*, and *Jubal*. He also considers *White Feather*, a Western that Daves co-wrote but did not direct. White contextualizes his analysis in the political turmoil of the House of Un-American Activities Committee, legislative fears over miscegenation, and the growing Civil Rights movement—all of which affected Hollywood. He considers Daves' auteur credentials in the face of studio constraints and through his screenwriting collaborations. Despite some of the associated screenwriters holding wildly differing political attitudes, White demonstrates that they all worked with Daves to produce films that espoused a signature commonality of the director's own liberal sentiments: sympathy for different races and compassion for the class struggles of the working poor against industrial capitalism. Furthermore, White's discussion of Daves and his work with different screenwriters emphasizes the complexities of the genre's so-called "classical" period.

Józef Jaskulski examines *Broken Arrow* and *Drum Beat*, considering the perspective that the latter perpetuates the very Native American stereotypes that the former attempted to amend. He links these two narratives through a contrastive analysis of their respective Native American protagonists: firstly, the noble, articulate Cochise and the obstinate, inarticulate Modoc, Captain Jack; secondly, the female characters of Sonseeahray and Toby. Though it is easy to discard *Drum Beat* as an essentialist step back in Hollywood's century-long struggle with the so-called "Indian problem," Jaskulski suggests that *Drum Beat* serves as a latent supplement to *Broken Arrow*, which can be read as an important document of Hollywood's conflicted sentiments toward Native Americans in the late-Truman/early-Eisenhower eras—in particular, reflecting a critique of the major about-face in Federal Indian Policy during the 1940s.

Adrian Danks points out that, although it is relatively common to examine the collaborations between various actors and directors working in the 1950s Western—John Wayne/John Ford, James Stewart/Anthony Mann, etc.—the series of three varied films made by Daves and Glenn Ford between 1956 and 1958—*Jubal*, *3:10 to Yuma*, and *Cowboy*—have seldom attracted attention. While at least one of these films, *3:10 to Yuma*, has been championed in terms of Daves' spatially and tonally expressive direction and of Ford's morally ambiguous but effortlessly genial characterization, this extraordinary trio of films has seldom been examined in relation to one another. Danks reads the collaboration between Ford and Daves as symptomatic of the work of both actor and director, and their sympathetic, subtle, "benevolent," and relatively unadorned approach to various subjects and character types. In the process, he helps pinpoint some of the key reasons why both of these important but workaday figures have remained relatively underestimated, and why they need to be brought to the forefront of a more complex understanding of the variations possible in the "classical" Western.

Sue Matheson engages with the common perception that Delmer Daves is a competent but conventional studio man. She argues that his work with the "adult" Western is actually that of an auteur filmmaker. Placing *Cowboy* within the context of the director's 1950s Westerns, she interprets it as his scalding critique of the coming-of-age Western. In what she sees as a radical departure from the "classical" Western, Matheson details how *Cowboy* critically interrogates classical notions of frontier manhood, deconstructs the celebration of individualism, and empties the Western landscape of its usual symbolic significance. In short, she forwards *Cowboy* as an example of genre critique, suggesting that it gleans mythic images and styles from films like Howard Hawks' *Red River* and John Ford's *Stagecoach* only to contrast them with its presentations of a more "authentic" West. Overall, Matheson considers Daves a mythoclast who examined the darker, more selfish side and appetites of the national character.

Joseph Pomp offers an analysis of *Spencer's Mountain*, a film Daves adapted from the novel by Earl Hamner Jr. He observes that Daves' lack of recognition by auteur theorists was due to the fact that he often delved into melodramatic themes in his Westerns, themes out of favor with those who preferred the coarse masculinity of a John Ford or a Raoul Walsh, and who associated the melodrama with a female audience. Pomp suggests that *Spencer's Mountain* provides a key window into Daves' views on American family values, education, and class, arguing that Daves deconstructed melodrama's "classic realist" paradigm by considering a nascent feminist agenda that undermines the patriarchal underpinnings of the source novel. This, argues Pomp, creates an unusual mix—rendering *Spencer's Mountain* different from most other Westerns of the period, but also different from most melodramas. Ultimately, Pomp argues, *Spencer's Mountain* suggests that fierce, heroic individualism has no place in Daves' cinematic universe.

Fran Pheasant-Kelly argues for the status of Delmer Daves as an exemplary filmmaker by offering an in-depth analysis of *3:10 to Yuma*. She considers the film in relation to its aesthetics, critical reception, and cultural significance, illuminating Daves' involvement throughout. Whilst acknowledging the film as one among several significant Westerns Daves directed, her primary focus remains on *3:10 to Yuma* as she tries to explain its cultural significance. Overall, her analysis examines the film's textual aspects, archival material in respect of its critical reception, and its historical contexts. In so doing, it deeply enriches our understanding of the film's significance in relation to the Hollywood Western genre as a whole.

Fernando Gabriel Pagnoni Berns argues that the clash between different cultures is a key element of the films of Delmer Daves. He offers a dialectical account of these cultural clashes, suggesting that Daves dramatizes social progress by conceiving it as the passage from one social stage to another that supplants, in an act of improvement, the preceding one. Through analysis of three of his films from three different decades, representing three different genres—*The Red House*, *The Hanging Tree*, and *Spencer's Mountain*—Berns demonstrates the sustained and consistent authorial concern that Daves felt for the betterment of society. What was required, Daves felt, was a community constantly willing to work to achieve social concord. In this regard, Berns' analysis is one that is contextualized in America's post-war years, representing a period in which hope was held out for a better society.

Andrew Howe provides this collection's sole account of one of Daves' war films. *Task Force* is a biopic of General Billy Mitchell who, during the 1920s, tirelessly advocated for the concept of the aircraft carrier as the future of naval warfare. In his analysis, Howe posits three central figures: Daves as writer-director, Billy Mitchell as historical inspiration, and lead actor Gary Cooper, who plays Mitchell's fictional treatment in the film, Jonathan L. Scott. The chapter situates its analysis of Mitchell within the context of the early Cold War years and of the Hollywood of the time. In the case of the latter, it discusses Hollywood's post-war obsession with the subject of aerial warfare. In contrast to other contributors in this collection, Howe suggests Daves' greater quality was as a writer, rather than a director, and ranks his best scripting efforts—*Task Force* included—alongside those of Alfred Hitchcock and Nicholas Ray.

Finally, Matthew Carter closes this collection by offering an in-depth examination of Delmer Daves' *Jubal*. He contextualizes the film within both the Western genre and Hollywood more generally and argues that, both formally and thematically, it and other prominent Westerns of the time are more closely aligned with film noir than is generally acknowledged to be the case. Applying a psychoanalytically-informed feminist analysis that considers the ideological intent of *Jubal*'s use of the femme fatale, he evaluates its critical-, or, counter-ideological capacity. From such a reading, he argues that the film's narrative focus on repressed sexual desire and on the plight of the main female protagonist provides enough material to justify *Jubal* as constituting a critique of the excesses of patriarchal power.

When reading this collection, and as these chapter outlines suggest, the reader will no doubt make the quite correct observation that most of the contributors take Daves' Westerns as their primary object of study. This genre bias is justified on the grounds that the majority of his most successful and accomplished films were Westerns, or at least films that situated themselves in a frontier setting. If we accept as fact the observation that Delmer Daves is an underappreciated Hollywood filmmaker—not only as a director, but also as a writer and producer—then it is also fair to accept as fact that such an observation is, as noted above, more often than not made in relation to his role as a "creator" of Western genre films.

When discussing questions of influence with respect to the development of the Western, particularly during the 1950s when Daves made the greater majority of his, our recourse is still frequently to the work of the genre's so-called "great directors." Often analyzed are the films and personalities of John Ford, Anthony Mann, and Budd Boetticher. Of the three, Ford has received the most attention, and it is no exaggeration to say that he and his works have dominated scholarly discussion to the extent that as far as many are concerned, John Ford *is* the Western.[178] Many also regard Howard Hawks as a filmmaker of note, although given the nature of his work across multiple genres, his name has not been so inextricably linked to the Western.[179] Several hundred Westerns were made in Hollywood during the 1950s, by many talented filmmakers—directors, writers, producers, and their collaborators: actors, cinematographers, and so on. And yet, as is apparent, scholarship on this period of the genre has been dominated by discussions of the work of a small group of individuals.

Of course, our contention—which is also in keeping with the broader spirit behind the ReFocus series and expressed through the ten chapters that constitute this collection—is that Daves was more than a competent studio man, a *metteur-en-scène*. We suggest that his work does evidence an individual vision in a manner comparable to the signatures and predilections detected in the work of the other Western filmmakers so far mentioned.

As we have already discussed, film scholarship has often defined the Western by the conflict between the opposing forces of wilderness and civilization.[180] Kitses for one believes that this conflict endures in the American collective consciousness due to the mythologization of America's historical nineteenth-century frontier experience—its expansion across the North American continent. It is in the Western that this frontier myth is explored and its structural conflict resolved, with the genre typically providing an imaginary reconciliation embodied by the attributes and actions of the prototypical Western hero. In this conception, the Western hero—who is derived from numerous mythical, historical, and literary sources—is neither fully integrated into civilization nor wholly a part of the wilderness. The hero figuratively straddles the divide between the two sides, embodying the best attributes of each—and is therefore superior to both. The long-standing infatuation with the cowboy in American culture is thus taken as a reflection of society's ambivalence about the human and environmental costs of progress, and a valorization of a mythical figure that embodies the "best of both worlds."[181]

Of course, and as Kitses' study demonstrates, not every filmmaker has engaged with the myth in the same way. "Where Ford and Peckinpah generate an epic historical canvas," he writes, "Mann, Boetticher and Eastwood explore archetypal and existential aspects of the frontier experience."[182] It is worth pointing out, however, that the mythological approach does not define the Western, and as much as some frontier tales are not Westerns, it is equally apparent that some Westerns criticize the myth, or seemingly have very little to do with it. Furthermore, as Steve Neale suggests, the danger of interpreting a genre too broadly, as in the mythological approach to the Western, often "stresses the former's overarching characteristics . . . rather than the latter's local features."[183] Excepting *Broken Arrow* and *Drum Beat*, most of Daves' Westerns seem to embody a non-mythological approach; that is to say, they do not appear to engage with the frontier myth in terms of civilization and wilderness, painting neither "an epic historical canvas" nor exploring mythic archetypes. This might explain, in part, their relative neglect by Western film scholars. And at least two of our contributors alert the reader to the fact that the Western genre does not define Daves. Primarily, Daves was an innovator, and whilst this is especially true of his 1950s Westerns, it can also be argued as being true of his non-Western output. Consider *Dark Passage* (1947), starring Humphrey Bogart and Lauren Bacall, which Daves directed from a screenplay he adapted from the novel by David Goodis.

DARK PASSAGE AND DAVES' GENERAL THESIS

One of the least regarded (certainly least discussed) of the four Bogart-Bacall films of the 1940s, *Dark Passage* would appear to align itself with several of the traits one readily attributes to film noir. The plot involves a convict, Vincent Parry (Humphrey Bogart), who has been wrongly convicted of murdering his wife and has recently escaped from San Quentin prison. Vincent is aided by a mysterious woman, Irene Janson (Lauren Bacall). Along the way there is romance, murder, betrayal, and the presence of a femme fatale, Madge Rapf (Agnes Moorehead), a former lover of Vincent's whom he had spurned and who, it is revealed, had framed him for the murder of his wife. However, the film has several characteristics that both distinguish it from the typical noir style and assist in the task of identifying an authorial "signature" for Daves.

For a start, Bogart's Vincent is not a heroic figure—not in the same mold as Sam Spade in John Huston's *The Maltese Falcon* (1941) or Philip Marlowe in Howard Hawks' *The Big Sleep* (1946). Instead, Daves writes his protagonist as an everyman, thrust into an extreme situation and in way over his head. Then, there is an unusual (for a film noir) faith in teamwork and the altruism of strangers: aside from Irene there is the taxi driver, Sam (Tom D'Andrea), who assists Vincent in his efforts to evade the police by setting him up with an extremely strange but effective off-the-record plastic surgeon. The film ends with Vincent, now in exile in Peru, reuniting with Irene in an unambiguous "happy ending"—typical of Hollywood at the time, perhaps, but less typical of film noir.

Figure I.3 Subjective camera in *Dark Passage*.

Whilst these aspects of *Dark Passage* might align it thematically with the kind of signature style we have described for Daves above, they are not sufficient to mark the film as particularly noteworthy, or even interesting. What does mark it out as potentially noteworthy, and certainly interesting, is its peculiar visual style. Apart from the moment of the surgery scene when Vincent is anaesthetized—which descends into outright surrealism and is, alone, worthy of a Freudian analysis—many of the opening sequences use subjective camera, as the audience adopts Vincent's point of view and experiences events from his perspective, helped at times by Vincent's expository voiceover narration.

Pre-production notes in Daves' personal papers indicate that the director and his team had been experimenting with the practical application of extensive subjective camera techniques with different camera equipment in preparation for *Dark Passage*, including the development of a harness to ameliorate issues of vibration caused by hand-held cameras.[184] Even when the film largely abandons Vincent's direct point of view, long shots and deep shadows keep his face hidden from view. The effect is sometimes jarring, as it denies us the conventional third-person perspective of the protagonist with whom were are supposed to identify, but it serves a purpose. The post-plastic-surgery scene—nearly forty minutes into the film—substitutes more traditional establishing shots and shot-reverse-shots for the erstwhile point-of-view shots, but still leaves Vincent's face bandaged up. The removal of the bandages—over one hour into the film—provides the "great reveal" to accompany a well-known voice. It shows us Vincent's new face—that of Humphrey Bogart.

Such extended use of subjective camera was extremely unusual for its time, but it was not unique. Several months before the release of *Dark Passage*, another film had employed the technique to an even greater extent: actor Robert Montgomery's directorial debut *Lady in the Lake* (1947), adapted from the Raymond Chandler novel with Montgomery playing Philip Marlowe. Montgomery's film was shot *in its entirety* using the subjective camera techniques that Daves employs in *Dark Passage*. The similarity did not go unnoticed by the press, and thus what might have—in fact, what *should have*—been noted as an innovation in cinematic storytelling was described as a copy of an earlier effort by another filmmaker. A typescript note by Daves attached to his original screenplay reveals that, after Daves turned his screenplay in to Warners on 24 May 1946, a conflict emerged between himself and Jack Warner. Daves' note details that, upon reading his script, Warner "was startled to find the CAMERA was to be Bogart through to page 77." The fact that Bogart's head would be covered by bandages for several pages more apparently gave Warner "cold feet," worrying that "the exhibitors would accuse [them] of making a "fake Bogart" film . . . so he called off the film." The note reveals that Daves subsequently had dinner with Montgomery, where he told him his "CAMERA-AS-MAN plan for the film—and all the other things I had figured out." It was at this stage that Montgomery revealed that "he had a script he didn't like—*but* if he made 'lady of the lake' on this pattern, with HIM as the detective-camera, he would make it." Daves gave his consent, and soon afterwards, Montgomery began shooting *Lady in the Lake*. Daves then notes what happened next:

> Ironically, after Bob started shooting in this new fashion—and the papers spoke about the technique he was using as "something new"—Warner RELENTED—said "if Bob will make a WHOLE film using this technique, we should be able to tell the exhibitors they have a precedent!" I wanted NO precedent, but now was stuck with the apparent use of "Bob's technique" for no one would know it was mine.

The director consoled himself with the fact he was getting to use the handheld Aeroflex camera, "the first ever used in a major film feature"—a camera, Daves concludes his annotation by noting, which would be used to enduring acclaim several years later by Jean-Luc Godard et al. in the films of the French New Wave.

If this note is anything to go by, Daves, it would seem, earned an unacknowledged status as an innovator three years before *Broken Arrow* ushered in the pro-Indian Western. Here one could ask with reason why his later melodramas in particular, and charges of creative decline in general, have, as suggested above, overshadowed and obscured Delmer Daves' earlier accomplishments and proved such an impediment to film critics and historians taking him seriously. After all, the work of many celebrated filmmakers has included, or even been defined by, opulent post-war melodramas that were popular with audiences but reviled by critics. Consider Nicholas Ray, Vincente Minnelli, and especially Douglas Sirk. Moreover, the latter years of the careers of many of Daves' contemporaries, including Ford, Hawks, and Mann, are also marked by appraisals of decline.

Daves' wholesale shift to melodrama in the 1960s does distinguish him from these other filmmakers who, as much they may be defined by their association with particular genres, continued to work in multiple genres until the ends of their careers. Even Anthony Mann, who, like Daves, abandoned the Western in the 1960s, explored a range of genre subjects in his final films. Viewed in tandem with Daves' earlier embrace of the Western in the 1950s (after not having scripted a single Western in the 1930s or 40s), it risks giving the impression of a director who went with the flow rather than forged his own path, in contrast to a director like Hawks, who claimed, with justification, that *Rio Bravo* helped reinvigorate the movie Western at a time when its popularity was waning. Moreover, while Daves' melodramas include many of the characteristics critics have detected in the celebrated films of Sirk and Minnelli—intergenerational conflict within the middle-class family, an emphasis on the protagonist's feelings over his or her actions, Freudian tropes and symbolism (e.g. repression, Oedipal conflict, alcoholism), and so on—they appear to lack the elaborate, symbolic critique of post-war American society detected in the "excessive" mise-en-scene of *All that Heaven Allows* (Douglas Sirk, 1955) or *The Cobweb* (Vincente Minnelli, 1955). Daves, by contrast, was judged at his best to be stylish and old-fashioned. As the *New York Times* review of *The Battle of the Villa Fiorita* averred, "[Daves] is just about the only man around who still makes good old-fashioned tearjerkers for the feminine trade, and does it with a sense of humor and a certain flair."[185] Yet those who have identified "progressive" elements in Daves' war films and Westerns have failed to see them in his melodramas. As critic Dave Kehr argues, *A Summer Place* helped to redefine the way sex was portrayed in American cinema at a time when the sexual revolution was influencing popular novels and magazines.

> Daves not only suggested actual physical relations between the lovers, but also went to the scandalous length of condemning the sexual hypocrisy of the older generation while suggesting that teenage sex was natural and healthy (if still likely to lead to consequences) . . . To an America that

needed to believe that "nice girls don't," Daves' melodramas responded, "Nice girls do"—or did at least sometimes, when the appropriate distinctions had been made between lust and love, predatory older males and sincere young men, casual encounters and lifetime commitments.[186]

Of course, scholarship on the melodrama was helped immeasurably by Sirk himself, who proved to be an articulate, charismatic commentator on his own work, confirming that he had, indeed, intended everything that critics had gleaned from his films. Similarly, nearly all of the directors discussed above—Ford, Hawks, Welles, along with others like Alfred Hitchcock—found receptive audiences in young film critics and filmmakers eager to learn at the altar of their heroes. Daves, expectedly, did not.

Another of the reasons given by Tavernier for Daves' neglect is that "he had given few interviews by the time he died in 1977." Unlike the enduring auteurs of American cinema, Daves had no advocate in the critical establishment—no Peter Bogdanovich, Joseph McBride, François Truffaut, or Jon Halliday to record his thoughts and transmit them to the world. Aside from quotations in various newspaper and magazine articles and promotional studio materials, Daves, to our knowledge, gave only one extended interview: to Christopher Wicking in the film journal *Screen* in 1969. In it, Daves speaks energetically of his entry into the industry, his concern for history and authenticity—"I will never subordinate mere fact for dramatic use," he says—and of his penchant for crane shots and how he developed specialized camera-crane equipment. As Hawks often did, he mentions a potential "next film," a restaging of *Broken Arrow* in China as part of his ongoing, personal interest in understanding different cultures and religions. And he even acknowledges the influence of his work, describing *Broken Arrow* as "the father of the so-called adult Western. It was literally the first sound film to show the Indian as an intelligent human being."[187] Yet Daves' recognition of his own influence and innovations is overshadowed by the final lines of the interview, lines that come close to perfectly encapsulating everything we hope to convey about the films of Delmer Daves: "I much prefer the audience not to know that there's a director. That's my general thesis in regard to directing."

It is our earnest wish that this collection will go some way toward rectifying Daves' heretofore neglected status and acknowledging his significance in the history of American cinema.

In short, that you will know it was his.

NOTES

1. Quoted in Christopher Wicking, "Interview with Delmer Daves," *Screen*, 10:4/5 (1969), p. 66.
2. Andrew Sarris, *The American Cinema: Directors and Directions, 1929–1968* (New York: Da Capo, [1968] 1996), pp. 176–7.
3. Jean-Pierre Coursodon, *American Directors, Volume 1* (New York: McGraw-Hill, 1983), p. 81.
4. Delmer Daves Papers, box 65, folder 34, Department of Special Collections, Stanford University Libraries.
5. Delmer Daves, "Nimbus Beyond the Footlights," in Edith R. Mirrielees and Patricia F. Zelver (eds.), *Stanford Mosaic: Reminiscences of the First Seventy Years of Stanford University* (Stanford, CA: Stanford University Press, 1962), p. 130.
6. Bertrand Tavernier, "The Ethical Romantic," *Film Comment*, January–February 2003, <http://www.filmcomment.com/article/delmer-daves-bertrand-tavernier> (last accessed 11 November 2015).
7. Ibid.
8. "Delmer Daves," in John Wakeman (ed.), *World Film Directors Volume 1: 1890–1945* (New York: The H. W. Wilson Co., 1987), p. 199.
9. Coursodon, p. 87.
10. Ibid. p. 88.
11. Interview with Michael Daves. *Icons Radio Hour*, 29 January 2007, <http://www.podcasts.com/icons_radio_hour/episode/michael_daves_son_of_director_delmer_daves>.
12. Material on *Mothers and Daughters* and *Seventeenth Summer* can be found in Delmer Daves Papers, boxes 61, 62, and 63.
13. Quoted in Marilou McCarthy, "Shoot-Out at Jackson Hole," *Chicago Tribune*, 21 July 1963: <http://archives.chicagotribune.com/1963/07/21/page/125/article/shoot-out-at-jackson-hole> (last accessed 11 November 2015).
14. Susan Sontag, "Notes on 'Camp'" [1964], in Susan Sontag, *Against Interpretation and Other Essays* (New York: Picador, 2001), pp. 272–92.
15. Thomas Meehan, "Not Good Taste, Not Bad Taste—It's 'Camp'," *New York Times*, 21 March 1965, p. 30.
16. Ibid. p. 113.
17. Joan Didion, "Movies: 'Youngblood Hawke'/'Joy House'," *Vogue* 155:6 (1 October 1964): p. 110.
18. Bosley Crowther, "The Screen: Corny and Cliché-Ridden: "Susan Slade" Arrives at Two Theaters, Connie Stevens Stars in Soap-Sudsy Drama,' *New York Times*, 11 November 1961, <http://www.nytimes.com/movie/review?res=9903E7DB1E3DE733A25752C1A9679D946091D6CF> (last accessed 11 November 2015).
19. McCarthy, "Shoot-Out at Jackson Hole."
20. Paine Knickerbocker, "'A Summer Place' on the California Coast,' *New York Times*, 5 April 195, p. X7.
21. See Pauline Kael, "Raising Kane," *The New Yorker*, 20 February 1971, pp. 43–89, and 27 February 1971, pp. 44–81.
22. For an account of the production history of *The Magnificent Ambersons*, see Robert L. Carringer, *The Magnificent Ambersons: A Reconstruction* (Los Angeles: California University Press, 1993).
23. Alexandre Astruc, "Du Stylo à la Caméra et de la Caméra au Stylo" ("The Birth of a

New Avant-Garde: The Camera-Pen"), *L'Écran française*, 144 (1948), reprinted in Peter Graham (ed.), *The New Wave* (London: Secker and Warburg, 1968), pp. 17–23.
24. Astruc, "Du Stylo à la Caméra," p. 18.
25. Ibid.
26. François Truffaut, "Une Certaine tendence du cinéma français" ("A Certain Tendency of the French Cinema"), *Cahiers du cinéma*, 31 (1954), reprinted in Bill Nichols (ed.), *Movies and Methods: Volume I* (Berkeley and Los Angeles: University of California Press, 1976), pp. 224–36.
27. Susan Hayward, *French National Cinema* (London: Routledge, 1993), p. 208.
28. Pam Cook and Mieke Bernink (eds.), *The Cinema Book*, 2nd edition (London: British Film Institute, 1999), p. 81.
29. Ibid. In one particular essay published in *Cahiers*, entitled "Les taches du soleil" ("Sun Spots"), Fereydoun Hoveyda describes how the auteur develops and combines aspects of *mise-en-scène* to form a "language":

> The originality of an *auteur* lies not in the subject matter he chooses but in the technique he employs, in the *mise-en-scène*, through which everything is expressed on the screen . . . a film-maker's thought appears through *mise-en-scène*. What counts in a film is the striving toward order, harmony, composition, the placing of the actors and objects, the movements within the frame, the capture of a movement or a look; in short, the intellectual operation which has set to work an initial emotion and a general idea. *Mise-en-scène* is nothing other than the technique which each auteur invents in order to express himself and establish the specificity of his work.

—Hoveyda, "Sun Spots," reprinted in Jim Hillier (ed.), *Cahiers du cinéma 2: 1960 to 1968, Neo-Wave, New Cinema, Reevaluating Hollywood* (Cambridge, MA: Harvard University Press, 1986), pp. 135–46, quote on p. 142.
30. André Bazin, "L'évolution de la langue du cinéma" ("The Evolution of the Language of Cinema") [1950–5], in André Bazin, *What is Cinema? Vol. I*, essays selected and translated by Hugh Gray (Los Angeles: University of California Press, 1967), pp. 23–41.
31. Ibid. pp. 39–40.
32. Cook and Bernink, *The Cinema Book*, p. 240.
33. Ibid. Cook also identifies the "contradictory position" Bazin took, "given his admiration for Hollywood directors such as Orson Welles and Alfred Hitchcock." Bazin's insistence on the "transparency of cinematic language" in promoting "objective reality" was, indeed, contradicted by his lauding directors like Welles and Hitchcock – both filmmakers having come to be understood as manipulators of *mise-en-scène par excellence*. In 1957, Bazin clarified his position with respect to some of his perceived conflicts with the *Cahiers* group as something akin to that of a "family quarrel" that revolves around the idea of the work transcending the director, as one that "concerns the relationship between the work and its creator":

> *Cahiers du Cinema* is thought to practice the *politique des auteurs*. This opinion may perhaps not be justified by the entire output of articles, but it has been true of the majority, especially for the last two years . . . Nevertheless, our readers must have noticed that this critical standpoint – whether implicit or explicit – has not been adopted with equal enthusiasm by all the regular contributors to *Cahiers*, and that there might exist serious differences in our admiration, or rather in the degree of our admiration. And yet the truth is that the most enthusiastic among us nearly always win the day . . . It follows that the strictest adherents of the *politique des auteurs* get

the best of it in the end, for, rightly or wrongly, they always see in their favourite directors the manifestation of the same specific qualities. So it is that Hitchcock, Renoir, Rossellini, Lang, Hawks, or Nicholas Ray, to judge from the pages of *Cahiers*, appear as almost infallible directors who could never make a bad film.

I would like to avoid a misunderstanding from the start. I beg to differ with those of my colleagues who are the most firmly convinced that the *politique des auteurs* is well founded, but this in no way compromises the general policy of the magazine. Whatever our differences of opinion about films or directors, our common likes and dislikes are numerous enough and strong enough to bind us together; and although I do not see the role of the *auteur* in the cinema in the same way as François Truffaut or Eric Rohmer for example, it does not stop me believing to a certain extent in the concept of the *auteur* and very often sharing their opinions, although not always their passionate loves. I fall in with them more reluctantly in the case of their hostile reactions; often they are very harsh with films I find defensible – and I do so precisely because I find that the work transcends the director (they dispute this phenomenon, which they consider to be a critical contradiction). In other words, almost our only difference concerns the relationship between the work and its creator. I have never been sorry that one of my colleagues has stuck up for such and such director, although I have not always agreed about the qualities of the film under examination. Finally, I would like to add that although it seems to me that the *politique des auteurs* has led its supporters to make a number of mistakes, its total results have been fertile enough to justify them in the face of their critics. It is very rare that the arguments drawn upon to attack them do not make me rush to their defence.

So it is within these limits, which, if you like, are those of a family quarrel, that I would like to tackle what seems to me to represent not so much a critical mistranslation as a critical "false nuance of meaning."

—Bazin, "La politique des auteurs" ("On the Politique des Auteurs") [1957], reprinted in Jim Hillier (ed.), *Cahiers du Cinéma: The 1950s: Neo-Realism, Hollywood, New Wave* (Cambridge, MA: Harvard University Press, 1985), pp. 248–59; quote on pp. 248–9.

34. James Monaco, *The New Wave* (New York: Oxford University Press, 1976), p. vii.
35. Robert Lapsley and Michael Westlake, *Film Theory: An Introduction* (Manchester: Manchester University Press, 1988), p. 107.
36. Ibid.
37. Ibid.
38. Ibid.
39. Ed Buscombe, "Ideas of Authorship," *Screen*, 14:3 (1973): 75–86; quote on p. 77.
40. Ibid. p. 83.
41. Ibid. p. 78.
42. Ibid.
43. Bazin, "La politique des auteurs," quoted in Buscombe, "Ideas of Authorship," p. 78.
44. Ibid. (emphasis in original).
45. Ibid. (emphasis in original).
46. Ibid.
47. Ibid.
48. Ibid. pp. 78–9.
49. Andrew Sarris, "Notes on the Auteur Theory in 1962" [1962], reprinted in Leo Braudy and Marshall Cohen, *Film Theory and Criticism*, 5th edn. (New York and Oxford: Oxford University Press, 1999), pp. 515–19.

50. Andrew Sarris, "Toward a Theory of Film History" [1968], reprinted in Nichols (ed.), *Movies and Methods: Volume I*, pp. 237–50.
51. Ibid. pp. 155–71. Sections on John Huston and William Wyler, pp. 156–8 and 167–8, respectively.
52. Ibid. p. 171.
53. As Bazin puts it himself: "Eric Rohmer put his finger on the reason in his reply to a reader in *Cahiers* 63: when opinions differ on an important film, we generally prefer to let the person who likes it most write about it." —Bazin, "La Politique des auteurs," quoted in Hillier, *Cahiers du Cinéma*, p. 248.
54. Despite his fostering of appreciative criticism, it is important to point out that Bazin was himself critical of the idea that auteurs always made "good" films. "So it is that Hitchcock, Renoir, Rossellini, Lang, Hawks, or Nicholas Ray, to judge from the pages of *Cahiers*, appear as almost infallible directors who could never make a bad film."—Bazin, "La politique des auteurs," quoted in Hillier, *Cahiers du Cinéma*, pp. 248–9. See also fn. 8, above. Perhaps more so, Buscombe criticizes the notion of authorial infallibility: "[Jacques] Rivette declares that [Vincente] Minnelli is not a true auteur, merely a talented director at the mercy of his script. With a bad script he makes a bad and uninteresting film. Fritz Lang, on the other hand, can somehow transform even indifferent material into something personal to him (and this, Rivette assumes, makes it interesting)."—Buscombe, "Ideas of Authorship," p. 76.
55. Buscombe, "Ideas of Authorship," p. 78.
56. Ibid. p. 79.
57. Helen Stoddart, "Auteurism and Film Authorship Theory," in Joanne Hollows and Mark Jancovitch (eds.), *Approaches to Popular Film* (Manchester: Manchester University Press, 1995), pp. 37–57; quote on p. 43.
58. Ibid. In all fairness to Sarris, he was not blind to the commercial–industrial processes of Hollywood filmmaking. Stoddart does dilute Buscombe's critique by reminding us that Sarris "widely acknowledges that Hollywood cinema is a commercial enterprise." In this sense, Sarris does consider Buscombe's (and Bazin's) appeal for "historical determinism." However, in accordance with Buscombe, Stoddart is also quick to point out that "the value he places on certain directors none the less depends wholly on the way in which they defiantly transcend this cluttered environment"—Stoddart, "Auteurism," p. 43.
59. Ibid. This recurring notion of transcendence harks back to the writings of Astruc and the *Cahiers* group, specifically their original, romanticized conception of the director as individual artist. To reiterate, despite studio constraints on artistic autonomy and the primacy of market considerations, *Cahiers*, and others who developed their approach— namely Sarris and those writing for the British film journal *Movie* during the 1960s (most notably, Robin Wood)—argued that Hollywood auteurs such as Ford, Hitchcock, and Renoir left their signature on their films in the form of characteristic motifs or striking compositions. Additionally, as Lapsley and Westlake summaries, while auteurist critics "can be applauded for having opened up popular culture to serious study . . . it did so in order to elevate one small section of it to the status of high art" (Lapsley and Westlake, *Film Theory*, p. 107). Furthermore, they suggest that through Sarris, auteurism became "an extraordinary plea for the superiority of American cinema over that of the rest of the world, specifically through the agency of a hierarchy of directors from 'the Pantheon' downwards" (ibid. p. 106).
60. Writes Buscombe: "The *auteur* theory was never, in itself, a theory of the cinema, though its originators did not claim that it was . . . The translation of [the *politique*] into 'the

auteur theory' appears to be the responsibility of Andrew Sarris. In an essay entitled 'Notes on the Auteur Theory in 1962' he remarked, 'Henceforth, I will abbreviate "*la politique des auteurs*" as the auteur theory to avoid confusion.' Confusion was exactly what followed when the newly christened 'theory' was regarded by many of its supporters and opponents alike as a total explanation of the cinema." Buscombe, "Ideas of Authorship," p. 75.

61. Ibid.
62. Ibid. p. 76.
63. Ibid. p. 75.
64. Lapsley and Westlake, *Film Theory*, p. 106.
65. Ibid.
66. Stoddart, "Auteurism," p. 44.
67. Richard DeGeorge and Fernande DeGeorge (eds.), *The Structuralists from Marx to Lévi-Strauss* (New York: Anchor Books, 1972), p. xi.
68. Ibid. p. xii.
69. Ibid.
70. Ibid.
71. Ibid.
72. Claude Lévi-Strauss, *The Raw and the Cooked*, trans. John and Doreen Weightman (London: Jonathan Cape, 1970), p. 12. Lévi-Strauss discussed in Lapsley and Westlake, *Film Theory*, p. 109, and Cook and Bernink, *The Cinema Book*, pp. 328–30.
73. Lévi-Strauss, *The Raw and the Cooked*, p. 12.
74. Lapsley and Westlake, *Film Theory*, p. 108.
75. Ibid. p. 109.
76. Peter Wollen, *Signs and Meaning in the Cinema* [1969], 3rd edition (Bloomington: Indiana University Press, 1972).
77. Vladimir Propp, *Morphology of the Folktale* [1928], trans. Laurence Scott [1968] (Austin: University of Texas Press, 2005).
78. Peter Wollen, "The Auteur Theory," in Wollen, *Signs and Meaning*, pp. 91–3.
79. Ibid., p. 94.
80. Ibid., p. 93.
81. Ibid.
82. Ibid.
83. Ibid.
84. Ibid., p. 96.
85. Ibid.
86. This is itself derived from the culture/nature binary, which Lévi-Strauss argued occurs in the interaction between human subjects and the environment.
87. Lapsley and Westlake, *Film Theory*, p. 110.
88. Wollen, "The Auteur Theory," pp. 94–5. Stoddart, "Auteurism," p. 46.
89. Stoddart, "Auteurism," p. 46.
90. Wollen, "The Auteur Theory," p. 96.
91. Ibid. p. 104.
92. Ibid.
93. Ibid. (emphasis in original).
94. Ibid. pp. 113, 115.
95. Ibid. pp. 113–15.
96. Stoddart, "Auteurism," p. 47.
97. Wollen, "The Auteur Theory," p. 104.

98. Ibid. p. 104.
99. Ibid. p. 102.
100. Wollen, "Conclusion," in Wollen, *Signs and Meaning*, p. 167.
101. Ibid.
102. Ibid.
103. Ibid.
104. Ibid.
105. Ibid.
106. Ibid. pp. 167–8.
107. Ibid. p. 168.
108. Ibid.
109. Brian Henderson, "Critique of Cine-Structuralism Part 1," *Film Quarterly*, 27:1 (1973): 25–34, reprinted in John Coughie (ed.), *Theories of Authorship* (London: Routledge, 1981), pp. 166–83; quote on p. 176.
110. Ibid.
111. Ibid. p. 171.
112. Ibid. pp. 176–7.
113. Ibid. p. 177.
114. Ibid.
115. Lévi-Strauss, *The Raw and the Cooked*, p. 12. Discussed in Cook and Bernink, *The Cinema Book*, p. 328.
116. Henderson, "Critique," p. 177.
117. Stoddart, "Auteurism," p. 47.
118. Buscombe, "Ideas of Authorship," p. 83.
119. Ibid.
120. Ibid.
121. Stoddart, "Auteurism," p. 47.
122. Ibid. p. 83.
123. Quoted in Stephen Heath, "Comment on 'The Idea of Authorship'," *Screen*, 14:3 (1973): 86–91; quote on p. 89.
124. Buscombe, "Ideas of Authorship," p. 84.
125. Ibid.
126. Ibid.
127. Ibid., p. 85.
128. Ibid.
129. Lapsley and Westlake, *Film Theory*, p. 111.
130. Ibid.
131. Stoddart, "Auteurism," p. 48.
132. Roland Barthes, "La mort de l'auteur" ("The Death of the Author") [1967], reprinted in Roland Barthes, *Image-Music-Text*, essays selected and translated by Stephen Heath (London: Fontana, 1977), pp. 142–8.
133. Ibid. p. 143.
134. Ibid. p. 147.
135. Ibid. p. 146.
136. Ibid. This notion was perhaps best summed up by the celebrated American novelist, Cormac McCarthy. In an interview with Richard B. Woodward, McCarthy said that "the ugly fact is that books are made out of other books. The novel depends for its life on the novels that have been written"—R. B. Woodward, "Cormac McCarthy's Venomous Fiction," *New York Times Magazine*, 19 April 1992, p. 36.

137. Barthes, "La mort de l'auteur," p. 147.
138. Ibid. p. 148 (emphasis added).
139. Ibid.
140. Ibid. p. 143.
141. Ibid. Barthes' declaration of the death of the author in full and in its original context is as follows:

> Thus is revealed the total existence of writing: a text is made of multiple writings, drawn from many cultures and entering into mutual relations of dialogue, parody, contestation, but there is one place where this multiplicity is focused and that place is the reader, not, as was hitherto said, the author. The reader is the space on which all the quotations that make up a writing are inscribed without any of them being lost; a text's unity lies not in its origin but in its destination. Yet this destination cannot any longer be personal: the reader is without history, biography, psychology; he is simply that someone who holds together in a single field all the traces by which the written text is constituted. Which is why it is derisory to condemn the new writing in the name of a humanism hypocritically turned champion of the reader's rights. Classic criticism has never paid any attention to the reader; for it, the writer is the only person in literature. We are now beginning to let ourselves be fooled no longer by the arrogant antiphrastical recriminations of good society in favour of the very thing it sets aside, ignores, smothers, or destroys; we know that to give writing its future, it is necessary to overthrow the myth: the birth of the reader must be at the cost of the death of the Author.

—Barthes, "La mort de l'auteur," p. 148.

142. Ferdinand de Saussure, *Course in General Linguistics* [1916], trans. Roy Harris (New York: Columbia University Press, 2013). See also sections on Saussure in, Peter Barry, *Beginning Theory: An Introduction to Literary and Cultural Theory* (Manchester: Manchester University Press, 1995), pp. 156–70; Terry Eagleton, *Literary Theory: An Introduction* (Oxford: Blackwell, 1983), pp. 91–127; Lapsley and Westlake, *Film Theory*, pp. 32–67.
143. Buscombe, "Ideas of Authorship," p. 84. See also Stephen Heath, "The Idea of Authorship," *Screen* 14:3 (1973): 86–91.
144. Cook and Bernink, *The Cinema Book*, p. 301. According to Cook and Bernink, "the idea of 'text' as constituted by the interaction of different historically specific codes" was taken up by the editors of *Cahiers* in their now famous "collectively authored" 1972 article on Ford's film *Young Mr. Lincoln* (1939). After 1968, the journal sought to incorporate post-structuralist theories by "reformulat[ing] its position on authorship and cinema" and developed a deconstructive methodology "which would approach cinema as an ideological system." *Cahiers* suggested that, in certain films, the dominant ideological position assumed often threatened to collapse under the weight of "internal contradictions." Essentially *Cahiers* focused not on the relationships between complete structures, but "attempted to uncover cracks in the system of the film, disjunctures between the different codes which made up the text." However, "while attempting to displace the author (Ford) as intentional source of the film, the *Cahiers* analysis ends up by confirming the Fordian authorial system [throughout] and by implication the continuing relevance of *auteur* analysis in the study of American cinema." As Lapsley and Westlake have it, the spirit behind the idea was that "by applying a process of 'active reading' the text could be made to yield up what was left unsaid." There is, however, "an evident tension between two trends. On the one hand the film is discussed in traditional

auteurist terms, with its ideological project attributed to Ford and repeated references to the Fordian oeuvre"—on the other hand, and citing Ben Brewster, "the 'active reading' does 'not hesitate to force the text, even to rewrite it, insofar as the film only constitutes itself as a text by integration of the reader's knowledge.'" See Cook and Bernink, *The Cinema Book*, pp. 301–2; Lapsley and Westlake, *Film Theory*, pp. 120–3; and Ben Brewster, "Notes on the text '*Young Mr. Lincoln*' by the editors of *Cahiers du Cinéma*," *Screen*, 14:3 (1972): 29–43.

145. Cook and Bernink, *The Cinema Book*, p. 301.
146. Ibid.
147. Michel Foucault, "What is an Author?," trans. Donald F. Bouchard, *Screen*, 20:1 (1979): 13–29. Foucault discussed in Lapsley and Westlake, *Film Theory*, pp. 125–6.
148. Lapsley and Westlake, *Film Theory*, p. 126.
149. Ibid. p. 124. See also Heath, "Comment on 'The Idea of Authorship'," pp. 86–91.
150. Ibid.
151. Ibid.
152. Richard Slotkin, *Gunfighter Nation: The Myth of the Frontier in Twentieth-Century America* (Norman: University of Oklahoma Press, 1992).
153. Ibid. p. 665, fn. 12.
154. Ibid.
155. Ibid.
156. Ibid.
157. Jim Kitses, *Horizons West: Anthony Mann, Budd Boetticher, Sam Peckinpah; Studies of Authorship in the Western* (London: British Film Institute, 1969).
158. Kitses, *Horizons West* (1969), p. 60.
159. Jim Kitses, *Horizons West: Directing the Western from John Ford to Clint Eastwood* (London: British Film Institute, 2004), pp. 12–3.
160. Kitses, *Horizons West* (1969), p. 26.
161. Kitses, *Horizons West* (2004), p. 23, fn. 8.
162. Ibid., p. 14.
163. Ibid., p. 10.
164. Ibid. To reiterate briefly, and as summarized by Sam Rohdie, the theory which makes auteurs "scared . . . has no concepts for the social or the collective, or the national. The primary act of *auteur* criticism is one of dissociation—the *auteur* out of time and history and society is also freed from any productive process." (Sam Rohdie, "Education and Criticism," *Screen*, 12:1 (1971): 9–13; quote on p. 10.
165. Kitses, *Horizons West* (2004), p. 10.
166. Ibid. p. 14.
167. Ibid.
168. Ibid.
169. Ibid. pp. 14–5.
170. Ibid. p. 15.
171. Ibid. p. 22.
172. Richard Maltby, *Hollywood Cinema* [1995] (London: Wiley Blackwell, 2003), p. 506.
173. Ibid.
174. Eagleton, *Literary Theory*, pp. 75, 89.
175. Ibid. p. 89.
176. Ibid.
177. Delmer Daves Papers, box 41, folder 3.
178. Ford's significance in relation to the Western is by no means restricted to the 1950s and

such celebrated films as *Wagon Master* (1950), *Rio Grande* (1950), and *The Searchers* (1956). He also made Westerns during the silent era, most notably *The Iron Horse* (1924). Toward the end of the 1930s, he directed the much-lauded *Stagecoach* (1939), which among other things is often credited with elevating the Western from its erstwhile "B" movie status into a major, lucrative Hollywood genre. In the immediate post-war years, he made two classics of the genre, *My Darling Clementine* (1946) and *Fort Apache* (1948). Ford rounded off his prolific career in the 1960s, with critical and introspective works like *Sergeant Rutledge* (1960), *The Man Who Shot Liberty Valance* (1962), and *Cheyenne Autumn* (1964).

179. Hawks' importance to the genre's development through the 1950s is generally "confirmed," as it were, by two well-crafted films, *Red River* (1948) and *Rio Bravo* (1959)—accepting of course that, given it was released in 1948, *Red River* is not strictly speaking a 1950s Western. However, it does foreshadow many of the themes that would feature in the genre during that decade.
180. Kitses, *Horizons West* (2004), pp. 12–13.
181. Various critics have interrogated the negative consequences of the Western's role in shaping popular historical memory in the United States through recourse to the frontier myth. To name but two, there is Slotkin's *Gunfighter Nation* (mentioned above) and, more recently, Robert B. Pippin's *Hollywood Westerns and American Myth: The Importance of Howard Hawks and John Ford for Political Philosophy* (New Haven, CT: Yale University Press, 2010).
182. Kitses, *Horizons West* (2004), p. 14.
183. Steve Neale, *Genre and Hollywood* (London: Routledge, 2000), p. 136.
184. Delmer Daves Papers, box 23, folders 3 and 4.
185. Eugene Archer, "'Battle of the Villa Fiorita' Begins Engagement at Palace,' *New York Times*, 27 May 1965, p. 28.
186. Dave Kehr, "New DVDs: Romance Classics," *New York Times*, 26 January 2009, <http://www.nytimes.com/2009/01/27/movies/homevideo/27dvds.html> (last accessed 11 November 2015).
187. Wicking, "Interview," p. 63.

CHAPTER 1

Don't Be Too Quick to Dismiss Them: Authorship and the Westerns of Delmer Daves

Andrew Patrick Nelson

Delmer Daves' 1950 film *Broken Arrow* is credited in histories of the Western genre with inaugurating a cycle of "pro-Indian" (or "liberal" or "adult") Westerns that began in the early 1950s and lasted until the early 1960s.[1] Based on true events, the film follows former Army Scout Tom Jeffords (played by James Stewart) as he is initiated into the Chiricahua Apache tribe led by the respected chief Cochise (Jeff Chandler). Overcoming bad actors on both sides of the racial divide and the murder of his Apache wife, Sonseeahray (Debra Paget), Jeffords ultimately brokers a peace treaty between the Apache and the U.S. Government.

Though *Broken Arrow* was not the first post-war Western to take a compassionate view of American Indians—consider John Ford's *Fort Apache* from 1948 and *She Wore a Yellow Ribbon* from 1949—the film initiated a wave of Indian-themed films in the 1950s and 60s, the majority of which, as Edward Buscombe has observed, offer a positive interpretation of Indian history and culture (within, of course, the limits of generic constraints).[2] Like most Westerns of the period, *Broken Arrow* takes liberties with its representation of people and events from American history. This includes the portrayal of its Indian protagonist, Cochise, who is, among other things, played by a Caucasian actor—in accordance with Hollywood's standard casting practices.[3]

Broken Arrow and the films that followed it, including titles like *Apache* (Robert Aldrich, 1954), *Broken Lance* (Edward Dmytryk, 1954), *White Feather* (Robert D. Webb, 1955), *Run of the Arrow* (Samuel Fuller, 1957), *Flaming Star* (Don Siegel, 1960), and *Cheyenne Autumn* (John Ford, 1964), featured sympathetic, and at times heroic, portrayals of Indian characters as well as attempts to portray Indian customs with a greater degree of authenticity and detail. In *Broken Arrow* the Apache are depicted, accurately, as residing in wikiups rather than in tipis. The narrative includes the depiction of Apache customs, including the girls' puberty rite and the social dance, which is performed by members of the White Mountain Apache Tribe of Arizona's Fort Apache Reservation. The Apache characters also speak in standard (if formal) English, a significant change from Indians speaking in broken, pidgin English, as was conventional at the time.

Reviews of the picture generally praised its efforts to offer a more balanced and complete depiction of American Indians than Hollywood's previous portrayals, though some found these new depictions overly idealistic, replacing one set of stereotypes with another. Wrote Bosley Crowther in the *New York Times*, "[I]n trying to disabuse the public of a traditional stereotype, the producers have here portrayed the Indian in an equally false, romantic white ideal. Why couldn't the Indians in this picture be as natural, inelegant and unkempt as Mr. Stewart and the other white men?"[4] This is a fair question that raises a host of issues around Western fiction's—and, indeed, Western history's—often-idealized representation of America's past. Addressing the ideological shortcomings of these stereotypes has been the principal focus of subsequent criticism and debate about the pro-Indian Western, yet, paradoxically, such criticism has at times led readers *away from* the Indian characters of the films.

In one vein of criticism the focus falls on the story's white protagonist, who learns the ways of the natives and comes to straddle the divide between their society and his own: the figure influentially termed the "man who knows Indians" by cultural historian Richard Slotkin. Citing James Fenimore Cooper's character Hawkeye as the model for future versions of this frontier hero, Slotkin describes the man who knows Indians as standing "between the opposed worlds of savagery and civilization, acting sometimes as a mediator or interpreter between races and cultures but more often as civilization's most effective instrument against savagery—a man who knows how to think and fight like an Indian, to turn their methods against them."[5] The longevity, and hierarchical implications, of this figure in American culture, and especially in Hollywood Westerns, is for Slotkin important evidence of the enduring influence of a racialist theory of white hegemony in twentieth-century American popular culture.

By contrast, a second vein of criticism treats these films' Indian characters not historically but allegorically. Here it is claimed that Indians in the Western function as an empty signifier for some other group or concern. As film historian Richard Maltby observes, "Critical interpretation of the postwar Western has made much of the idea that the genre and its signs, and the sign of the Indian in particular, are highly mutable and open for transfer to a variety of other contexts."[6] Thus, American Indians in the Western have been cast as advocates for ecology in the 1990s; analogs for Vietnamese victims of American military aggression in the 1970s; and, in the case of the pro-Indian Western of the 1950s and 60s, surrogates for African Americans. As Brian Henderson has influentially argued of John Ford's *The Searchers* (1956)—in which a Confederate veteran searches across the American West for his niece, who has been kidnapped by Comanche Indians and made the wife of their chief—these films offered a "mythical displacement of present day white–black relations onto historical white–red relations," motivated by contemporary struggles over black civil rights and fears about miscegenation, particularly in the wake of the Supreme Court's May 1954 ruling against segregation in public schools in the case of *Brown v. Board of Education*.[7]

Against this allegorical interpretation, others have argued that pro-Indian Westerns like *Broken Arrow* advocated for the continued engagement of white authorities in shepherding American Indians toward eventual integration, a position that was relevant in the context of the 1950s when pressure was mounting on the government to remove itself from Indian affairs entirely.[8] Cochise in *Broken Arrow* thus advocates the cause of integration. As he tells a group of Apache leaders assembled to debate the signing of a peace treaty:

> Now I say this. The Americans keep cattle but they are not soft or weak. Why should not the Apache be able to learn new ways? It is not easy to change but sometimes it is required. The Americans are growing stronger, while we are growing weaker. If a big wind comes a tree must bend or be lifted out by its roots. I will make a test of it for three moons. I break the arrow! I will try the way of peace.

In his analysis, Buscombe acknowledges that films like *Broken Arrow* are the product of a limited 1950s mindset that saw only two options available to Indians: either adapt or perish, because history is on the side of the white race. Using this as grounds for criticism, however, fails to acknowledge the contextual and social factors shaping film production, including a typical inability at the time to imagine a third-way solution to the "Indian problem."[9]

Regardless of whether or not we agree that these films did, in fact, reflect contemporary concerns about American Indians, or instead used Indians as "stand-ins" for other ethnic groups, there is little question about their influence in shaping popular perceptions of America's native peoples. *Broken Arrow*'s portrayal of Cochise, in particular, established a template for the "good" Indian character in the following decades: stoic, wise, and a skilled fighter—in many ways the equal of the white hero—yet ultimately willing to acknowledge that his people must adapt in the face of historical change, or risk extinction.

When discussing questions of influence with respect to the development of the Western genre, particularly over the course of the 1950s, our recourse is frequently to the work of the genre's great directors like John Ford, Anthony

Figure 1.1 Cochise breaks the arrow in *Broken Arrow*.

Mann, and Budd Boetticher. Hundreds of Western features were made during the decade—861, according to one source—but histories of the genre are dominated by discussions of the work of a few men.[10] As detailed in the introduction to this book, a key, influential work here is Jim Kitses' 1969 monograph *Horizons West*, in which he observed that a fundamental "structure" underlay the Western: a dynamic opposition between wilderness and civilization.

Kitses was not the only scholar at around this time to articulate similar ideas about the appeal of the Western genre. John Cawelti, Peter Wollen, and Will Wright also invoke the wilderness/civilization binary in their work—a reflection of the growing influence of structuralist analysis at this point in time. Among other things, structuralism provided a means of justifying the study of popular literature and culture by treating its artifacts as akin to the myths of earlier societies, which, as anthropologist Claude Lévi-Strauss influentially argued in the 1950s, provided imaginary resolutions to real questions, problems and contradictions. In the case of the Western, the conflict between civilization and wilderness is resolved in the American imaginary by the mythical frontier hero who embodies the best attributes of each side. What distinguished Kitses' study, however, was his linking of structural analysis with auteurism, an approach that privileges the influence of a film's director and foregrounds stylistic and thematic continuities observed across his body of work.

The claim that films—or at least some films—are art because they are the product of an artist or "author" may today seem simple, even axiomatic, but the significance of this premise in legitimizing the study of cinema in the 1950s cannot be overstated. Nearly two decades later, structuralist analysis in the form of genre study offered a means of bringing critical attention to films that did not have the benefit of an "auteur" director—but this didn't really happen. Instead, the study of film genres largely emphasized and valorized the work of particular filmmakers already established to be auteurs. One of the unintended consequences of Kitses' auteur-structuralism, which he tacitly acknowledges in the introduction to the revised edition of *Horizons West*, has been the creation of an authorially-defined canon of "great Westerns" to which scholarship returns time and again, as opposed to using the approach to examine the work of *other* filmmakers.

There are, of course, a few notable exceptions: influential and enduring films like *High Noon* (Fred Zinnemann, 1952) and *Shane* (George Stevens, 1953), made by directors whose involvement with the Western was limited to one or two films. Where, then, in this configuration might we situate *Broken Arrow*, a successful picture that inaugurated one of the most significant trends in Western moviemaking in the 1950s and early 60s and, along with it, established an Indian stereotype that persists to this day in popular culture?

Broken Arrow is nearly always discussed in a manner comparable to *High Noon* and *Shane*, its importance established and asserted on the basis of its influence in the development of the genre, or how it typified the Western's reflection of socially or psychically significant transformations in American society. Unlike *High Noon* or *Shane*, however, *Broken Arrow* was directed by a man, Delmer Daves, who would go on to direct a remarkable series of Westerns over the course of the 1950s, equaling or even exceeding the output of the filmmakers named above.

Following *Broken Arrow*, Daves wrote and directed *Drum Beat* (1954), about an Indian fighter enlisted by the government to help make peace between white settlers and a band of renegade Modoc Indians on the California–Oregon border; he wrote the screenplay for *White Feather* (Robert D. Webb, 1955), about the resettlement of the Cheyenne in Wyoming; and he co-wrote and directed *The Last Wagon* (1956), in which the survivors of an attack by Apaches on a wagon train must rely on a wanted murdered and Indian sympathizer, and *Jubal* (1956), a Western reworking of *Othello* about a loyal cowhand who must fend off the advances of the unfaithful wife of his boss. Daves then directed *3:10 to Yuma* (1957), about a poor rancher who agrees to help escort a dangerous outlaw to the train that will take him to prison; *Cowboy* (1958), about a tenderfoot who joins a cattle drive and learns countless hard lessons at the hands of an experienced cowman; *The Badlanders* (1958), a Western version of *The Asphalt Jungle* about a pair of ex-convicts who plan a gold robbery in

Mexico; and finally *The Hanging Tree* (1959), about a reclusive frontier physician's complicated relationships with two of his patients, a young male thief and a crippled female victim of a stagecoach holdup.[11]

It is on account of these films, and in particular *Broken Arrow* and *3:10 to Yuma*, that Daves is remembered today principally as a maker of Westerns, even if he was much more than that. As William R. Meyer writes in *Warner Brothers Directors*, "Daves participated in the making of war films, comedies, Westerns, swashbucklers, crime films, soap operas, musicals—every genre of film that Hollywood ever produced—but it is as a director of Westerns that his place in the pages of film history has been justified."[12] That may be so, but it must be said that the *number* of pages dedicated to Daves as a Western filmmaker has been small.

A survey of the limited literature on Daves' Westerns suggests a key reason for this: their variety. Jean-Pierre Coursodon states that Daves' Westerns

> are characterized by an amazing, almost disconcerting diversity. Whereas Anthony Mann and Budd Boetticher tended to return to the same thematic material over and over again and had definite preferences for specific types of locations, plots, and protagonists, Daves seemed intent upon investigating a broad range of topics and themes within the scope of the genre.[13]

This variety, observes Michael Walker, has led many to claim that Daves' Westerns "are difficult to talk about collectively."[14] Consistency across a number of films is clearly helpful in positing the presence of singular creative force behind those works, as has been the case with Mann and Boetticher, and Daves' Westerns certainly never attain the topical or thematic consistency of Mann's five collaborations with James Stewart, or of Boetticher's seven films with Randolph Scott. We might observe, though, how some films by Mann and Boetticher that fail to conform to established authorial parameters—say, Mann's *The Last Frontier* (1955) and *Cimarron* (1960), or the six Westerns Boetticher made prior to *Seven Men from Now* (1956), and his final Western, *A Time for Dying* (1969)—are not those that come readily to mind when discussing the Westerns of either filmmaker.[15]

In "The Westerns of Delmer Daves," the first comprehensive study of the subject, Walker offers a rejoinder to claims about the lack of authorial vision in Daves' Westerns, arguing that they "are distinguished by highly personal themes and preoccupations which mark him, in this genre at least, as a distinctive *auteur*."[16] Yet the recurring themes and preoccupations detected by Walker manifest less across the totality of Daves' Western oeuvre than within two groupings of his films: "those in which Indians play a significant role" and "those in which they do not." Walker further divides his second group in two: *3:10 to Yuma* and *Jubal* focus "on the relationship between two men, one of whom . . . is the leader of an all-male group, the other is struggling to perform a task of which he has no experience," while *Jubal* and *The Hanging Tree* "show the hero entering an already established community . . . and being rather uneasily integrated." *The Badlanders*, a fifth "non-Indian" film, is judged "the outsider," "the least marked by Daves's authorship."[17] In an otherwise insightful and nuanced examination of Daves' Westerns, these divisions, subdivisions, and qualifications ultimately work against establishing the unity of theme and purpose that characterizes auteurist analyses.

To be sure, simply making a lot of Westerns does not an auteur make. Explaining his choice not to include "prolific filmmakers . . . of prominent Westerns" like Daves or John Sturges in his Western pantheon, Kitses writes,

> Such a decision reflects the belief that not all the work of those directors who favored the genre is equally distinctive and distinguished. My goal has not been to provide a comprehensive account of the genre's veterans, but to explore how the genre has functioned as a creative canvas for those directors who achieved a body of work at the highest levels.[18]

But could the sociocultural significance of a film like *Broken Arrow* in fact be an indication of broader tendencies evident in Daves' filmmaking? That is, could it reflect Daves' authorial vision in a manner comparable to the signatures and predilections detected in the work of other Western filmmakers like Ford, Mann, and Boetticher?

As Walker's classification of Daves' Westerns indicates, the director's films do evidence an interest in American Indian subject matter. If we include the 1955 film *White Feather*, for which, again, Daves wrote the screenplay, then four of his Westerns are about conflicts between Indians and white settlers on the American frontier. Daves, it is often noted, spent three months living among the Hopi and Navajo in 1926 following his graduation from Stanford University, which may have later influenced his decision to make Indian-themed Westerns. Yet none of Daves' writing or directing efforts in the 1930s and 1940s was a Western. Materials in Daves' personal papers held at Stanford University do reveal that he began developing *Drum Beat* in the late 1930s: these include a synopsis dated 20 March 1939, a completed screenplay titled *Modoc Ambush*, and a revised version titled *Warpath*. Neither screenplay is dated, but information in the foreword to "Modoc Ambush" indicates it was completed around 1940—after the start of the Second World War, but before America's entry into the conflict.[19] The early development of what would become *Drum Beat* thus shows that Daves' interest in dramatizing historical conflicts between Indians and settlers predates *Broken Arrow* by over a decade. Yet nothing in Daves' materials suggests there was any further movement on the picture until after the completion of *Broken Arrow*.²⁰ Also, the initial appearance of the project in 1939 coincided with the dramatic resurgence of the Hollywood "A-Western," with the releases of *Stagecoach* (John Ford, 1939), *Jesse James* (Henry King, 1939), *Dodge City* (Michael Curtiz, 1939), *Union Pacific* (Cecil B. DeMille, 1939), and *Destry Rides Again* (George Marshall, 1939). We may thus infer that a commercial imperative, in addition to personal interest, played some role in the initial development of the film. Moreover, in the foreword to "Warpath," Daves pitches the film based on its resonance with contemporary geopolitics rather than its depiction of Native American culture, writing:

> [T]his story is a true one, the problem a real one, and, because I have spent so many months of effort toward the end of making "WARPATH" an honest and dramatic screen play, I hope the parallel to current events will not be mis-construed as betraying dramatic license . . . there was no need to change history. It happened this way. And—I think the reader will agree—it casts its shadow far ahead! Captain Jack, Modoc Chief, lived . . . not in 1940 . . . but 70 years ago!²¹

It also bears noting that none of Daves' Westerns made after *Broken Arrow* feature an Indian protagonist like Cochise. Indeed, the later films in some ways appear to offer *regressive* portrayals of Native American characters. The most important Indian character in these films, in terms of influencing the film's plot, is Modoc Chief "Captain" Jack in *Drum Beat* (played by Charles Bronson), but he typifies the "bad Indian" archetype of the genre: hostile, deceitful, eager for war, and predictably defeated by the white hero in the film's climax and sentenced to hang. *The Last Wagon* features Apaches and Comanche as a looming if generally peripheral threat to the film's imperiled heroes, and also engages with issues of prejudice and racism. Yet, as Coursodon observes, the film's "by-then familiar indictment" of these evils "curiously coexists with a thoroughly conventional presentation of the Indians . . . as bloodthirsty savages with no other apparent purpose than the killing of white men, women, and children."²²

Walker explains the "ideological difference" in the presentation of Indians between *Broken Arrow* and *Drum Beat* as a reflection of shifting political currents. He writes,

> In 1950, the political climate was more amenable to a liberal film like *Broken Arrow*. By 1954, after four years of Joseph McCarthy's attacks on the Left, even liberalism could seem politically suspect. *Drum Beat*, with its depiction of the failure of liberalism (the peace council) and the necessity for direct military action against the Indian (read communist) enemy, registers the shift only too clearly.

John H. Lenihan also reads *Drum Beat* in light of the Cold War, as offering "a historical account to substantiate the naiveté of compromise with a treacherous aggressor."[23] But, in a footnote, Lenihan relates that in an interview he conducted with Daves in 1973 the director said he wanted to offer the settlers' side of the frontier narrative after having presented the Indian perspective in *Broken Arrow*. And whereas the director may have originally intended his dramatization of the Modoc War to have some resonance with the events of the Second World War, with respect to the completed film Daves "had no recollection of intending any analogy with contemporary problems. Only in retrospect did Daves acknowledge the likelihood of unconsciously fashioning *Drum Beat*."[24]

Daves' explanation to Lenihan of his intention with *Drum Beat* is in keeping with other comments the director made about his Westerns, which he described as "gradually making a whole composite of the west," moving from the initial conflict between Indians and settlers, to films that dealt with the later challenges in the settled west, to, finally, *Spencer's Mountain* (1963), about "what happened to the sons of the pioneers."[25] This does not dismiss so much as qualify Daves' treatment of Native Americans. *Broken Arrow* is an important film for the way it helped to transform how American Indians are represented in cinema. In *Drum Beat*, most of the other Indian characters oppose the renegade Captain Jack's violent actions. Even *The Last Wagon*, as Walker argues, adopts and endorses the Indian perspective, albeit as represented by Comanche Todd (Richard Widmark), a "man who knows Indians" figure who has lived most of his life among the Comanche and who is, at the start of the film, a prisoner on his way to be tried for the murder of three white men—men who, we learn at the end of the movie, raped and murdered Todd's Indian wife and killed his two young sons. In contrast to the celebrated Westerns of Mann and Boetticher, in which the "moral change" occurs within the hero (often thanks to the influence of a good woman), here the opposite is true. Writes Walker, "It is the terms under which the changes occur that makes the film so remarkable for its time. Whether dealing with the killing of enemies, the learning of survival skills, the seduction of the heroine or a critique of racism, it is the way of the Indian that is consistently validated."[26] Yet if Daves' treatment of Indians was, on balance, sympathetic and at times nuanced, it also reflects the director's interest in examining different points of view, even within similarly-themed films, and in dramatizing a range of experiences and events that occurred during the settlement of America's western frontier. Had Indian characters like Cochise appeared throughout Daves' other Westerns, or had those films offered as patently "liberal" positions as *Broken Arrow* on Native American history and culture, there is no doubt that, somewhere along the line, Daves would have been posited as the auteur behind these works, rather than simply the filmmaker who happened to direct a socially significant Western. But while none of Daves' other Westerns offer a variation on Cochise, what *Broken Arrow* does share in common with almost all of Daves' other Westerns—all except *Drum Beat*—is the central dynamic between two protagonists of seemingly incompatible backgrounds and points of view.

In advance of the advent of the "professional Western" of *Rio Bravo* (1959), *The Magnificent Seven* (1960) and *The Professionals* (1966), which feature groups of heroes operating outside of society, the Westerns of Delmer Daves consistently emphasize the importance of cooperation between multiple heroes over the actions of a lone hero. From this perspective, Cochise *is* a common character in Daves' Westerns: the secondary hero who steadies, strengthens, and ultimately defers to the mildly neurotic leading man. In the case of *The Last Wagon* and *The Hanging Tree*, this second hero doubles as the romantic interest. In all cases, the dynamic between the heroes is predicated upon complementarity and reciprocation.

In *Broken Arrow*, Jeffords earns the trust, respect, and then friendship of Cochise. But in the end it is Cochise who reminds the grieving Jeffords, clutching to his murdered wife and wanting to break the peace treaty in order to avenge her death, of the values that united them:

> Are you a child, that you thought peace would come easy? You who taught me so well? Is it my brother who asks me to spit on my word? [. . .] You will hear me now. You will bear this. This was not done by the military. Geronimo broke the peace no less than these whites. As I bear the murder of my people so you will bear the murder of your wife. I am Cochise! I do not betray my people or their children. And no one on my territory will open war again. Not even you.

Though our first inclination may be to read this dialogue ideologically—as Cochise, enlightened savage, again advocating the cause of integration—it takes on a different meaning when considered as a Delmer Daves Western, most of which end in scenes of cooperation and exchange between the heroes.

At the conclusion of *3:10 to Yuma*, for example, rancher Dan Evans (Van Heflin) and outlaw Ben Wade (Glenn Ford) stand in the rail yard in Contention City as the 3:10 train to Yuma Prison begins to pull out. Opposite them is Wade's gang, intent to free him from Evans' custody. One of the gang, Charlie Price (Richard Jaeckel), yells at Wade to drop to allow him a clear shot at Evans. As the train slowly rolls past, Wade surveys the situation and says to Evans, "Let's us get out of here." "Us?" Evans replies. "How do I know you'll jump?" "You'll have to trust me on this one. Jump!" The pair leap into an open railcar. Wade's gang runs after them, firing into the car. Evans returns fire, killing Price, and the rest of the gang give up their pursuit. Now safe, Evans asks,

"Why did you do it, Ben?" "I don't like owing anybody any favors," Wade responds. "You saved my life back at the hotel." He smiles, and then adds, "It's all right. I've broken out of Yuma before." Wade's motivations are in fact more ambiguous than pat reasons like not wanting to owe anybody anything, or his confidence in being able to escape from Yuma Prison. His placid, calculating nature is part of what makes the character compelling, especially in the way the film repeatedly signals to the viewer that Wade is sizing up a situation without explicitly tipping its hand to what actions he will take. What is clear, however, is that Wade's respect, even admiration, for the overmatched Evans grows over the course of the narrative. It doesn't lead the outlaw to renounce the way of the gun—far from it, as his final lines indicate—but it does lead him to side with Evans, nominally his adversary, over his own kind.

This partnership between heroes is a manifestation of what is arguably the signature aspect of Daves' Westerns: rather than being natural or instinctual agents, the protagonists proceed based on reason and often pragmatism. The willingness to work to understand and cooperate with others in equal partnership—indeed, the acknowledgment that such cooperation is necessary for survival—suggests both faith in civilization and skepticism of mythical, individual action. This outlook places Daves starkly at odds with the 1950s Westerns of Ford, Mann and Boetticher, with their continued valorization of the lone Western hero, as reflected in the close associations between these filmmakers and their leading men—John Wayne, James Stewart, and Randolph Scott respectively—who play variations of the same character in film after film, providing imaginary reconciliations of the archetypal conflict between civilization and wilderness. As noted in the introduction to this volume, Daves' Westerns do not evidence Hollywood's typical brand of frontier mythology (beyond geographical setting) but instead seem to embody a non-mythological approach to the people and events of America's frontier past, neither painting an epic historical canvas nor examining mythic paradigms. As critic and filmmaker Bertrand Tavernier argues,

> Daves does not mythologize Nature but befriends it, the way his characters do, at least those who live or survive in it . . . To befriend Nature, however, is not to idealize it. While Daves's Nature may provide a field for apprenticeship . . . it isn't necessarily a realm of purification and redemption counterposed to a corrupt and corrupting civilization.[27]

The "failure" of Daves' Westerns to conform to the tenets of genre—whether those consciously employed by filmmakers or retrospectively asserted by critics—explains, at least in part, their relative neglect. Re-conceiving of *Broken Arrow*'s Cochise as a "Davesian" character is thus an important step toward reclaiming the pivotal role played by Delmer Daves in the development of the Western film in the 1950s. It may also help us to reconsider his entire body of work from an auteurist perspective.

Yet another film that could be enlisted as evidence of Daves' interest in American Indians is *Bird of Paradise* (1951). Based somewhat loosely on the 1932 film of the same name about the adventures of a white man among the Polynesians on a south Pacific island, *Bird of Paradise* is obviously set far away from the American West. Yet it was fashioned with *Broken Arrow* in mind, most obviously in the casting of Jeff Chandler as Tenga, the college-educated son of the island's chief who has grown disillusioned with the "civilized" world, and Debra Paget as Tenga's beautiful sister Kalua. Rounding out the cast is Louis Jourdan as André Laurence, a French college friend of Tenga's who accompanies him to the island on vacation but falls in love with Kalua.

As portrayed by Chandler, Tenga is a near-facsimile of Cochise, from his formal diction to his role as noble, compassionate intermediary between his people and his foreign friend. But though the larger historical conflict between the islanders and Euro-American visitors is alluded to throughout the film, it does not instigate events in the way that the historical conflict between the Apache and the U.S. Government forms the backdrop of *Broken Arrow*. Instead, the film's conflict arises from the white hero's ongoing struggles to understand the culture and religion of the Pacific Islanders, which, unlike in *Broken Arrow*, continue after he has wed the native princess. Kalua does not become pregnant in the first three months of her marriage to André, and so she brings her younger sister to him to be his "second wife" and bear him a child. Patiently, and with difficulty, André refuses the offer. Then, in the film's climax, the island's volcano erupts, and the tribe's shaman, the Kahuna, says that only the sacrifice of the chief's oldest daughter will satisfy the gods and quell the volcano. André protests, but Kalua, satisfied that she has "loved and known love," does her duty. She ascends to the mouth of the volcano and, after a loving glance back at her husband, jumps into the fire. The volcano is extinguished, the island's inhabitants are saved, and, in voiceover, André tells us that he left the island, taking with him only his fond memories of Kalua, Tenga, and their people.

Aside from its superficial similarities to *Broken Arrow*, it is not easy to assimilate *Bird of Paradise* with that film. Both *Broken Arrow* and *Bird of Paradise* end with the hero leaving his adopted culture after the death of his wife and returning whence he came. While that death brings about salvation in both films, there is a significant difference between being murdered and sacrificing oneself to the gods. The challenge, again, is how to account for the "broad range of topics and themes" examined by Daves, even within films that cover similar subject matter. His willingness to adopt different perspectives, without judgment, frustrates the auteurist impulse to detect an underlying, unifying vision. Yet, though *Bird of Paradise* lacks the concluding act of cooperation and exchange that typifies Daves' Westerns, it does throughout emphasize those values, and arrives in a similar place of mutual acceptance and respect.

In a 1969 interview Daves relates how his father, in matters of religion, always advised him to consult as many different perspectives as possible before making a decision.

> Ever since I've had a respect for the other man's religion. Don't be too quick to dismiss them. I respect other people's religions around the world and seek to find out what has great meaning to them, and I've done a great study on the religions of the world and I always will.[28]

Daves' own perspective on religion could certainly account for the lack of judgment leveled against the "primitive" beliefs of the islanders in *Bird of Paradise*, including the necessity of ritual sacrifice. Like the director himself, his characters frequently confront challenges that present no single obvious answer. They must proceed based, again, on reason and pragmatism in the face of circumstances that defy their own beliefs and, in a sense, place men of all backgrounds on similar footing. As Meyer observes of Daves' war films *Destination Tokyo* (1943) and *Pride of the Marines* (1945), both of which confront anti-Semitism, "war equalizes all races, colors, and creeds."[29] And if Daves' Westerns appear to question the rightness or naturalness of mythical masculine action, their alternative conception of masculinity—sensitive, sensible, and, if more fragile, then still resilient—is equally found in his war films and, crucially, his later melodramas like *A Summer Place* (1959) and *Parrish* (1961).

Much work remains to be done in order to do justice to the Westerns of Delmer Daves, let alone the many films he made outside of the genre. However, the re-evaluation of influential aspects of his Westerns, like the character Cochise in *Broken Arrow*, as reflecting less contemporary social trends than the director's own interests and perspectives can open up his larger body of work to greater study and, ultimately, appreciation. Whether with regard to his Westerns, war films, or later melodramas, we should heed the director's own words and not be too quick to dismiss them.

BIBLIOGRAPHY

Buscombe, Edward, *"Injuns!": Native Americans in the Movies* (London: Reaktion Books, 2006).

Coursodon, Jean-Pierre, *American Directors, Volume 1* (New York: McGraw-Hill, 1983).

Crowther, Bosley, "Film Flummery: Inspecting Some Pictorial Wool That Is Pulled Over Audiences' Eyes," *New York Times*, 23 July 1950: p. X1.

Fenin, George N., and William K. Everson, *The Western: From Silents to the Seventies*, rev. edn. (New York: Penguin Books, 1982).

French, Philip, *Westerns: Aspects of a Movie Genre* (Manchester: Carcanet Press, [1973] 2005).
Henderson, Brian, "*The Searchers*: An American Dilemma," *Film Quarterly*, 34 (1981): 9–23.
Lenihan, John H., *Showdown: Confronting Modern America in the Western Film* (Urbana, IL: University of Illinois Press, 1980).
Maltby, Richard, "A Better Sense of History: John Ford and the Indians," in Ian Cameron and Douglas Pye (eds.), *The Movie Book of the Western* (New York: Continuum, 1996).
Meyer, William A., *Warner Brothers Directors: The Hard-Boiled, the Comic, and the Weepers* (New Rochelle, NY: Arlington House Publishers, 1978).
Neale, Steve, "Vanishing Americans: Racial and Ethnic Issues in the Interpretation and Context of Post-war 'Pro-Indian' Westerns," in Edward Buscombe and Roberta E. Pearson (eds.), *Back in the Saddle Again: New Essays on the Western* (London: British Film Institute, 1998), pp. 8–28.
Slotkin, Richard, *Gunfighter Nation: The Myth of the Frontier in Twentieth-Century America* (Norman: Oklahoma University Press, [1992] 1998).
Tavernier, Bertrand, "The Ethical Romantic," *Film Comment*, January–February 2003, <http://www.filmcomment.com/article/delmer-daves-bertrand-tavernier> (last accessed 11 November 2015).
Wicking, Christopher, "Interview with Delmer Daves," *Screen*, 10:4/5 (1969): 60.

FILMOGRAPHY

Badlanders, The, director Delmer Daves, featuring Alan Ladd, Ernest Borgnine, Katy Jurado, Claire Kelly (Metro-Goldwyn-Mayer, 1958).
Bird of Paradise, director Delmer Daves, featuring Louis Jourdan, Jeff Chandler, Debra Paget (20th Century Fox, 1951).
Broken Arrow, director Delmer Daves, featuring Jimmy Stewart, Jeff Chandler, Debra Paget, Basil Ruysdael (20th Century Fox, 1950).
Cowboy, director Delmer Daves, featuring Glenn Ford, Jack Lemmon, Anna Kashfi, Dick York (Columbia Pictures, 1958).
Drum Beat, director Delmer Daves, featuring Alan Ladd, Audrey Dalton, Marisa Pavan, Charles Bronson (Warner Bros., 1954).
Hanging Tree, The, director Delmer Daves, featuring Gary Cooper, Maria Schell, Karl Malden, George C. Scott (Warner Bros., 1959).
Jubal, director Delmer Daves, featuring Glenn Ford, Valerie French, Rod Steiger, Ernest Borgnine (Columbia Pictures, 1956).
Last Wagon, The, director Delmer Daves, featuring Richard Widmark, Felicia Farr, Susan Kohner, Tommy Rettig (20th Century Fox, 1956).
Spencer's Mountain, director Delmer Daves, featuring Henry Fonda, Maureen O'Hara (Warner Bros., 1963).
White Feather, director Delmer Daves, featuring Robert Wagner, John Lund, Deborah Paget, Jeffrey Hunter (20th Century Fox, 1955).

NOTES

1. See, for example, Fenin and Everson, *The Western*, pp. 18–19, 281–3; Lenihan, *Showdown*, pp. 55–89; French, *Westerns*, pp. 47–50; Buscombe, *"Injuns!"*, pp. 101–50.

2. Buscombe, *"Injuns!"*, p. 118.
3. The practice of having non-Native actors perform Native American roles—sometimes called "redface"—remains a staple of the Western genre to the present day, and so is not, in and of itself, a particularly compelling criticism of the film.
4. Crowther, "Film Flummery."
5. Slotkin, *Gunfighter Nation*, p. 16. Also see pp. 125–7.
6. Maltby, "A Better Sense of History.", p. 36.
7. Henderson, "*The Searchers*: An American Dilemma." Also see Walker, "The Westerns of Delmer Daves," for a reading of *Broken Arrow* and Daves' other Indian-themed Westerns as reflections of contemporary racial attitudes.
8. See "Chapter 2: The Liberal Western" in Buscombe, pp. 101–50, and especially pp. 101–11. Also see Neale, "Vanishing Americans," pp. 8–28.
9. Buscombe, pp. 116–17.
10. For production figures, see the various tables in the appendix to *The BFI Companion to the Western*, pp. 425–8.
11. Daves also completed uncredited work on the screenplays for *The Badlanders* and *The Hanging Tree*. The shooting script for *The Badlanders*—the one Daves had with him on set—is credited "by Delmer Daves." On it Daves has handwritten, "NOTE: I waived writing credit" (Delmer Daves Papers, Department of Special Collections, Stanford University Archives, box 50, folder 2). In an annotation on a draft of *The Hanging Tree*, Daves wrote that he was responsible for "blending" the drafts of writers Wendell Mayes and Halstead Welles into the final draft (Delmer Daves Papers, box 49, folder 2).
12. Meyer, *Warner Brothers Directors*, p. 109.
13. Coursodon, *American Directors*, p. 84.
14. Walker, "The Westerns of Delmer Daves," p. 159.
15. Kitses, to his lasting credit, offers readers of *Horizons West* comprehensive accounts of his chosen directors' bodies of work, and emphasizes the need to "be prepared to entertain the idea that *auteurs* grow, and that the genre can help to crystallize preoccupations and contribute actively to development" (pp. 26–7).
16. Walker, "The Westerns of Delmer Daves," p. 125. Original emphasis.
17. Ibid. p. 123.
18. Kitses, *Horizons West* (2004), p. 16.
19. Delmer Daves Papers, box 39, folders 1 and 2.
20. A casting memo is dated 19 April 1950. Delmer Daves Papers, box 40, folder 2.
21. Delmer Daves Papers, box 39, folder 2.
22. Coursodon, *American Directors*, p. 85.
23. Lenihan, *Showdown*, pp. 40–1.
24. Ibid. p. 41.
25. Quoted in Wicking, "Interview," p. 60.
26. Walker, "The Westerns of Delmer Daves," p. 141.
27. Tavernier, "The Ethical Romantic."
28. Quoted in Wicking, "Interview," p. 55.
29. Meyer, *Warner Brothers Directors*, p. 111.

CHAPTER 2

Trying to Ameliorate the System from Within: Delmer Daves' Westerns from the 1950s

John White

During the 1950s Delmer Daves wrote and directed a series of Westerns, but the two that have received the most favorable critical and popular acclaim—*Broken Arrow* (1950) and *3:10 to Yuma* (1957)—were not written by him. This chapter assesses these generally more well-known films and two others for which the credits make no mention of Daves having contributed to the screenplay—*Cowboy* (1958) and *The Badlanders* (1958)—alongside two Westerns he not only directed but for which he is credited with having written the screenplay—*The Last Wagon* (1956) and *Jubal* (1956). Some attention will also be given to a Western he wrote but did not direct, *White Feather* (1955). Although the focus will be on these films, the suggestions being made here are seen as being relevant to other Westerns Daves directed in this period—namely, *Return of the Texan* (1952), *Drum Beat* (1954) and *The Hanging Tree* (1959). An attempt will be made to isolate for consideration a distinctive and consistent liberal imprint achieved by Daves in association with a series of screenwriters.

In the 1995 documentary *A Personal Journey with Martin Scorsese through American Movies*, Scorsese describes Daves as one of those "directors that are sadly forgotten today." A cursory survey of online lists of "best" Westerns would seem to confirm this. Daves' *Broken Arrow* and *3:10 to Yuma* often receive a mention, although never within the really elite echelons, and *Cowboy* figures only very occasionally in a lowly position in the "top" 100. The rest of the director's Westerns are almost never alluded to. This is despite the fact that the Western genre is one to which critics have considered Daves to have been well suited. At the same time, despite the lack of widespread acclaim from some cinephiles, his work continues to hold real interest. A series of screenings titled "Fortunes of the Western" shown in 2014 at the Harvard

Film Archive Cinematheque, for example, included two of Daves' Westerns, *The Hanging Tree* and *Jubal*.[1] And, according to Kent Jones, Daves was "a true artist, a western specialist, and a Hollywood pro whose work was respected by insiders but received little in the way of official recognition."[2] This chapter will not, primarily, seek to answer the question of why there may have been a lack of plaudits for Daves' work from within the industry, nor why there continues to be little public awareness of his Westerns, though possible responses to both of these questions may suggest themselves along the way. Instead, the focus here will be on the role of Daves as an auteur within Hollywood. In particular, the effort will be to come at the work through a consideration of the politics and ideologies placed with deliberation, it will be suggested, within the films.

Bertrand Tavernier, who knew the man, tells us Daves was a Republican but he also links his work to "progressive, liberal cinema," and it is this aspect of his work that this chapter will seek to investigate.[3] In the post-war period, nobody working in Hollywood could place intimate interracial relationships on the screen in the way Daves did, without explicitly engaging with race issues as they relate to African Americans in contemporary society. Similarly, it was not possible for a director working in the film industry at that time to locate films in mining towns as Daves did, and not be aware of the fact that what they were presenting to audiences was related to a wider social debate around the relationship between capital and labor. This is the period in which the Civil Rights campaign was developing momentum, and in which a massive internal fear of communism was surging through the social and political fabric of the country. Certainly, it is not possible that somebody as deftly aware as Daves was of the creation of meaning through cinematic language could have been unaware of these contexts. And to these two primary areas of interest—race and labor—we might add a third of secondary relevance to the argument here: sexuality. Through his films, Daves makes it abundantly clear that he is in favor of society taking a much more liberal attitude toward sex.

In one of Daves' most well-known films, *Broken Arrow*, James Stewart plays Tom Jeffords, a gold prospector in Arizona in 1870, a period of bloody conflict between the U.S. Army and the Chiricahua Apaches. Jeffords finds an Apache boy dying of gunshot wounds and saves his life despite the fact that "for ten years we'd been in a savage war with his people: a bloody, no-give, no-take war." The boy is concerned that his mother will be crying because he has gone missing, and we are given Jeffords' response: "Funny, it never struck me that an Apache woman would cry for her son like any other woman. Apaches are wild animals, we all said." An Apache war-party spares Jeffords' life as a result of his having saved the boy's life, but he is forced to watch as the war-party attack passing gold prospectors, killing two immediately and then torturing to death three others, with two of them left hanging from trees. The response of Jeffords to all of this is: "I learned things that day."

Similar events and responses, reconfigured according to the narratives of particular films, re-appear through a series of Daves' Westerns during the 1950s. He is interested in the brutality of war and the possibilities for peace. (The image of bodies hanging from trees haunts his work.) He sees any opportunity for peace as lying in the realization of our common humanity, and he emphasizes the necessity of learning from experience. Alongside his central characters, the audience is asked to "learn things."

The script for *Broken Arrow* was provided by Albert Maltz, but the same sentiments recur throughout Daves' work.[4] Either Daves had a larger part to play in adjusting the screenplay for *Broken Arrow* than is generally acknowledged, Maltz had a profound effect on Daves and his outlook on the world that is reflected in the director's later work, or Maltz and Daves had a shared political perspective.

As the film develops, further aspects of Daves' work as a whole in this period are revealed: his concern for history and for taking account of different sides of a debate, for example.[5] The realities of "a bloody, no-give, no-take war" are apparent: "the Apaches burned my house last month: my wife was inside" says one man. But, Jeffords' response is: "Hold on, let's just get the facts straight here. Cochise didn't start this war, a snotty little lieutenant, fresh out of the East, started it. He flew a flag of truce which Cochise honored and then he hanged Cochise's brother and five others under the flag." The details of the events mentioned here, the Lieutenant Bascom Affair of 1861, and the sequence of how things played out remains a matter of some dispute, but Daves' interest in recognizing the problems posed by the genuine difficulties of conflicting senses of reality, particularly in a war situation, and his interest in attempting to establish some sense of historical reality, remain.[6] Again, these things could be said to be attributable to the influence of Maltz as the scriptwriter, but, again, the evidence is that these twin interests continue to be shown throughout the extended group of Westerns under discussion.[7]

When, in an effort to find the common humanity in which Daves is interested, Jeffords begins to learn the Apache language, we might notice that he does so beneath a portrait of George Washington, who wrote (in an earlier period) that, "The Government of the United States are determined that their administration of Indian affairs shall be directed entirely by the great principles of justice and humanity."[8] The film's interest in history continues when General Oliver Otis Howard—known as "Bible-reading Howard"—is introduced in the final third of the film. It was this general, a real historical figure, who (with the help of the real Tom Jeffords) negotiated a treaty with Cochise in 1872. The dialogue that is used in the film propounds a fairly straightforward, liberal Christian ideology that is consistently followed by Daves in the rest of his Westerns from the 1950s:

Howard: The Bible I read preaches brotherhood of all God's children.
Jeffords: Suppose their skins aren't white. Are they still God's children?
Howard: My Bible says nothing about the pigmentation of the skin.

The historical figure, General Howard, was in charge of the Freedmen's Bureau after the Civil War, established to help former slaves to take a full role in society, and also founded Howard University in Washington as an institution open to all races. In this light, the connection of all of this talk of Native Americans and race to African American civil rights in the 1950s is abundantly clear.

Under the ultra-conservative studio system, Daves may not have been able to show a mixed race couple surviving through to the end of the film, and both partners may have been played by white actors; but, before Sonseeahray's death, Daves does succeed in forcing (or allowing) the audience to watch the intimacy of a (supposed) interracial relationship in close-up on the screen.[9] Jimmy Stewart is shown stretched full-length across the screen, lying intimately with his Apache wife. Furthermore, the shot is framed with a classic "American" (Western) landscape behind them. The vital context for this is that at the end of the Second World War, most states still had laws against miscegenation. It only became legal for whites to marry blacks or Asians in California after 1948. In Arizona it was not legal until 1962, and in Texas and a host of other states not until 1967.

Writing in 1973, Jean-Loup Bourget says: "the freedom of the Hollywood director is not measured by what he can openly do within the Hollywood system, but rather by what he can imply about American society in general and about the Hollywood system in particular. He can describe in extensive detail how a given social structure operates, but cannot do so openly unless the society in question is remote in time and space."[10] Bourget specifically includes *Broken Arrow* when he discusses films that posit some utopian vision of what life could be like. He claims that "a Utopian world which calls itself Utopian is not escapist in the derogatory sense of the word; rather it calls the viewer's attention to the fact that his [sic] own society is far removed from such an ideal condition."[11]

If we move to look at *The Last Wagon*, another story based around the relationship between whites and Native Americans, we find the same patterns repeated. The idea that all people are "human beings" and should be treated as such is again emphasized and, essentially, debated within the narrative. When the central character, "Comanche" Todd (Richard Widmark), a white man who lives among Native Americans, is seen in chains and being pulled along on a rope, the woman who becomes his love-interest puts the issue in simple, straightforward terms: "He's a human being and you're treating him like an animal."[12] The debate, however, is again complex. When all those on the wagon-train stop to pray before eating a meal and end the prayer with, "Teach us to love with open hearts and to share with our fellow man Thy infinite goodness each according to his needs," it feels like a sentiment to be endorsed. When the leader of the wagon-train tells the sheriff who has captured Todd that he has to treat his prisoner with more humanity, saying, "We're Christian. We like to think we're civilized. We'd be neither if we let a fellow man thirst and starve," it feels like a sentiment to applaud. But, within a short time, this man and most of the men, women, and children on the wagon-train have been slaughtered by Apaches. Neither humanity, nor civilized attitudes, nor Christian charity has been enough to save these people. And the sheriff's berating of them as "Christers" in danger of getting "soft-bellied" seems to have some truth to it.

The issue of miscegenation is again addressed in this film. Colonel Normand (Douglas Kennedy), who is leading the wagon-train, has two daughters, one of whom was born as a result of his relationship with a Navajo woman. When the white daughter, Valinda (Stephanie Griffin), spits the words "Indian lover" with venom, the mixed-race daughter, Jolie (Susan Kohner), says that she makes it sound "filthy." "It is something filthy," responds Valinda. "It was something filthy when my father took your mother as his woman." The absolute intensity of right-wing hatred for this sexual transgression of boundaries is embodied in Griffin's delivery of the words. But Daves pushes those boundaries as far as he can within the controls of the studio system and within the social context of the period. The film ends with a white woman, Jenny (Felicia Farr), riding off to live with "Comanche" Todd. This may be someone who is nominally a white man and whom the audience may see (given his portrayal by Richard Widmark, a well-known white actor) as such, but we should recall that earlier the sheriff warned us, as well as those on the wagon-train, about Todd: "Don't be fooled by the color of his skin. He may be white, but inside he's all Comanche." So when Todd and Jenny consummate their relationship earlier in the film and he is wooing her with talk of living in wikiups, is not Daves again, as in *Broken Arrow*, presenting us with the challenge of an interracial sex act?[13]

If we return to the massacre of those on the wagon-train in this film, one of the features of this episode is that Daves again, as with the deaths of the gold prospectors in *Broken Arrow*, uses images of the dead being left hanging from trees. The Colonel's daughters, for example, look up and react to something, presumably his body, that we do not see (apart from a boot) but are left to imagine. It is clear to us, and would have been abundantly clear to cinema audiences in the 1950s, that where we find bodies hanging from trees in America is in the Deep South. This may be an ironic reversal in the sense that what we have here are people of color "lynching" whites (and may well have, in Daves' mind, some linkage to Goya's sequence of drawings, "Disasters of War"[14]), but the contemporary reference for the United States in the period is to the black experience and to the "strange fruit" Billie Holiday sang about that could be found throughout the first half of the twentieth century "swinging in the southern breeze."[15] Some of us might, like the Colonel's daughters, turn in horror from such a sight, but there is plenty of evidence that many in America did not. *Without Sanctuary: Lynching Photography in America* displays around 100 photographs and postcards documenting the gruesome business.[16] By the 1950s lynching, the figures suggest, had dropped off, but violence against blacks demanding democratic rights was intensifying. The Civil Rights movement was getting under way, and a real struggle over segregation in schools and on public transport was gaining momentum. Whites were rallying beneath placards that announced that "Race mixing is Communism." The race issues that are at the heart of Daves' film were making their way to the top of the political agenda.[17]

In 1955—the year before *The Last Wagon* was released—two voting rights activists, the Reverend George Lee and Lamar Smith, were both murdered in Mississippi. Smith was killed in front of plenty of people, but no witnesses came forward, and a jury of white men later refused to indict three suspects. In the same year, Emmett Till, a fourteen-year-old from Chicago who was in Mississippi to visit relatives, was abducted and murdered. The trial of two men accused of Till's murder ended with both men being acquitted by the all-male, all-white jury.[18] And what does Todd say to the judge in his defense toward the end of *The Last Wagon*? "You show me a white man jury that'd hang four white men for killin' an Indian squaw and two Comanche boys." Todd may be put in chains and hauled along on a rope behind his horse by Sheriff "Bull" Harper (George Matthews) as part of the given Western narrative, but the sub-narrative image created is that of an escaped slave who has been hunted down and re-captured. What we see in the film is Todd, an expression of the savage feared Other ("a savage like you wouldn't know what goes on in the hearts of human beings," says Valinda), breaking those chains and reclaiming his freedom from the white man in a liberal Hollywood studio director's 1950s equivalent of Quentin Tarantino's *Django Unchained* (2012).

Daves is given on-screen credit for the script of *The Last Wagon*, alongside Gwen Bagni (who is credited as the originator of the story) and James Edward Grant. In rather a contrast to Maltz, Grant was John Wayne's favorite screenwriter, who the star frequently brought on board film projects to rewrite his lines.[19] From working with Maltz on *Broken Arrow*, Daves seems to have gone to the opposite end of the political spectrum for a screenwriter partner.[20] In the previous year, Daves had worked with Leo Townsend on the script for *White Feather* (1955), directed by Robert D. Webb. Townsend had joined the Communist Party in the 1940s, but then named those he knew to be members of left-wing organizations when called before the House of Un-American

Activities Committee in 1951.[21] Because he was a studio professional and, perhaps, as a consequence of his own liberal politics, Daves worked with a series of scriptwriters of different political persuasions during a time of political turmoil in Hollywood and in the country as a whole. Thematically, though, the ideas being dealt with and the positions being taken up are remarkably consistent throughout these three films dealing with relationships between different races. At the end of *White Feather* a full interracial marriage is achieved. The central character and Daves, both of whom are again attempting to bridge the divide between the races, achieve the aim of their narrative trajectories. Although what we end up with, it seems, is assimilation, with the Cheyenne warrior chief living to see his grandson "enter the military academy at West Point." Referring to *Broken Arrow* and questioning the liberal politics to be found there, Angela Aleiss suggests that beneath the "message of tolerance was an attempt to erase Indian identity."[22] Aleiss sees such filmic unions of the races in bleak terms for Native American culture:

> postwar movies had ventured into new territory by suggesting a commonality between Indians and whites. But mutual co-existence demanded a sacrifice of Indian identity, and prospects of Native American cultural survival became bleak indeed. As more Westerns depicted a lasting romantic union between Indians and whites, they simultaneously suggested that civilization would absorb Native American autonomy.[23]

But Daves (or is this Maltz?) is not unaware of the difficulties. In *Broken Arrow*, Cochise (Jeff Chandler) counsels Jeffords about his relationship with Sonseeahray:

> It will not be easy for you. You're an American. Where will you live? Here? There will always be Apaches who have suffered from white men, who will hate you for it. Tucson, maybe? Will there not always be whites who will hate your wife because of the color of her skin?

What Daves/Maltz is dealing with here is an issue facing all interracial marriages in post-war America, but it is not something that stops this series of films advocating those cross-cultural unions.

In the films *Jubal* (1956), *3:10 to Yuma* (1957), *Cowboy* (1958) and *The Badlanders* (1958), Daves shifts the main focus of attention from race to the harsh world of work as experienced by the poorest in society. In the first of these films, for example, when Jubal Troop (Glenn Ford) arrives on the farm owned by Shep Horgan (Ernest Borgnine), he is immediately quizzed by Pinky (Rod Steiger) over his past and challenged about how he ended up working sheep.

Figure 2.1 Jeffords and Sonseeahray embrace in *Broken Arrow*.

Jubal: I hired out to a sheep ranch 'cos it was the only job I could get.
Pinky: But most cowhands would die before they would herd sheep.
Jubal: Show me one.

In *3:10 to Yuma* the man who ends up escorting the dangerous outlaw, Ben Wade (Glenn Ford), to catch the 3:10 train is a poor homesteader, Dan Evans (Van Heflin), who is desperate for money to try to save his farm in the face of catastrophic drought.

According to Kent Jones, both Daves and Columbia's vice-president, Jerry Wald, were unhappy with Russell S. Hughes' early script for *Jubal* and Daves undertook an extensive rewrite, with the final script being based on only a small part of the original Paul I. Wellman novel.[24] In Daves' story, "Jube" becomes an outsider, a loner who, because of his past, has never been able to trust anybody. "How many men you known in your life you could trust, complete?" Shep asks him, and Jube replies, "One, just one. That was my father." In a later scene in which Shep is helping a calf to learn to suckle, Daves has him say to Jube, "Nobody learns without help." And this is Jube's situation: he needs help, and he needs to learn. He has to learn that the strong, silent hero of the Western is a myth and that, as Naomi tells him: "you mustn't be ashamed of needing somebody. Everybody does." But, interestingly, when Naomi, who is moving through the country on a Christian wagon-train, suggests to Jube, "Say a prayer, Jube: let God help," Jube rejects this advice. In the end the narrative demonstrates that it is not prayer that decides the outcome of events, but Jube's own decisive actions and determination to face things rather than to run away. He learns that you need the support of a community (the Christian community shelters him), that you need people like Naomi within that community that you can trust, and that then, within that context, it is your own actions that determine outcomes. In other words, what we are shown (and, maybe, learn) is that the individualistic ideology of the Western (and of free-market capitalism) is insufficient for real human beings living in the real world.

It is in *Badlanders*, a film that for much of the time appears to be little more than a churned-out caper movie, that Daves' position in opposition to exploitative capitalism becomes most clear. The opening scenes, set in a prison with a brutal regime, continue the director's interest in chains, both real and metaphoric. At one point a group of prisoners, linked together in the equivalent of a chain gang, make their way to the river to wash and, if you were in the audience, you might reflect that even in the worst of prisons this is surely unlikely to be the way prisoners washed. But then you might remember that throughout his work Daves makes reference to the films of others working in the same period; and as one of the men, in order to escape the inhumanity with which he is surrounded, tries to take his own life by drowning himself, you might realize that what we have here is an ironic reference to John Ford's use of the hymn, "Shall We Gather at the River." "Have mercy, Jesus," the man pleads as he allows himself to drop into the raging waters—but Jesus does not have mercy, and he is pulled from the river alive.[25] These chained-together prisoners are for Daves images of the poor, some of those at the bottom of the heap in society, and their experience in "Arizona Territorial Prison, 1898" expresses their lot in life. And, if you do not think this film, for Daves, is about the poorest of the poor, take note of the line he gives to Alan Ladd as Peter van Hoek, "the Dutchman," when five minutes later in the film this character enters the town of Prescott on a stagecoach. "On the left," he says to the ladies traveling with him, "is the Mexican part of the town: the mine owners brought them in as cheap labor." A little later, John McBain (Ernest Borgnine), who has come out of prison at the same time as van Hoek, enters the office of the businessman, Sample, and virtually begs him for a job, for the chance to be able to work. "I don't want a sermon, I want a job," he says.

Race, notice, continues to be an issue. Sample, for example, says, "I don't trust Mexes," and the term "Mexican-lover" is spoken with as much venom as "Indian-lover" in Daves' earlier Westerns. But the main focus is on poverty, its expression in society, and its effects. "There's no money for doctors here," says Anita (Katy Jurado), talking about the poor Mexican quarter. And, McBain is given the cryptic line that is as near to "ownership is theft" as you

Figure 2.2 Anita rallies the Mexicans against the rich businessmen in *The Badlanders*.

are likely to get in a Hollywood studio film: "Seems like everybody around here is stealing from everybody else." The literal *pièce de résistance* comes in the final minutes of the film, as Anita rallies the Mexicans and they rebel against the rich businessmen who have ruled the town. We are given two shots of a tricolor behind Anita, who is dressed in a red headscarf, white blouse, and red skirt, with a blue sash tied around her waist.

The flag should carry the colors of the Mexican flag, since this is all taking place in the middle of their fiesta, but at this point the flag actually carries the blue, white, and red of the French flag. Anita leads the Mexicans in the same way Eugene Delacroix's *Liberty Leading the People*[26] shows the national emblem of France, Marianne—an icon of freedom and democracy against all forms of dictatorship—leading the Parisians in the July Revolution of 1830. Revolution becomes a celebratory festival of liberation. The mine owner, Lounsberry, and the overweight businessman, Sample, are manhandled in a manner that references Sergei Eisenstein's treatment of similar characters in *Strike* (1925). If anything, Daves has become more radical over the period of the 1950s. *Badlanders* utterly subverts a simple Hollywood caper into a moment of revolution. Daves revels in his ability to outflank the businessmen and studio bosses of Hollywood, so that Lounsberry and Sample are not only representatives of big business who find their way into a supposedly light-weight Hollywood caper film, and not only Eisenstein's buffoons, but also the very men who run Hollywood.

Prescott, where the events in *Badlanders* take place, is an actual mining town in Arizona where gold was discovered in 1863. But just over thirty miles north-east of there is Jerome, another mining town where in 1930 a census showed 57 per cent of the population to be Latino,[27] and from where in 1917 more than sixty leaders of the Industrial Workers of the World trade union were rounded up by vigilantes on behalf of the mine owners, loaded into railroad cattle trucks, and taken out of town. Most were offloaded somewhere near the California state line.[28] The details of trade union relations and the demographic make-up of Arizona mining towns was clearly much more complex than these few sentences allow, and much more complex than a Hollywood caper Western was ever likely to be able to reveal. However, there can be no doubt that through this film and others in the second half of the 1950s, Daves is expressing an interest in the experience of ordinary working-class Americans not only in the late nineteenth century but also in the first half of the twentieth century. Glenn Ford, who worked with Daves on three films from this period, said that "Nothing happened in a Delmer Daves film that wasn't intentional, from the camera set-ups to the wardrobe."[29] It would be strange, therefore, if he paid any less attention to the inherent ramifications of script, historical context, and location.

In *Cowboy* (1958), the script of which was nominally written by Edmund H. North but actually written by blacklisted Dalton Trumbo, Daves offers a film that sets itself up as a light-hearted romantic comedy but challenges the viewer on a number of levels. It is still about the working conditions of ordinary men, in this case cowboys; but it also confronts the whole genre industry of the Western. Cattleman Tom Reece (Glenn Ford) immediately challenges Frank Harris's (Jack Lemmon) romantic notions of what life on the cattle trail is like. "Do you know what the Trail is really like?" he asks. "Dust storms all day and cloudbursts all night. A man's gotta be a fool to want that kinda life." Some of the exquisite cinematography unfortunately works to counter this anti-romantic view of the cowboy's life, with an exciting intensity to the work with horses conveyed particularly through low-level close-up, and a calm beauty given to peaceful river scenes and dramatic evening skies. Daves is also unable to pass up the chance to echo camera shots by John Ford and, beyond that, paintings by Frederic Remington and Charles Marion Russell. At one point, he has Paco (Victor Manuel Mendoza) ride his horse to the top of a steep bluff and raise his hat for no other reason than to achieve a shot of aesthetic beauty (which is not necessarily to be decried). Furthermore, when there is an Indian attack, in best Hollywood style the cowboys all become expert marksmen, able to shoot with amazing precision from horseback. Referring to *Cowboy*, Richard Whitehall recognized something of the difficulty only a few years after the film was released when he wrote that, "A few films have tried to penetrate the legend and touch on historical truth but the legend, I fear, has been too strong for them."[30] Even more of a problem, or just the simple reality, is that Daves is clearly working within the demands of Hollywood for a saleable product and his own desire to find an audience for his work.[31] Nevertheless, and although the very last scenes re-assert the opening light, comedic touch, it remains the case that by the end of the cattle drive Frank has become unrecognizable from the weak and rather insubstantial character we first encountered. Some real sense of the dust and hardship of the Trail has been given. A sub-plot involving Brian Donlevy as "Doc" Bender, a former sheriff who ends up hanging himself after shooting his best friend, is allowed to carry the key thematic line in the whole film for Trumbo/Daves: "A man has to have something other than a gun and a saddle: you just can't make it all by yourself." This is, again, a direct assault on the Western legend and on the American (capitalist) focus on the individual.

The attempt by Daves to look (and to get his audience to look) at the hardships of life for the poor is very apparent in perhaps his most well-known film, *3:10 to Yuma*. The key change made to the original Elmore Leonard short story is that, rather than having a deputy trying to load a prisoner on to the 3:10 train, we have a poor dirt farmer.[32] We are also given this person's backstory in considerable detail, both through the script and the visuals. The screenplay is by Halsted Welles but everything in the script is backed up, underlined, and emphasized by the images we are given on screen. In particular, dust is everywhere in the opening shots. A stagecoach crosses a vast plain that has the aridity of a desert. When it is brought to a halt by cattle across the trail, there are clouds of dust that clear only slowly.[33] Moments later, when Dan Evans (Van Heflin) arrives with his two sons, the dust is still settling. So, when we learn of the Evans family's struggle in the face of drought, we have already been prepared for it. Could any of the adults watching this film in the United States in the late 1950s not at this point begin to think of the Dust Bowl of the 1930s and the resulting poverty and dislocation of people's lives? Minutes later, when his wife looks at Dan and says, "Dan, you have to do something. You can't just stand by and watch. You worked so hard. I worked so hard, and the boys," can we avoid reflecting on the powerlessness of so many poor families in that period? Can we avoid seeing in the face of Dan's wife, Alice (Leora Dana), a deliberate echo of Dorothea Lange's most famous photograph, "Migrant Mother"?[34] Of course, when Alice comes out beneath the porch to look for her men returning, there is a reference to Martha in *The Searchers* (Ford, 1956), but Daves shoots his porch altogether differently. It is a space encompassing a poignant, vast emptiness and loneliness.[35]

3:10 to Yuma is set initially in and around Bisbee, a mining town in Arizona that had—at the time this film is supposedly set, in the 1880s—just recently been founded. The town is most (in)famous for the time in 1917 when local vigilantes put in place a deportation of striking miners that dwarfed the Jerome deportation of the same year.[36] *3:10* is about the attempt to load one outlaw under armed guard onto a cattle truck as it pulls out of Contention. The Bisbee "deportation" involved 900 ordinary townspeople having their civil rights ignored as they were loaded at gunpoint on to box-cars, transported 200 miles into New Mexico, held against their will for weeks, and warned not to return to Bisbee.[37] The outlaw gang in *3:10*, led by Ben Wade (Glenn Ford), is of course attempting to intercept a shipment of gold being taken out of Bisbee, a shipment of precious metal coming out of a mining town in which poor people extract precious metals and hand them over to a wealthy elite. Ben sees the choices for a "cowpoke" like him, or Dan, as being limited. "You gotta have money behind you," he says.

As with Budd Boetticher in *The Tall T* (1957), Daves makes use of the town of Contention as a location in *3:10 to Yuma*, and some of the suggestions made here may be considered contentious, but they are deliberately so and are made in the spirit of attempting to push toward a re-assessment of the politics found in Daves' Westerns. The evidence of the films is that Daves was the ultimate liberal. He was prepared to work with screenwriters like Albert Maltz and Leo Townsend, and to work productively with both. Maybe because he could see the liberal "truth" of both men's positions in relation to HUAC: Maltz refused to betray others and was determined to hold to democratic rights, while Townsend recognized that communism as practiced by the Communist Party was tantamount to Stalinism. There are problems with liberalism as an ideology attempting to confront the worst excesses of capitalism, but let us establish Daves' credentials in the field as a liberal before we engage more confrontationally with the politics to be found in his films.

BIBLIOGRAPHY

Aleiss, Angela, *Making the White Man's Indian: Native Americans and Hollywood Movies* (Westport, CT: Praeger, 2005).

Allen, James (ed.), *Without Sanctuary: Lynching Photography in America* (Santa Fe, NM: Twin Palms, 2000).

Arnesen, Eric (ed.), *Encyclopedia of U.S. Labor and Working-class History* (New York and Abingdon: Routledge, 2007).

Behlmer, Rudy (ed.), *Memo from Darryl F. Zanuck: the Golden Years at Twentieth-Century Fox* (New York: Grove Press, 1993).

Bourget, Jean-Loup, "Social Implications in Hollywood Genres," *Journal of Modern Literature*, 3:2 (1973): 191–200.

Casty, Alan, *Communism in Hollywood: the Moral Paradoxes of Testimony, Silence and Betrayal* (Lanham, MD: Scarecrow Press, 2009).

Ceplair, Larry, and Steven Englund, *The Inquisition in Hollywood: Politics in the Film Community, 1930–1960* (Berkeley: University of California Press, 1983).

Clements, Eric L., *After the Boom in Tombstone and Jerome, Arizona: Decline in Western Resource Towns* (Reno: University of Nevada Press, 2003).

Eckstein, Arthur M., and Peter Lehman (eds.), *The Searchers: Essays and Reflections on John Ford's Classic Western* (Detroit, MI: Wayne State University Press, 2004).

Falconer, Pete, "3:10 Again: A Remade Western and the Problem of Authenticity," in Rachel

Carroll (ed.), *Adaptation in Contemporary Culture: Textual Infidelities* (London and New York: Continuum, 2009).
Filler, Louis, *American Anxieties: a Collective Portrait of the 1930s* (New Brunswick, NJ: Transaction Publishers, 1993).
Herzberg, Bob, *Savages and Saints: the Changing Image of American Indians in Westerns* (Jefferson, NC: McFarland, 2008).
Horne, Gerald, *Class Struggle in Hollywood, 1930–50: Moguls, Mobsters, Stars, Reds and Trade Unionists* (Austin: University of Texas Press, 2001).
Jones, Kent, "*Jubal*: Awakened to Goodness," The Criterion Collection (2013a), <http://www.criterion.com/current/posts/2765-jubal-awakened-to-goodness> (last accessed 11 November 2015).
Jones, Kent, "*3:10 to Yuma*: Curious Distances," The Criterion Collection (2013b), <http://www.criterion.com/current/posts/2766-3-10-to-yuma-curious-distances> (last accessed 11 November 2015).
Joyner, C. Courtney, *The Westerners: Interviews with Actors, Directors, Writers and Producers* (Jefferson, NC: McFarland, 2009).
Leonard, Elmore, *Three-Ten to Yuma and Other Stories* (New York: HarperTorch, [1953] 2006).
Lindquist, John H., "The Jerome Deportation of 1917," *Arizona and the West*, 11:3 (1969): 233–46.
Maltz, Albert, "What Shall We Ask of Writers?" *The New Masses*, 12 February 1946.
Moloney, Deirdre M., *National Insecurities: Immigrants and U.S. Deportation Policy since 1882* (Chapel Hill: University of North Carolina Press, 2012).
Raheja, Michelle H., *Reservation Reelism: Redfacing, Visual Sovereignty, and Representations of Native Americans in Film* (Lincoln: University of Nebraska Press, 2010).
Scorsese, Martin, and Michael Henry Wilson (1995), *A Personal Journey With Martin Scorsese through American Movies*, film, directed by Scorsese and Wilson (London: British Film Institute).
Stanfield, Peter, Frank Krutnik, Irian Neve, and Steve Neale (eds.), *"Un-American" Hollywood: Politics and Film in the Blacklist Era* (Piscataway, NJ: Rutgers University Press, 2007).
Tavernier, Bernard, "The Ethical Romantic," *Film Comment*, January–February 2003, <http://www.filmcomment.com/article/delmer-daves-bertrand-tavernier> (last accessed 11 November 2015).
Whitehall, Richard, "The Heroes are Tired," *Film Quarterly*, 20:2 (1966–7): 12–24.

FILMOGRAPHY

Badlanders, The, director Delmer Daves, featuring Alan Ladd, Ernest Borgnine, Katy Jurado, Claire Kelly (Metro-Goldwyn-Mayer, 1958).
Broken Arrow, director Delmer Daves, featuring Jimmy Stewart, Jeff Chandler, Debra Paget, Basil Ruysdael (20th Century Fox, 1950).
Cowboy, director Delmer Daves, featuring Glenn Ford, Jack Lemmon, Anna Kashfi, Dick York (Columbia Pictures, 1958).
Drum Beat, director Delmer Daves, featuring Alan Ladd, Audrey Dalton, Marisa Pavan, Charles Bronson (Warner Bros., 1954).
Hanging Tree, The, director Delmer Daves, featuring Gary Cooper, Maria Schell, Karl Malden, George C. Scott (Warner Bros., 1959).

Jubal, director Delmer Daves, featuring Glenn Ford, Valerie French, Rod Steiger, Ernest Borgnine (Columbia Pictures, 1956).
Last Wagon, The, director Delmer Daves, featuring Richard Widmark, Felicia Farr, Susan Kohner, Tommy Rettig (20th Century Fox, 1956).
Return of the Texan, director Delmer Daves, featuring Dale Robertson, Joanne Dru, Walter Brennan, Richard Boone (20th Century Fox, 1952).
Searchers, The, director John Ford, featuring John Wayne, Natalie Wood, Jeffrey Hunter, Vera Miles (Warner Bros., 1956).
Strike, director Sergei Eisenstein, featuring Maxsim Shtraukh, Grigori Aleksandrov, Mikhail Gomorov, I. Ivanov (1925).
Tall T, The, director Budd Boetticher, featuring Randolph Scott, Richard Boone, Maureen O'Sullivan, Arthur Hunnicutt (Columbia Pictures, 1957).
3:10 to Yuma, director Delmer Daves, featuring Glenn Ford, Van Heflin, Felicia Farr, Leora Dana (Columbia Pictures, 1957).
White Feather, director Delmer Daves, featuring Robert Wagner, John Lund, Deborah Paget, Jeffrey Hunter (20th Century Fox, 1955).

NOTES

1. The Harvard Film Archive is housed at the Carpenter Center for the Visual Arts, Cambridge, MA. Bertrand Tavernier gave an interesting interview for the promotion of this series of films, available at <hcl.harvard.edu/hfa/films/2014janmar/western.html> (last accessed 11 November 2015).
2. Jones, "*3:10 to Yuma*: Curious Distances."
3. Tavernier, "The Ethical Romantic."
4. Maltz was one of the "Hollywood Ten" who refused to answer questions when brought before the House of Un-American Activities Committee (HUAC). He appeared before the Committee in 1947, claimed the First Amendment gave him the right not to answer, and was sentenced to twelve months' imprisonment and fined $1,000. His plays from the 1930s are described by Louis Filler as "bluntly anti-capitalistic, pro-radical labor, pro-peace" (Filler, *American Anxieties*, p. 106), but he had also been critical of the Stalinist line of the Communist Party in the States and had been criticized on the left for his article "What Shall We Ask of Writers?" published in *New Masses* in 1946, which suggested writers could be reactionary, might not have didactic left-wing political aims, and could still produce valid artistic work (Stanfield et al., *"Un-American" Hollywood*, p. 12; Horne, *Class Struggle*, 81). Maltz had also worked with Daves on the script for *Destination Tokyo* (1943) and so his influence on the director may have been greater than is generally suggested. In "What Shall We Ask of Writers?" Maltz stated: "much of left-wing artistic activity—both critical and creative—has been restricted, narrowed, turned away from life, sometimes made sterile because the atmosphere and thinking of the literary left has been based upon a shallow approach" (pp. 19–22).
5. Entirely predictably, Daves' (and/or Maltz's) enthusiasm for the idea of having debates within the film was not shared by studio heads. Darryl F. Zanuck is quoted as saying, "I saw from the very beginning that the tempo in the dialogue scenes was hopelessly slow and that we would have to find ways and means of speeding up, cutting dialogue etc." (Behlmer, *Memo*, p. 186).
6. See, for example, Douglas C. McChristian, *Fort Bowie, Arizona: Combat Post of the*

Southwest, 1858–1894 (Norman: University of Oklahoma Press, 2005), pp. 20–35; Bruce Vandervort, *Indian Wars of Canada, Mexico and the United States, 1812–1900* (New York: Routledge, 2006), pp. 192–210; and Edwin R. Sweeney, *Cochise: Chiricahua Apache Chief* (Norma: University of Oklahoma Press, 2005), pp. 142–65.

7. The debates over history and its interpretation, of course, continue. Bob Herzberg, for example, referring to Maltz, suggests, "The communist scenarist promptly turned the usual homespun western townsfolk into a fascist mob, and ignored Cochise's real-life atrocities" (Herzberg, *Savages and Saints*, p. 113). And the debate over the representation of Native Americans on screen remains complex. For Michelle H. Raheja, "Even in films that express admiration for Native Americans, such as Cecil B. DeMille's *The Squaw Man* (1914) or Delmer Daves's *Broken Arrow* (1950), seemingly respectful and balanced representations are often rooted in uncritical, problematic racial ideologies that reflect unexamined notions of Native American culture on the part of the director and on the part of North American society as a whole" (Raheja, *Reservation Reelism*, p. x).

8. "George Washington to the Secretary of State, 1 July, 1796," *The Writings of George Washington*, 35:112, quoted in Richard Harless, "Native American Policy," George Washington's Mount Vernon (2014), <http://www.mountvernon.org> (last accessed 11 November 2015). But Harless goes on to recognize the difficulties in this position and concludes that: "By 1796 even Washington had concluded that holding back the avalanche of settlers had become impossible, writing that 'I believe scarcely anything short of a Chinese wall, or a line of troops, will restrain land jobbers, and the encroachment of settlers upon the Indian territory.'"

9. The ending offers an interesting case in point in relation to Maltz's essay, "What Shall We Ask of Writers?" If Sonseeahray lives and goes off happily with Tom Jeffords at the end, we succeed in defying both the Hollywood system and the wider dominant ideology. However, if she dies in an Ophelia-like moment that suggests, as in Shakespeare's *Hamlet*, that in some sense she is too good for this world, and if Daves is then also able to replicate the earlier camera shot of the two lovers but this time with Sonseeahray dead, and if Jeffords is then able to exclaim, as he does, "Oh no, God in heaven!", with the implied question, "Is there a God in heaven?", then do we not, in fact, end up with a stronger artistic piece?

10. Bourget, "Social Implications," p. 193.

11. Ibid. p. 200.

12. For much of the film, Todd is presented in a much more ambivalent light than Jeffords in *Broken Arrow*. The opening sequence, for example, shows him killing a man as if he is on a hunting trip, shooting the man at distance precisely as if he were an animal.

13. The act itself is played out through Daves' cinematography as he manoeuvres Farr and Widmark into an ever closer coupling within the frame.

14. See *Los Desastres de la Guerra*, No. 39, "Grande hazana, con muertos," for example, and No. 36, "Tampoco." Images can be seen online, for example, at Cedar Rapids Museum of Art: <http://www.crma.org/exhibition/Detail/Past/Goyas-Disasters-of-War.aspx> (last accessed 11 November 2014).

15. "Strange Fruit," a poem by Abel Meeropol, a member of the Communist Party, written around 1937, was made famous as a song by Billie Holiday, available at <http://www.youtube.com/watch?v=h4ZyuULy9zs> (last accessed 11 November 2015); or see Nina Simone, available at <http://www.youtube.com/watch?v=P8Lq_yasEgo> (last accessed 11 November 2015).

16. See Allen, *Without Sanctuary*.

17. "... in western films of the 1950s, Indians are often substituting for the social question of black-white relations" (Eckstein and Lehman, *The Searchers*, p. 220).

18. On these events, see, for example, Michael Vinson Williams, *Medgar Evers: Mississippi Martyr* (Fayetteville: University of Arkansas Press, 2011), pp. 117–27; and Simeon Booker, *Shocking the Conscience: a Reporter's Account of the Civil Rights Movement* (Jackson: University Press of Mississippi, 2013), pp. 49–83.
19. See Ronald L. Davis, *Duke: The Life and Image of John Wayne* (Norman: University of Oklahoma Press, 1998) for a sense of Jimmy Grant's relationship with Wayne.
20. Though the pacifism of *Angel and the Badman* (1947), written and directed by Grant and starring Wayne, might suggest further complications for our too simplified approach.
21. Ceplair and Englund, *The Inquisition in Hollywood*, pp. 374–5. Townsend is even quoted as saying at the time, "Several years ago all of us fought with all our might against German and Italian fascism. Today there is a section of people who shut their eyes to Soviet fascism." See Casty, *Communism in Hollywood*, p. 17.
22. Aleiss, *Making the White Man's Indian*, p. 91.
23. Ibid. p. 99.
24. Jones, "*Jubal*: Awakened to Goodness."
25. The hymn, written by Robert Lowry in 1864, refers to the anticipation of rewards in heaven with which Christian teaching consoles those who have had it tough in life: "Yes, we'll gather at the river,/The beautiful, the beautiful river,/Gather with the saints at the river,/That flows by the throne of God."
26. "July 28: Liberty Leading the People," <http://www.louvre.fr/en/oeuvre-notices/july-28-liberty-leading-people> (last accessed 11 November 2015). The caption, given online, tells us "The Paris uprising . . . was initiated by the liberal republicans for violation of the Constitution by the Second Restoration government."
27. Clements, *After the Boom*, p. 316.
28. Lindquist, "The Jerome Deportation of 1917."
29. Joyner, *The Westerners*, p. 18.
30. Whitehall, "The Heroes Are Tired," p. 19.
31. Trumbo/Daves do allow themselves one episode in which they challenge the audience to consider the nature of reality in relation to the more usual Hollywood representation of reality. Horseplay with a rattlesnake ends abruptly when it bites one trail-hand (who has been standing innocently to one side). The immediate reaction of the audience might be that the trail-hand is continuing the joking and is only pretending to have been bitten; but it soon becomes clear this is not the case. In the next scene, the man lies dying in the foreground of the shot as the others sit around the camp casually talking. The effect is bizarre, surreal, jolting.
32. Falconer, "*3:10 Again*," p. 61.
33. See storyboards by Daves for the opening and some of the shots in this film at "Drawings by Delmer Daves," The Criterion Collection, 2013, <http://www.criterion.com/current/posts/2772-drawings-by-delmer-daves> (last accessed 11 November 2015).
34. See Lange's photographs of migrant families at <http://www.historyplace.com/unitedstates/lange> (last accessed 11 November 2015).
35. See Daves' drawings referred to in n. 33 above.
36. See Eric Arnesen (ed.), *Encyclopedia of US Labor and Working-class History* (New York and Abingdon: Routledge, 2007), pp. 155–6.
37. Moloney, *National Insecurities*, pp. 165–7.

CHAPTER 3

Bent, or Lifted Out by Its Roots: Daves' *Broken Arrow* and *Drum Beat* as Narratives of Conditional Sympathy

Józef Jaskulski

Stanley Corkin described the 1950s as the "golden age of the golden age" of Westerns.[1] This decade also saw Delmer Daves at his most prolific. Between 1950 and 1959, Daves delivered fifteen of his thirty movies. This included a run of nine Westerns, two of which recounted some of the endmost episodes in the long history of the Indian Wars.[2] Daves' first and arguably most covered Western, *Broken Arrow* (1950), recounts the story of the famous Apache chief Cochise and his friendship with Army scout and Indian agent Tom Jeffords. Conversely, in *Drum Beat* (1954) Daves turned his attention to a conflict far more obscure, recalling the U.S. Army's brief albeit bloody feud with the Modoc tribe of northern California.

Frequently described as the first Western to depict Native Americans in a thoroughly sympathetic manner, *Broken Arrow* may indeed serve as one of Hollywood's earliest comprehensive attempts to portray them as individuals rather than the usual feathered props. While it may not have been the first major Western to cast Native American characters in a more favorable light— John Ford's *Fort Apache* (1948) would likely stake this claim—*Broken Arrow*'s groundbreaking significance stems from its dwelling on the eagerly repressed history of broken treaties and encroachments on Native lands. It is often said that *Broken Arrow* critically engages with the myth of Manifest Destiny—and makes serious efforts to comprehensively represent Apache traditions.[3]

Compared with *Broken Arrow*, the legacy of *Drum Beat* has not proved nearly as lasting or apologetic. Several decades after its premiere, the film remains the sole Hollywood movie covering the largely forgotten Modoc War, yet its chief merit is that of visual craftsmanship. Shot in the then-cutting-edge CinemaScope widescreen format—as opposed to the standard spherical lens used in *Broken Arrow*—*Drum Beat* presents us with some of the most glamorous images in all Western movies. As to compassion for its Native American characters, *Drum Beat* stands in stark contrast to its famed antecedent, making virtually no pretence of veiling its director's political affiliations with ethnographic insight.

Though it may be tempting to discard *Drum Beat* as an essentialist step back in Hollywood's century-long struggle with the so-called "Indian problem," I suggest that *Drum Beat* can be read as a latent supplement to *Broken Arrow*. Together, the two films can serve as an important document of the industry's conflicted sentiments in the late Truman/early Eisenhower eras. Edward Buscombe referred to this entanglement of condescending sympathy to Native Americans as "benevolent paternalism," that is, an exhortation of continuous involvement of the federal government in the gradual integration of tribes in post-war society, even if such supervision necessitated considerably greater expenditure in the sector.[4] Daves' benevolently paternalist stance toward Native American affairs reflected a critique of the major about-face in the governmental policy implemented during the 1940s.

During U.S. engagement in the Second World War, the federal government began to withdraw from the assistance program adopted by the Bureau of Indian Affairs (BIA) under the Indian Reorganization Act and the Johnson-O'Malley Act (both 1934). Proposed by John Collier, the head of the BIA under President Franklin D. Roosevelt, the program was designed to counter the impact of long-lasting assimilationist practices through restitution of tribal land and the provision of publically funded services such as education, medical care, and new job positions on reservations. The program assumed that these improvements would assist the revival of a broadly (and generically) defined aboriginal culture. Starting early in the 1940s, Washington abandoned its relief policies—at the time outweighed by the pressing concerns of the War—and reinstated rapid assimilation in what became known as Termination Policy. The BIA was marginalized following its transfer to Chicago, and the subsequent collapse of federal assistance served as an efficient tool of "integration" through the imposition of harsh economic pressure on the Native American population. It also restored the government's hopes of gaining commercial access to tribal land, thus sparking protests from sympathizers such as Daves (a sentiment he clearly pronounced in *Broken Arrow* by casting Will Geer as the money-driven white villain). Most importantly, though, proponents of Termination saw it as a durable resolution of the perennial "Indian problem" by means of their ultimate acculturation. In the words of Steve Neale, "for conservatives, assimilation would ensure conformity and the ultimate superiority of Euro-American rules, norms, and laws."[5]

Although himself a Republican, Daves was apparently among those in opposition to Termination Policy. As a Republican, he was progressive and opposed right-wing radicalism; as an individual, his approach to Native

Americans was no doubt affected by the experience of living next to a reservation for an extended period. Daves' films are informed by a friendly yet condescending humanitarianism toward Native Americans, as they promote gradual assimilation combined with stipulated cultural autonomy. In the eyes of a prudent progressive, Termination failed to guarantee either.

As Neale reminds us, most critics typically elucidate "pro-Indian" Westerns in a twofold manner, that is, as allegories of contemporary racial debates (where Native Americans serve as substitutes for African Americans) and/or as parables of American involvement in the Cold War.[6] Thus are Hollywood's Indians frequently revealed as props in a catalogue of stories dealing with the ascension of the Civil Rights Movement and American imperialism. In this essay, I wish to recalibrate the focus on these narratives and study them as allegories of contemporary social and cultural conditions of Native Americans. Bearing in mind the fact that most discussions of Daves' "Indian Wars" Westerns tend to focus on *Broken Arrow*,[7] this essay shifts the emphasis toward *Drum Beat*. This approach will be taken with a view to examining how the changing socio-political prospects dictated by the post-war Indian policy reforms were reflected on the silver screen. It may also be illustrative of the inconsistencies that characterized Hollywood's probing of the so-called "Indian problem." This is due to the fact that, as Angela Aleiss observes, the evolution of representations of Native Americans in the movie industry has been historically inconsistent, proceeding in tides rather than in a linear pattern, and dependent on current political circumstances.[8] When read together with *Broken Arrow*, *Drum Beat* seems to reflect one such tidal change.

Premiering in 1950, *Broken Arrow* echoed with post-war optimism and appreciation of Native American war efforts, much as it also evinced disgust for McCarthyite witch-hunts—a sentiment shared by many, regardless of their otherwise diverse political sympathies (including progressive Republicans such as Daves).[9] Released in 1954, *Drum Beat* coincided with the federal withdrawal from the above-mentioned paternalistic, pre-war New Deal policies. While it reiterates the pro-reservation agenda presented in *Broken Arrow*, Daves' second pro-Indian Western also seems to possess an underlying tone of miscegenation anxiety, perhaps linked to the prospect of increasing racial integration. In addition, *Drum Beat* saw the progressive Republicanism of Daves[10] coalesce with the staunch conservatism of the film's producer and lead actor, Alan Ladd.[11] This resulted in a far more reactionary picture and, consequently, the original sympathy for the historical plight of the Apaches in *Broken Arrow* wanes in *Drum Beat*. Forced to leave the area that was once allotted to them, Captain Jack's (Charles Bronson) Modocs are ascribed with an inability to coexist peacefully with whites within a segregationist social contract. *Drum Beat* seems to imply that termination's mistake has been letting the jejune indigene "loose," instead of overseeing their steady "maturation" as citizens by a fatherly federal government.

That the above contradictions in political attitudes arose in the span of a mere four years, and within the body of work of a single director, only seems to amplify Jacquelyn Kilpatrick's observations on 1950s American cinema: "Films of the fifties," she contends, "ran the gamut from racist political propaganda to a type of enlightenment not seen in Hollywood since the days of the early silent films."[12] Analysing *Drum Beat* in the context of the themes of *Broken Arrow*, I argue that the two films reflect the ambivalent perception held by many in the U.S. toward Native Americans in the early phase of the Cold War. *Broken Arrow* evidently sympathizes with the historical plight of the quaintly picturesque and peaceful Apaches (represented by Cochise and Sonseeahray, Jeffords' Apache wife). While striving to render their material tradition with Remingtonian flair, it also advocates the reservation system as a guarantor of separate but equal coexistence, a means of sustaining tribal customs while under the supervision of civic development. In *Drum Beat*, the issue of assimilation is presented from a radically different angle. Appointed as peace commissioner by President Ulysses S. Grant, and aided by the accommodating "Indian maiden" Toby (Marisa Pavan), experienced Indian fighter Johnny MacKay (Alan Ladd) sets off for northern California to negotiate a truce with Captain Jack and his Modocs (who have left their reservation to wreak havoc on nearby white settlements). In portraying Jack as a throwback "Indian villain," the film projects onto the benign Native American citizens-in-the-making a racialist anxiety instilled in the vision of the mass disbandment of Native American tribes and their imminent "encroachment" upon white communities. This slip from the optimistic near-mysticism of *Broken Arrow* to a defensively harsh naturalism apparent in *Drum Beat* will be examined through the movies' respective uses of the (ig)noble savage and Indian princess archetypes. This amounts to a diptych of narratives of conditional sympathy, contingent on the changing legal status of Native Americans in U.S. society.

I shall consider the above archetypes in light of cultural history and postcolonial theory. To paraphrase a famous passage from Edward Said's *Orientalism*, I will read the two films as examples of a discourse entailed in the Western genre, which had become both a corporate institution for dealing with otherness, and a means of structuring, dominating, and imposing authority on otherness.[13] Pervading that discourse are generalizations of the other, a fascination with their exoticized material culture, and an assumption of what we may call a "caring authority" over the studied object. I shall further buttress these parallels by assuming the analogical position of the Western as the dominant cultural device in 1950s America. As noticed by Stanley Corkin, the Western acted as the prevalent tool for promotion of American selfhood on the brink of the Cold War.[14]

A HURT DEER ... OR A SNAKE: THE (IG)NOBLE SAVAGERY OF COCHISE AND CAPTAIN JACK

The end of the Second World War saw many of the over 25,000 Native American men and women who served in the armed forces, and still more of those involved in the war industry, return to their home country. With the government yet again effectively backtracking on its Indian policy, their homecoming was not a happy one. Washington's abandonment of the welfare programs it had adopted before the war, together with its push for Indian transformation, was met by a surprisingly abundant display of Native American patriotism.[15] Many in the U.S. greeted the radical character of this transformation with suspicion, as the rapid influx of Native Americans to urban areas spurred racialist fears and/or concerns for potential integration problems.

While both *Broken Arrow* and *Drum Beat* do envision the eventual assimilation of Native Americans into mainstream U.S. society, Daves seems to oppose the radicalism of the Termination Policy. Instead, he pleads for the maintenance of the reservation system, seeing it as a vessel that ensures controlled pluralism without disrupting the racial status quo.[16] Such a stance likely reflects what Howard Zinn dubbed the post-war "consensus . . . of conservatives and liberals, Republican and Democrats, around the policies of cold war and anti-Communism."[17] Zinn argues that this negotiable alliance revolved around a concurrent appeasement of conservatives and liberals through the fragmentary institution of Truman's Fair Deal welfare programme at home, which eventually congealed following the outbreak of the Korean War.[18] As noted by Philip Deloria, the sweeping experience of the Great Depression and the Second World War also induced many white Americans toward reconsidering the notions of cultural diversity, class divisions, and racial oppression.[19] Still, as far as the economics of the Native American issue were concerned, these reconsiderations also worked to the advantage of Termination Policy, enabling the government to cut down on federal assistance and thus force Native Americans to conform to Anglo-American norms under the cloak of emancipatory slogans.

Broken Arrow arrived at this historical juncture, addressing the aforementioned issues from a prudently progressive vantage point. Having developed a strong bond with the Southwest, where he spent some time on the Hopi Reservation, it was only natural for Daves to build his case around one of the most famous Native American leaders of the Southwest: Cochise of the Chiricahua Apache. Daves' Cochise set the standard for a number of nostalgic Hollywood representations of Native American heroes. Given Anglo-America's affection for a courageous other safely removed into the past,[20] the preferable choices for Hollywood screenwriters were the leaders uncompromising and articulate in their long-standing resistance to colonization. Still, the genre's nostalgia for the past was not one of sheer sentimentalism, since directors used the "cult of the Indian" to mediate the present and project the future.²¹ In *Broken Arrow*, such sentimental imagery acts as a catalyst for a sympathetic reconsideration of America's historical relations with Native Americans, a reassessment of its racialist prejudices, and a melioristic vision of their future.

Sympathy for this cause is generated through Cochise (Jeff Chandler) as an amalgam of the Indian sage and the noble savage. The prematurely gray-haired Chandler creates a "Good Indian" that Anglo-America loved to love, to paraphrase Kathryn Shanley.²² Cochise's nobility, eloquence, and honesty are a calming presence to the tense peace-making process, and a challenge to the popular anti-Indian convictions of the era. Conversely, his resigned rationality and quiet internalization of America's westward expansion embody the period's condescendingly racialist outlooks. Through Chandler as Cochise, Daves skillfully remodels the archetype of restrained masculinity, a figure that Lee Clark Mitchell attributes to James Fenimore Cooper's Leatherstocking Saga. Following in the footsteps of the founding father of the frontier epic, Daves manages to pack his picture with "mutually exclusive agendas: progressive and reactionary, liberal and conservative, forward-looking and nostalgic."²³

Although admittedly progressive in endowing Cochise with an unprecedented degree of dignity, *Broken Arrow* simultaneously declines to espouse the radical implementation of desegregation. Ever composed and aristocratic, Cochise beams with a confidence traditionally reserved for white frontiersmen. Cochise's credibility also lies in his physiognomy, mirroring Sherman Alexie's aphoristic history of indigenous representations in the Anglo-American discourse. In the eyes of the highly conservative moviegoers of the fifties, a white, blue-eyed Chandler was doubtless more appealing than a full-blooded Native American would have been.²⁴ This enabled Daves to command a greater degree of sympathy from Anglo-American audiences. The sanitization of Cochise's racial otherness bestows on him a twofold familiarity. Chandler's whiteness in *Broken Arrow* is both figurative and literal, since the correspondence of Cochise's conduct with American virtues is bolstered by his Caucasian visage, which distinguishes Chandler from the crowd of Native American walk-ons.²⁵

An embodiment of assimilationist ideals, the Apache chief acts as a link between the estranged cultures and helps domesticate the Native American other. This combination endows Cochise with an aura of exceptionality. To his fellow tribesmen, such as Juan (Billy Wilkerson), from whom Tom Jeffords (Jimmy Stewart) receives a brief lesson in Apache customs before heading into Indian Country, Cochise is "greater than other men, able to see through lies." The chief's near-supernatural brilliance also shines through in his masterful use of guerrilla tactics when the disciplined Apaches wipe out a reckless U.S. Army detachment on a mission to exterminate the tribe. Most of all, however,

Cochise turns his insight to aiding what we may provisionally call "reasonable submissiveness." This is evident in his and Jeffords' peace-making efforts, during which he shows a full understanding of assimilation. In an early overture of peace, Jeffords asks the Apache chief if their peoples "can live together as brothers." For Cochise, such a state of affairs is not only possible but also an ideal to be strongly encouraged. So is the treaty's implied stipulation that the Apache gradually adopt the white man's ways. Appealing to his fellow tribesmen at a council of Chiricahua chiefs, Cochise sincerely asks, "Why should not the Apache be able to learn new ways? It is not easy to change, but sometimes it is required ... If a big wind comes, a tree must bend, or be lifted out by its roots." In political-allegorical terms, Daves seems to be arguing here that assimilation ought not to be imposed in dramatic fashion. Instead, it should be patiently mediated, much the way Jeffords and General Howard (Basil Ruysdael) patiently liaise between Cochise's Apaches and the impatient white population of Tucson.

In light of the above, *Broken Arrow* may be seen as an extension of the liberal-conservative consensus of the Truman era into Native American matters. Arguing for controlled Indian dissidence, guaranteed by the maintenance of federally supervised reservations, Daves' vision entails welfare and segregation without imposing immediate acculturation. Such sentiments are reflected in Cochise's progressively conservative thinking. He internalizes Anglo-America's fear of miscegenation, fearing that Jeffords' marriage with Sonseeahray (Debra Paget) is bound to fail among Apache and Anglos alike. Cochise knows better than his infatuated friend, arguing that each should stick to his or her own in a system negotiated by way of a treaty that ensures the tribe's survival through governmental protectionism. Cochise's ultimate success in persuading most of his Apaches to honor the treaty thus confirms the paternalistic message of the film, a message foreshadowed by the opening sequence in which Jeffords stumbles upon and treats a wounded Apache boy. Cochise's sensibility in cooperation with his white counterpart and his better judgment with respect to the matters of racial separation make the fatherly Jeffords proud of his Indian protégé ("I was so proud of Cochise I was ready to burst," he says in voiceover) and grant both parties the luxury of durable peace.

Broken Arrow opens with Tom Jeffords riding into Apache territory as a prospector in search of gold. In the midst of a desert landscape, Jimmy Stewart's voiceover introduces us to his story. "The story started when I saw some buzzards circling in the sky. The buzzard is a smart bird. Something or somebody was getting ready to die. I figured it was a hurt deer or a rabbit or a snake." This "figuration" comes in handy when comparing the expressions of "pro-Indian" ideology pervading *Broken Arrow*. It is tempting to draw a figurative parallel between the sympathetic portrayal of Cochise as a hurt deer whom the compassionate Jeffords assists in evading annihilation, and the reactionary depiction of *Drum Beat*'s Captain Jack as a serpentine figure whose actions are far from predictable and hence call for governmental containment. If Cochise's rational "maturity" deserves assistance, Jack's infantile obstinacy requires strict surveillance.

Broken Arrow's anti-Termination stance stems from a belief in the long-lasting impact of federal subsidization on eventual assimilation of Native Americans. In contrast, *Drum Beat* projects the feared negative consequences of Termination. The film's imperative motto, "Peace doesn't come cheaply," reverberates throughout the picture *ad nauseam*, as if to reiterate the director's objection to reactionary decision-making. At the time of the film's premiere, the Eisenhower era had set in (fittingly, the film's plot is set in the Gilded Age, with Ulysses S. Grant at the helm), and with it came the solidification of congressional efforts to withdraw federal assistance to Native American tribes. By 1954 the government had intensified its relocation policy, disbanding a number of tribes across the country and overriding indigenous criminal jurisdiction on reservations. As Donald Fixico points out, such decisions presented themselves as antithetical to the pre-war protectionism, corresponding with the ever-present fluctuations in Indian affairs. Fixico vividly compares these inconsistencies to "an oscillating pendulum swinging between opposing poles: accommodation and dispossession, assimilation and segregation, acculturation and cultural pluralism, quasi-foreign and quasi-domestic status."[26] Whenever the pendulum swung forth, it also apparently instilled apprehension into the discourse of racial segregation, as reflected in the surprisingly conservative *Drum Beat*.

Although the film displays high production values, *Drum Beat*'s screenplay comes off as a set of tired clichés that retract the progressivism evident in *Broken Arrow*.[27] Were we to use Aleiss's provisional characterization of B-Westerns, *Drum Beat* would fit the bill to a large extent: the film's sympathy toward the Modocs is sketchy, its plot overtly formulaic, its "Indian villain" routinely one-dimensional, and the tribe's pidgin English riddled with grammatical errors.[28] Juxtaposed with the noble eloquence of *Broken Arrow*'s Cochise, Captain Jack comes across as an inarticulate savage bent on retaining tribal sovereignty in the face of unavoidable change (much like the stubbornly uncompromising Geronimo, played by Jay Silverheels, in *Broken Arrow*). In short, Jack proves undeserving of sympathy.

Rather than portraying him as the tragic figure he truly was—forced to choose between loyalty to fellow tribesmen and commitment to colonial legislation, and eventually duped by both[29]—Daves chooses instead to present Captain Jack as a childishly stubborn and dangerously anarchic figure, one incapable of grasping the elementary modalities of a modern society. Jack signs a treaty but goes on to break it for no good reason, dragging his people into needless war in the process. "Maybe I not want peace . . . I not sick of war," Jack exclaims when coaxed again into talking peace. A "two-bit tyrant," as described by his white adversary Johnny MacKay, Jack is a detestable renegade, killing defenceless settlers and retired military men for trinkets and gewgaws.

If Cochise's integrity was mirrored by the towering presence and luminous countenance of Chandler, Jack's running wild is amplified by the immense athleticism and atavistic physiognomy of Charles Bronson. "Bad" Indianness thus came to be represented by a white but ethnically "other" actor.[30] Bronson's face highlights Jack's incalculable savagery and furthers the point of paternalists who urged the maintenance of governmental supervision of Indians, its implications much more overt in *Drum Beat* than in *Broken Arrow*. A veteran Indian fighter, peace commissioner Johnny MacKay not only knows what is best for the Modocs but is also far more reluctant than Tom Jeffords to indulge in historical revisionism (irked at one point with his compatriots' belligerence toward Cochise, Jeffords accuses his people of being unwelcome guests in Indian Country). Johnny also remains far more skeptical of the Modocs' readiness for peace (i.e. desegregated coexistence with whites). Oblivious to Colonel Meek (Richard H. Cutting), who beseeches the chief to surrender to the commissioner's care—"Johnny will treat you right, Jack, you can trust him!"—Jack and his henchmen go on a rampage in the Lost River Valley, an area they had supposedly ceded to settlers in a treaty co-signed by Johnny.

Even putting aside the factual inaccuracies of what Kent Jones strangely considers a faithful account of the Lava Beds war,[31] it is easy to see *Drum Beat*'s historiographical backwardness when compared with its more progressive predecessor. Where Jeffords engages in critical scrutiny, Johnny accuses Jack of warmongering ("we could've saved a lot of lives if you hadn't grabbed the country that wasn't yours"). Johnny's accusation resurfaces at other times throughout the film, for instance in his debate with Dr. Thomas (Richard Gaines), an archetypal East Coast Indian sympathizer. Charged with turning to excessive violence, Johnny retorts, "When somebody shoots at my people, I shoot back." Fittingly, the debate takes place in the White House, as though in reiteration of the director's critique of uninformed Indian policy decision-making. Johnny's retort also carries a historiographical load, as it solidifies Anglo-America's self-righteously affirmative tale of westward expansion.

In line with Ward Churchill's remarks on the use of history in classical Westerns, there seems to be no "before" to the story in either *Broken Arrow* or *Drum Beat*.[32] As mentioned above, the former film opens with Jimmy Stewart's voiceover introduction, in which Tom Jeffords states that the story begins "here where you see me riding." Likewise, the history of the Modoc conflict in *Drum Beat* is traced back to Jack signing the treaty, rather than settler encroachment on tribal land. Also, the peace which Johnny struggles to secure is only reached once the Modocs internalize Anglo-America's fears and realize that, when not properly supervised, they pose a threat to their white neighbors. Thus they eventually surrender to white authority, admitting their "immaturity" as citizens of a desegregated society. "You treat us right, we quit," says Scarface Charlie (Rodolfo Acosta) when turning his band in to the stagecoach-driver-turned-Indian-fighter Bill Satterwhite (Robert Keith), as if in obsequious acknowledgment of the film's anti-termination sentiments—thus not only safeguarding federal custody over Jack's Modocs, but also their continued separation from whites.

For all of its shortcomings in this regard, *Drum Beat* does contain a scene in which Jack reveals a degree of the sort of self-reflection exhibited by Cochise, although this self-reflection is only stipulated by his imminent death. Shortly before his execution, the imprisoned Jack engages in conversations with a Christian minister and Johnny. Talking to the former, Jack mockingly responds to a series of clichéd consolatory remarks. "You say this heaven nice place, huh? You like this place heaven? . . . Then I tell you what, preacher. You like it so much, you take my place out there . . . You go to heaven instead of me." Moments later, Jack accepts a visit from Johnny:

> Jack: Red man think he go to good place when he die: good hunting . . . good shooting . . . no white man. None! You not like preacher who talk about pearly gates. You got sense. You tell me, Johnny, you believe there is place like this?
> Johnny: Yeah, I believe that, Jack, except I think it's open for all of us when we die. I think they, ah, even let white men in.
> Jack: If I see this for red men only up there, maybe some day I tell them "you let Johnny MacKay in, he good fighter."
> Johnny: Thanks, Jack. Maybe I'll see you then. Goodbye, and good luck. And good hunting.

Whether intentional or not, the ambiguity of the two prison scenes makes them stand out as a minor *tour de force* in an otherwise reactionary film. Jack and Johnny muse on the possibility of ultimate integration, concluding it is best that the two communities stick to their own, and that their coexistence is inconceivable in this world. And yet, despite their racialist tone, Jack's prison-cell conversations provide *Drum Beat* with a quasi-trickster quality, as the grandiose seriousness of this ignoble savage is, for once, overcome with bitterly ironic humor. Conversing with the preacher, Jack rejects his words of comfort, exposing the minister's hypocrisy and resisting his own relegation to history. For once, Bronson's volatile character displays traces of Native American tricksterism, a subversive trait displayed by Native American freedom fighters in order to tease the dominant discourse. Even with his

Figure 3.1 Johnny and Captain Jack converse prior to Jack's execution.

own execution pending, Jack seems ready to "outwit the missionaries," to use Gerald Vizenor's phrasing.[33] But then again, Jack's playful resistance to the dominant discourse—a feature which Vizenor sees as a key component of Native American survival strategies—ironically contributes to his eventual demise. In the words of Johnny MacKay, Jack lives and dies for a purpose, and his is to pinpoint the anxiety attending the imminent return of the vanishing American to a racially sanitized landscape.

ABOUT INDIAN WOMEN: THE FEAR OF MISCEGENATION IN *BROKEN ARROW* AND *DRUM BEAT*

In *Killing the Indian Maiden: Images of Native American Women in Film*, M. Elise Marubbio recognizes *Broken Arrow*'s Sonseeahray as the paragon of the post-war transformation of the Indian princess from the well-disposed and sensuous silent-period figure into a deeply spiritual mediator between races.[34] That transformation concludes with her eventual death, which symbolically seals the peace treaty between the U.S. and the Apaches. *Drum Beat*'s Toby to a certain extent replicates these features. Still, juxtaposed with Sonseeahray, Toby's character seems indicative of the regression that characterized the subsequent development of the Indian princess as the decade went on and civil rights conflicts inflamed.[35] Although critics such as Edward Buscombe remain skeptical of treating the era's compulsive interest in miscegenation as an assimilative allegory, preferring to see it as a dramatization of white sexual anxieties,[36] it is not unreasonable to trace the evolution of the Indian maiden in Daves to the juncture of both of the above lines. Together, they help interpret the regressive appropriation and fencing off of Native American women in *Broken Arrow* and *Drum Beat* as driven by both protectionist sympathy embedded in controlled assimilation, and intense miscegenation angst impelled by the prospects of Termination Policy.

Let us go back once more to the immensely rich and ideologically charged opening of *Broken Arrow*, and examine the remainder of Jimmy Stewart's voiceover introduction:

> This is the story of a land, of the people who lived on it in the year 1870, and of a man whose name was Cochise. He was an Indian—leader of the Chiricahua Apache tribe. I was involved in the story and what I have to tell happened exactly as you'll see it—the only change will be that when the Apaches speak, they will speak in our language. What took place is part of the history of Arizona and it began for me here where you see me riding.

From the outset, *Broken Arrow* sets the tone for what the film promises to be and stresses its ambition to faithfully recount an excerpt from the nation's troubled past; an episode in which a Native American leader will be cast as the lead protagonist. Simultaneously, however, the movie relapses into the familiar mode of Anglo-American historiography, since its storyline commences *in medias res*, thus blurring the origins of the U.S. feud with the Apache and presenting it as a tale of appropriative discovery. For Jeffords, as for the viewer, the story of the land begins with his entry to the Indian Country. In the grain of prototypical frontiersmen, Jimmy Stewart rides into unexplored territory, staking a claim to its history, land, and aboriginal inhabitants. This appropriative gaze resurfaces in the film's archetypal ending, where we see Jeffords ride off into the wilderness, gradually fusing with the misty sierras, once more backed by Stewart's voiceover ("As time passed, I came to know that the death of Sonseeahray put a seal on the peace"). Like his literary predecessors, Jeffords is thus depicted as innate to the landscape, emerging from and returning to it as his quest concludes. His totalistic vision appropriates the otherness it purports to recognize.

As if in a literal reading of Chief Eskiminzin's famous speech, Daves' film seems to stem from a conviction that the Apaches have no one to tell their own story,[37] and hence their cause requires ambassadorial validation in the form of a white voiceover.[38] The intermediation of Tom Jeffords—historically the first Indian agent on Cochise's reservation—thus acquires a dual significance. Jeffords' ability to negotiate peace serves as litmus test for Apache humanity in the eyes of his white brethren, while at the same time the voiceover casts this humanization within a grid of patronizing racialism. Thus, to paraphrase Armando José Prats, while dissociating itself from historical violence, *Broken*

Arrow continues to transmute the presence of contemporary Native Americans into an absence.[39] This measure returns in *Drum Beat*, which is likewise bracketed by its subtitled prologue: "The story you are about to see is based upon historical fact. Fictional incidents and characters have been introduced only where necessary to dramatize the truth"; and voiceover epilogue: "Thus ended the killing in the Modoc country, and a peace began among our peoples that lives to this day."

What may be inferred from both films is an unquestioned belief in the superiority of canonical history, one that subdues their declared revisionist effort. Alternate narratives offered by Native Americans (Geronimo and Captain Jack respectively) are discarded in their angry infantilism in ways that are in line with imperialist practices noted by Said in *Culture and Imperialism*. Despite their considerable humanism, Daves' "pro-Indian" Westerns fail to recognize the coexistence of ideological counter-narratives. Instead, they work to solidify the prevailing linear historiography, which instrumentalizes the "presence" of other cultures for its own affirmation. Pursuant to these practices, Said contends that the transformation of natives from a state of subservience to inferior humanity is accompanied by the transfiguration of the colonizer into an "invisible" and "objective" chronicler of their history, resulting in the silencing of the former.[40] Said argues that the well-intentioned silencing of the other in these transmutations involves the exertion of epistemic violence on the represented other. After all, those representations follow from what Said refers to as geographical notation. This is to say, "the theoretical mapping and charting of territory that underlies Western fiction, historical writing, and philosophical discourse of the time." Essentially, for Said, "there is first the authority of the European observer—traveller, merchant, scholar, historian, novelist."[41] The ultimate, albeit implied, task of Daves' Indian diptych is to strengthen his own narrative from a position of candid historical "revisionism," and to address his own anxiety inherent to the forthcoming American social reforms that characterized government policy in the 1950s. To that end, his stories reinforce the interrelation between the colonizer and the colonized implied by the Orientalist tradition, in which the white subject writes about and on behalf of the exotic other.

In this regard, Daves' paternalism may be further explicated in light of another post-colonial theorist. In Gayatri Chakravorty Spivak's critique of Julia Kristeva—specifically, her essay "About Chinese Women"[42]—Spivak contends that Kristeva's analysis is predicated upon philosophical narcissism, and that her essay reduces its subject to a trampoline for self-enquiry. She declares that "[Kristeva's] question, in the face of those silent women, is about her own identity rather than theirs."[43] Spivak also points out that by measuring radically divergent cultural experiences of her Chinese subjects with Western theoretical tools, Kristeva self-absorbedly compromises her recognition of difference,[44] thus enclosing third-world women with a condescendingly Eurocentric narrative.

While not overtly narcissistic, Daves' probing of otherness in *Broken Arrow* and *Drum Beat* does disclose a condescending, Eurocentric perspective. Advertised as movies about Indians, his two films are less about actual Native Americans than they are about contemporary Anglo-Americans (and those aligned with the dominant white power structure). The films' appropriative compassion takes for granted that, given their historical marginalization and silencing, the Native American subaltern cannot understandably speak for him or herself and requires white advocacy to audibly translate their case. At the turbulent time of Termination, Daves thus takes the role of a mildly condescending interpreter of the Native American cause and makes the assumption that they cannot narrate their own discourse. Concurrently, the director unwittingly instrumentalizes his Indian protagonists for the sake of his own argument. Due to their autotelic character, these translations in turn overshadow the subject whose message they aim to transmit.

In view of Marubbio's above-mentioned delineation of the Indian princess in the 1950s Western as a secondary character in the service of the racialist ideologies of the time, and of the genre's inherent focus on males, the marginalization of Indian females is hardly surprising. In both films, the shadow of colonial production is cast on their respective incarnations of the Indian princess from two slightly different angles. While Sonseeahray and Toby share some qualities as models for Indian assimilation—their eagerness to embrace Anglo-American culture reflected in their command of English and in the films' incidental music—the ways in which Daves uses them as allegories to address America's miscegenation anxiety are highly divergent. Sonseeahray's spiritualized pubescence may reflect the mildness of racialist undertones of Hollywood's prototypical "pro-Indian" Western, but Toby's full-blown sensuality seems to mirror the intensifying fear of a racially mixed society.

The main feature Sonseeahray and Toby share is their literal and metaphorical whiteness, manifested by their cultural receptiveness. As mentioned by Marubbio, within the rhetoric of "pro-Indian" Westerns such as *Broken Arrow* and *Drum Beat*, whiteness stands for civilization and thus stigmatizes Indian protagonists as savages. At the same time, the princess's desire for the white protagonist conveys a promise of assimilation and petrifies dominant historical narratives when it misrepresents "nation-building" as a universally endorsed process.[45] Sonseeahray's striking paleness[46] and her naïve amazement at the tokens and knowledge of white culture facilitate her presentation as an innocuous student of a superior civilization ("The world is so big and I know so little"). While Sonseeahray internalizes racialist ideology in a thoroughly intimate way, Toby—played by an Italian actress dressed in white buckskins—subsumes Indian agency to white supervision in a more publicized manner.

Toby renounces the prospects of Termination represented by Jack's prowling around the Lost River Valley when she says to Johnny that "he's a bad Modoc... I think it is best that you kill him." Toby arrives in town from the Klamath reservation, on which Captain Jack's people were placed and which they left to wreak havoc among white settlers. Assuming voice on behalf of her people, Toby implores Johnny to restore peace—a mission which she pledges to facilitate, along with the "good" Modocs led by her brother Manok (Anthony Caruso), the aim being to ensure that Jack's "bad Indians" are brought back to the reservation they had supposedly chosen for their settlement. Although both of Daves' "Native American" females are ultimately doomed to fail in their attempts to enter white society, white viewers of the era may have read the princesses' efforts sympathetically, especially given the enhancement of their physical whiteness and cultural submissiveness through incidental music and their standout command of English.

In terms of incidental music, and as Stam and Spence notice in their essay on colonialist representations of otherness, it is no secret that every film score carries an emotional dimension which powerfully affects the viewer's sympathies. Perhaps no other film genre has been as ostentatious as the Western in turning to these musical amplifications of otherness. In this respect, *Broken Arrow* and *Drum Beat* are no different, supplying their Apache and Modoc characters with two types of "Indian" motifs. Where their male counterparts are invariably heralded by the eponymous beating of drums and *forte-fortissimo* brass chords, the princesses move, talk, and die to the accompaniment of soothing *piano-pianissimo* woodwinds backed by the string quartet. To paraphrase Stam and Spence, such use of music acts as an acoustic synecdoche of neutralized Indian restlessness epitomized by the genre's white-painted ladies.[47]

The above strategy is complemented by the way in which Daves' Indian princesses communicate with the Anglo-American audience. In his linguistic analysis of India as a British colony, Braj B. Kachru examines how colonialist discourse elevated the ability to speak English to the status of an alchemic tool, enabling the Empire's colonial subjects to remodel their multifarious identities in accordance with "neutral" standards of a language imposed on them by the colonizer. While such neutralization allowed the ethnically diverse inhabitants of the subcontinent to articulate clearly what resisted expression in their native languages, it nonetheless detached them from the cultural and emotional connotations contained within those languages. Kachru further points to the ambivalent duality of what he calls "the alchemy of English" when he observes that while providing access to an empowering discourse, the colonizer's language also constituted a linguistic mechanism of discipline and deception.[48] Relating to the experience of colonization among Native Americans, Gerald Vizenor notices a similar ambivalence in their attitude to English:

> The English language has been the linear tongue of colonial discoveries, racial cruelties, invented names, the simulation of tribal cultures, manifest manners, and the unheard literature of dominance in tribal communities; at the same time, this mother tongue of paracolonialism has been a language of invincible imagination and liberation for many tribal people in the postindian world. English, a language of paradoxes, learned under duress by tribal people at mission and federal schools, was one of the languages that carried the vision and shadows of the Ghost Dance.[49]

The above remarks, when referred to *Broken Arrow* and *Drum Beat*, help expound the ideological implications behind the "neutralized" English of their Indian princesses. In the grain of Kachru's analysis, Sonseeahray's command of the colonizer's language (a matter of cultural convention, since we learn that what is presented to viewers is merely a translation from the Apache) facilitates the nullification of her difference and disconnects her from the cultural prejudices inherent in the Western genre. It thus assists in manufacturing conditional acceptance of the other. Likewise, Toby's English, which she applies to sustain peaceful yet separate coexistence of Modocs and whites, assists the linear discourse of American colonialism and paternalism toward Native Americans. This is especially evident since, in contrast to *Broken Arrow*, *Drum Beat* refuses to extend linguistic equality on all of its Indian characters, and indeed uses English as a stigmatizing tool by having its "bad" Indians speak pidgin English.[50]

While they both embrace the Anglo-American culture and white protectionism, Daves' Indian princesses differ in terms of their sexuality. Like everything else relating to Native Americans, this seems to point to the fluctuating racial mores of the period. Played by the then fifteen-year-old Paget, Sonseeahray's budding sexuality implies innocence appreciative of Jeffords' guidance, reverberating with the idea of supervised assimilation. The film idealizes her pubescence, introducing Sonseeahray in the midst of a female rite of passage. She is, as Cochise informs Jeffords, "in the holiest time of her life," about to be celebrated as "the mother of life." Pristine and untainted by sexual contact with "red" Indians, Sonseeahray immediately captivates Jeffords's imagination. Daves seems at first to have broken the spell of miscegenation by having the white scout and the Indian princess marry in a wannabe-Indian fashion (an "Apache" wedding prayer was scripted into the movie in the grain of Anglo-American authorial marital vows) and sending them off to their honeymoon. In the end, however, Sonseeahray dies at the hands of white rogues, forewarning the audience of the lack of acceptance for miscegenation in a segregated society.

Toby's death adheres to a similar pattern—she is killed by her own people as she tries to defend her white (unrequited) love. Still, her passing stems from more radical premises, perhaps spurred by the still distant yet increasingly likely prospects of desegregation augured by Native American migrations to urban areas and, far more so, by the rise of the Civil Rights movement in the 1950s. Sonseeahray's sexual naïveté is contrasted by Toby's allure as an Indian seductress. In the grain of the pre-war silent movies, Toby's sexuality is devoid of "soul," if not self-debasing. Confessing her love to Johnny, Toby forces herself upon him ("I will do all those things you wish me to do as your woman, and I will be very proud"). Johnny immediately quashes the idea as downright insane. Coupled with his earlier comment on interracial marriage as provisionally acceptable when no white women are available, Johnny's statement testifies to the increasing reluctance of white America to accept a renegotiation of the social contract.[51] In this respect, white America's refusal to even entertain the possibility of miscegenation compromises *Drum Beat* far more so than *Broken Arrow*.

CONCLUSION

As the above analysis suggests, the director's attempts to transcend the genre's ideological limitations in *Broken Arrow* and *Drum Beat*—while constituting a significant improvement over the long-standing tradition of racialist depictions of Native Americans in Hollywood films—came off as partly foiled by the dynamics of socio-political changes of the first half of the 1950s. From today's perspective, the historical value of Daves' two "pro-Indian" Westerns seems to lie mostly in introducing "indigenous" characters who, despite their numerous shortcomings, appear as more than ill-sketched imitations (even if these humanitarian efforts ultimately slipped into stock romances of Native American absence). At the time of their production, Daves' narratives helped reimagine America's identity by providing a stabilizing narrative in a time of increased uncertainty (the Cold War) and budding confidence (the nation's rise to the position of a global superpower). From the micro-perspective of Indian affairs at the time, Daves pitches to the white audiences an offer of equality safeguarded by segregation (*Broken Arrow*), and forewarns of potential social disquiet embedded in Termination Policy (*Drum Beat*). His films remain unwaveringly reassuring thanks to the employment of interracial peace-making committees capable of alleviating prospective crises—Jeffords, Sonseeahray, and Cochise in *Broken Arrow*, MacKay, Toby, and Manoc in *Drum Beat*.

BIBLIOGRAPHY

Aleiss, Angela, *Making the White Man's Indian: Native Americans and Hollywood Movies* (Westport, CT: Praeger, 2005).

Alexie, Sherman, "I hated Tonto (still do)," *Los Angeles Times*, 28 June 1998, <http://articles.latimes.com/1998/jun/28/entertainment/ca-64216> (last accessed 11 November 2015).

Almond, Ian, *The New Orientalists: Postmodern Representation of Islam from Foucault to Baudrillard* (London and New York: I. B. Tauris, 2007).

Brown, Dee, *Bury My Heart at Wounded Knee: An Indian History of the American West* (London: Vintage, 1991).

Buscombe, Edward, *"Injuns!": Native Americans in the Movies* (London: Reaktion Books, 2006).

Churchill, Ward, *Fantasies of the Master Race: Literature, Cinema and the Colonization of American Indians* (San Francisco: City Lights Books, 1998).

Corkin, Stanley, *Cowboys as Cold Warriors: The Western and U.S. History* (Philadelphia: Temple University Press, 2004).

Critchlow, Donald T., *When Hollywood Was Right: How Movie Stars, Studio Moguls, and Big Business Remade American Politics* (New York: Cambridge University Press, 2013).

Deloria, Philip J., *Playing Indian* (New Haven and London: Yale University Press, 1998).

Ebert, Roger, "Charles Bronson: 'It's just that I don't like to talk very much'", <http://www.rogerebert.com/interviews/charles-bronson-its-just-that-i-dont-like-to-talk-very-much> (last accessed 11 November 2015).

Eyman, Scott, *Empire of Dreams: The Epic Life of Cecil B. DeMille* (New York: Simon & Schuster, 2010).

Fixico, Donald, "Federal and State Policies and American Indians," in P. J. Deloria and N. Salisbury (eds.), *A Companion to American Indian History* (Malden and Oxford: Blackwell Publishers, 2002), pp. 379–96.

Fojas, Camilla, *Border Bandits: Hollywood on the Southern Frontier* (Austin: University of Texas Press, 2008).

Gandhi, Leela, *Postcolonial Theory: A Critical Introduction* (Crows Nest, NSW: Allen & Unwin, 1998).

Hearne, Joanna, "The 'Ache for Home': Assimilation and Separatism in Anthony Mann's *Devil's Doorway*," in P. C. Rollins and J. E. O'Connor (eds.), *Hollywood's West: The American Frontier in Film, Television, and History* (Lexington: University Press of Kentucky, 2005), pp. 126–59.

Jones, Kent, "*Jubal*: Awakened to Goodness," The Criterion Collection (2013a), <http://www.criterion.com/current/posts/2765-jubal-awakened-to-goodness> (last accessed 11 November 2015).

Kachru, Braj B., "The Alchemy of English," in B. Ashcroft, G. Griffiths, and H. Tiffin (eds.), *The Post-Colonial Studies Reader* (London and New York: Routledge, 2009), pp. 272–5.

Kilpatrick, Jacquelyn, *Celluloid Indians: Native Americans and Film* (Lincoln, NE, and London: University of Nebraska Press, 1999).

Lawrence, David Herbert, *Studies in Classic American Literature*, ed. E. Greenspan, L. Vasey, and J. Worthen (Cambridge: Cambridge University Press, 2003).

Lenihan, John H., *Showdown: Confronting Modern America in the Western Film* (Urbana, IL: University of Illinois Press, 1980).

Marubbio, M. Elise, *Killing the Indian Maiden: Images of Native American Women in Film* (Lexington: University Press of Kentucky, 2006).

Mitchell, Lee Clark, *Westerns: Making the Man in Fiction and Film* (Chicago and London: University of Chicago Press, 1996).
Moyers, Bill, "Sherman Alexie on Living Outside Cultural Borders," <billmoyers.com/segments/sherman-alexie-on-living-outside-borders> (last accessed 11 November 2015).
Neale, Steve, "Vanishing Americans: Racial and Ethnic Issues in the Interpretation and Context of Post-war 'Pro-Indian' Westerns," in Edward Buscombe and Roberta E. Pearson (eds.), *Back in the Saddle Again: New Essays on the Western* (London: British Film Institute Publishing, 1998), pp. 8–28.
Said, Edward, *Culture and Imperialism* (London: Vintage, 1994).
Said, Edward, *Orientalism* (London: Penguin Books, 2003).
Shanley, Kathryn, "The Indians America Loves to Love and Read," in G. M. Bataille (ed.), *Native American Representations. First Encounters, Distorted Images, and Literary Appropriations* (Lincoln, NE, and London: University of Nebraska Press, 2001), pp. 26–51.
Slotkin, Richard, *Gunfighter Nation: The Myth of the Frontier in Twentieth-Century America* (New York: Harper Perennial, 1993).
Spence, Louise, and Robert Stam, "Colonialism, Racism and Representation," in B. Ashcroft, G. Griffiths, and H. Tiffin (eds.), *The Post-Colonial Studies Reader* (London and New York: Routledge, 2009), pp. 109–12.
Spivak, Gayatri Chakravorty, "Can the Subaltern Speak?," in B. Ashcroft, G. Griffiths, and H. Tiffin (eds.), *The Post-Colonial Studies Reader* (London and New York: Routledge, 2009), pp. 28–37.
Spivak, Gayatri Chakravorty, "French Feminism in an International Frame," in Gayatri Chakravorty Spivak, *In Other Worlds: Essays in Cultural Politics* (London and New York: Routledge, 2006), pp. 134–53.
Tavernier, Bertrand, "The Ethical Romantic," *Film Comment*, January–February 2003, <http://www.filmcomment.com/article/delmer-daves-bertrand-tavernier> (last accessed 11 November 2015).
Vizenor, Gerald, *Manifest Manners: Narratives on Postindian Survivance* (Lincoln, NE, and London: University of Nebraska Press, 1999).
Zinn, Howard, *A People's History of the United States: From 1492–Present* (New York: HarperCollins, 2003).

FILMOGRAPHY

Broken Arrow, director Delmer Daves, featuring Jimmy Stewart, Jeff Chandler, Debra Paget, Basil Ruysdael (20th Century Fox, 1950).
Drum Beat, director Delmer Daves, featuring Alan Ladd, Audrey Dalton, Marisa Pavan, Charles Bronson (Warner Bros., 1954).
Fort Apache, director John Ford, featuring John Wayne, Henry Fonda, Miguel Inclán, Shirley Temple (RKO Radio Pictures, 1948).

NOTES

1. Corkin, *Cowboys as Cold Warriors*, p. 127.
2. These were, in chronological order: *Broken Arrow* (1950), *Return of the Texan* (1952),

Drum Beat (1954), *Jubal* (1956), *The Last Wagon* (1956), *3:10 to Yuma* (1957), *Cowboy* (1958), *The Badlanders* (1958), and *The Hanging Tree* (1959).
3. Jones, "*Jubal*: Awakened to Goodness."
4. Buscombe, *"Injuns!"*, pp. 108–9.
5. Neale, "Vanishing Americans," p. 19.
6. Ibid. p. 8.
7. Discussions of *Broken Arrow* have been numerous and sometimes mutually divergent, to mention just a few: Richard Slotkin (*Gunfighter Nation*) interprets the film as a parable of the post-war market, in which common economic interests enable a peaceful coexistence of mutually cognizant agents; Jacquelyn Kilpatrick (*Celluloid Indians*) argues that the film uses Indians in a metaphorical appeal for tolerance to otherness during the McCarthy era; Stanley Corkin (*Cowboys as Cold Warriors*) treats it as an indictment of the Western's inclination to lend itself to ideologizations of social violence and Cold War militarism; Angela Aleiss (*Making the White Man's Indian*) reads *Broken Arrow* as an endorsement of the post-war Indian termination policy; on the contrary, Edward Buscombe (*"Injuns!"*) sees the movie as an appeal for the preservation of state supervision over Native American reservations (a viewpoint which informs this contribution); M. Elise Marubbio (*Killing the Indian Maiden*) turns her attention to the discussion of the film as an exemplary case of the post-war re-emergence of the cinematic Indian princess as a token of racial integration model envisioned by the dominant discourse; Joanna Hearne ("The 'Ache for Home'") considers it a fantasy in which Indian characters submissively transfer their rights to land and self-determination in a treaty sealed by Cochise breaking the arrow of war.
8. Aleiss, *Making the White Man's Indians*, p. xvii.
9. Indicative of Daves' stand on Senator McCarthy's witch hunts was his reaction to Cecil B. DeMille's infamous anti-Communist remarks at the 22 October 1950 Directors Guild meeting, during which the director of *The Ten Commandments* insinuated that a number of signatories of the petition in support of Joseph Mankiewicz's Guild presidency represented anti-American interests, an allegation reportedly founded solely on their ethnic origin. Having listened to DeMille's rant, "Delmer Daves stood up and said, 'I am a Republican, too, Mr DeMille. My children are fourth-generation Californians, and I resent beyond belief the things you said as you summarized the 25 men . . . I think it was disgraceful" (Eyman, *Empire of Dreams*, p. 107).
10. Tavernier, "The Ethical Romantic."
11. Critchlow, *When Hollywood Was Right*, p. 143.
12. Kilpatrick, *Celluloid Indians*, p. 58.
13. Said, *Orientalism*, p. 4.
14. Corkin, *Cowboys as Cold Warriors*, p. 5.
15. Fixico, "Federal and State Policies and American Indians," p. 386.
16. While Native American intellectuals of the earlier generation, such as N. Scott Momaday or Leslie Marmon Silko, also saw reservations as crucial factor in their struggle to preserve identity, some representatives of the younger generation, such as Sherman Alexie, tend to be more outspoken on their historical ambivalence. "We didn't make reservations. The U.S. military and government made reservations and it was a place where we were supposed to be concentrated and die, and disappear. And I think it is only out of self-destructive impulses that Native Americans have turned reservations into sacred spaces . . . Often, the places where the reservations are aren't where the sacred locations were for tribes. I think Spokane, because it's where Spokane Falls is, I think the city is actually far more sacred than the reservation . . . Ironically, the reservations also saved us, 'cause they concentrated us" (Moyers, "Sherman Alexie on Living Outside Cultural Borders.").

17. Zinn, *A People's History of the United States*, p. 427.
18. As evident in the Truman administration's conflicted Indian policy, the consensus did not resolve continuing congressional pushing and shoving, resulting in mutually contradictory decisions. For example, despite the rehabilitation of the Navajo and Hopi tribes and the passing of the Indian Claims Commission Act in the hope of effectively settling tribal land claims, the era also saw an intensification of efforts toward withdrawal of federal support of the reservation system.
19. Deloria, *Playing Indian*, p. 132.
20. Fixico, "Federal and State Policies and American Indians," p. 383.
21. Slotkin, *Gunfighter Nation*, pp. 347–78.
22. Shanley, "The Indians America Loves to Love and Read," pp. 26–51.
23. Mitchell, *Westerns*, p. 54.
24. Alexie, "I hated Tonto (still do)."
25. Slotkin, *Gunfighter Nation*, p. 375. See also Fojas, *Border Bandits*. Fojas denotes the "whitening" of ethnic others as a common practice of the era, utilized to indirectly address racial issues without disturbing the conservative preconceptions of white audiences. "Because of the racial prejudices largely spread by dominant media, the races had particular types in the public imaginary, which were undermined by these mixed-race characters played by white actors. With these characters, attractive by dominant beauty standards, the 'race' question could be addressed and dramatized in portraits that were pleasing to the eyes of the audience" (p. 44). In line with this practice, Daves' representations of Native Americans employ physiognomies fitting in the paradigm of "whiteness," but exotically divergent from the Anglo-American canons of beauty. In both films, the main "Indian" characters are thus played respectively by the Jewish American Jeff Chandler and the Lithuanian American Charles Bronson.
26. Fixico, "Federal and State Policies and American Indians," pp. 385–7.
27. Lenihan, *Showdown*, p. 43. Lenihan reads this retraction as the director's attempt to provide a "balanced" account of the history of the West, as "having presented the Indian's point of view in *Broken Arrow*, Daves wanted to offer the settler's side of the story."
28. Aleiss, *Making the White Man's Indians*, p. xix.
29. Brown, *Bury My Heart at Wounded Knee*, pp. 219–41.
30. Born Charles Buchinsky, Bronson came from a coal-mining town in Pennsylvania, one of fifteen children to a Tartar-Lithuanian father and Russian mother. His mesmerizing, feline eyes made him a perfect fit for the role of the rapacious chieftain. See Roger Ebert, "Charles Bronson: 'It's just that I don't like to talk very much'."
31. Jones, "*Jubal*: Awakened to Goodness."
32. Churchill, *Fantasies of the Master Race*, p. 168.
33. Vizenor, *Manifest Manners*, p. ix.
34. Marubbio, *Killing the Indian Maiden*, p. 66.
35. Ibid. p. 81.
36. Buscombe, *"Injuns!"*, p. 125.
37. Brown, *Bury My Heart at Wounded Knee*, p. 192.
38. As Richard Slotkin points out, "the Indian arguments are authenticated and made accessible to us by the hero of the film, Tom Jeffords. Virtually the whole of the film is seen from his perspective" (*Gunfighter Nation*, p. 374).
39. Hearne, "The 'Ache for Home'," p. 132.
40. Said, *Culture and Imperialism*, p. 203.
41. Ibid. p. 69.
42. Spivak, "French Feminism in an International Frame."

43. Gandhi, *Postcolonial Theory*, p. 87.
44. Almond, *The New Orientalists*, p. 135.
45. Marubbio, *Killing the Indian Maiden*, p. 81.
46. Richard Slotkin astutely spots the gradual whitening of Debra Paget's complexion and the intensifying glow of her blue eyes, two visual effects which to him reflect the growing acceptance of the other facilitated by "denying difference" (Slotkin, *Gunfighter Nation*, p. 376).
47. Spence and Stam, "Colonialism, Racism and Representation," p. 112.
48. Kachru, "The Alchemy of English," pp. 273–5.
49. Vizenor, *Manifest Manners*, p. 105.
50. Rushing into a farm in the Lost River valley, a band of Jack's Modocs terrorizes a female settler, demanding that she feed them: "We hungry! Not hurt you! Not fight white woman!"
51. The same device remained in use throughout the rest of the century, its most famous exemplification to be found in Kevin Costner's *Dances with Wolves*, where the white protagonist's involvement with the "Indian" woman is palliated by her actual whiteness, thus enabling the romance to be a lasting one.

CHAPTER 4

This Room is My Castle of Quiet: The Collaborations of Delmer Daves and Glenn Ford

Adrian Danks

The theatrical trailer for Delmer Daves' episodic 1958 Western, *Cowboy*, opens in black and white and features a solitary, seated figure impatiently clicking through the channels of a television, all of which show the same generic Western situation of a posse riding through a rocky, dusty, and ill-defined landscape: "Pardner, I don't mind sayin' I'm plum sick of childish Westerns." The trailer then cuts to the figure of Jack Lemmon, in cowboy attire, introducing the film he co-stars in: "it's really the West." Such a playful approach to the advertising of a Hollywood film is not that unusual by the late 1950s, but this trailer also pushes some of the key ways in which we are meant to receive and respond to the film in question, as well as its adversarial relationship to television.

Cowboy was made on the cusp of the great boom in the television Western that reached its peak in the early 1960s, a shift of medium and scale that highlighted the mundane, domestic, serialized, largely historically comfortable and generic characteristics of the form that were soon to be busted apart, or hyperbolically restaged, in the revisionist Westerns of directors such as Sergio Leone, Sam Peckinpah, and Robert Altman. Although Daves' film is not a revisionist Western in this sense—its aim is more circumspect, less aggressive, and clearly attentive to the existing legacies and histories of the West—it is plainly being promoted as something of an antidote to the redundancies of the serialized Western and the form of television itself. This trailer also highlights *Cowboy*'s "adult," realistic, naturalistic, "diurnal," and large-scale interventionist ambitions in relation to the genre. Although it aims to highlight the workaday actualities of cowboy life, its approach and setting are distinct from the sanitized backlots, domesticity, interiorized and clapboard main-street dramas of the TV Western.

In this trailer *Cowboy* is not promoted in terms of its director—Daves was a respected figure by this stage, but hardly a household name—and it doesn't make too much of the presence of Glenn Ford in a starring role, either, although he was then one of the biggest box-office attractions in the world. Nevertheless, the qualities that are highlighted by this promotional device, including the scale or size of the film's vision ("big," but is it?), its emphasis on realistic or naturalistic detail ("*Cowboy* blazes a new trail in realistic Western adventure," claims the trailer), and its focus on providing a refreshing and complex image of the historical West, are characteristics that resonate in different ways across the broader, often outwardly unassuming careers of both Daves and Ford.

By this time Ford had developed a reliable, if sometimes brittle screen persona across a vast array of Westerns, genial comedies, romantic adventures, and films noir. He was one of the hardest-working, most resilient and calmly versatile actors in Hollywood from the 1940s to the 1960s. Frank Capra somewhat bitterly called him a "garden-variety star"[1] after caving into him as associate producer of *Pocketful of Miracles* (1961), while David Shipman relegated him to the status of a "second-string ... dependable and efficient actor."[2] Although Ford is a more intriguing and mercurial figure than these largely dismissive accounts imply, there is some truth and even appropriateness to these appeals to the efficiency and ordinariness of his star persona.

By the late 1950s, Daves himself had forged a reputation as a highly professional and sympathetic director as well as a documentarian of frontier life. Although it is now a little difficult to see what is so remarkable or unusual about the film's depiction of cowboy life or its careful rendering of specific generic events, *Cowboy* is still unusual for the emphasis it places on particular images and landscapes (the spare, vertiginous shots in the railway loading yard or of a solitary Spanish Mission are striking), its documentation of the quotidian life of the cowpuncher, its mixture of broad comedy and sudden violence, and the truly episodic nature of its narrative and its focus upon the rhythms of work.

Daves spent much of his time as a director in the 1950s exploring the Western through a series of eight varied films that offer an uncommonly detailed, historically engaged, and consciously unspectacular portrait of life in the West. In addition to *Cowboy* these films include *Broken Arrow* (1950), *Drum Beat* (1954), *Jubal* (1956), *The Last Wagon* (1956), *3:10 to Yuma* (1957), *The Badlanders* (1958), and *The Hanging Tree* (1959). Jean-Pierre Coursodon has rightly identified and championed the scope and scale of Daves' achievement, as well as some of the reasons why these films remain largely undervalued within auteur-centered understandings of the genre: "As a body of works, Daves's westerns are characterized by an amazing, almost disconcerting diversity ... Daves seemed intent upon investigating a broad range of topics and themes within the scope of the genre."[3] These diverse films are unusual for their sympathetic and detailed rendering of setting, location, and geography, and, as I will argue, for their focus on the theme of friendship and the quiet bonds between male characters. Although Daves' Westerns are characteristically concerned with issues pertaining to masculinity and male protagonists (only a few have truly significant female characters), they also contain moments of domestic quiet, sensuality, and deeply held affection. For example, several of the scenes in *3:10 to Yuma* between Ben Wade (Glenn Ford) and the film's two key female characters (who appear only intermittently, but soulfully), the interracial relationship between Tom Jeffords (James Stewart) and Sonseeahray (Debra Paget) in *Broken Arrow*, and that suggested between Comanche Todd (Richard Widmark) and his murdered Native American wife in *The Last Wagon* are also unusual for the depth of feeling and even despair they communicate. The environments or settings created in Daves' Westerns also have a lived-in feel that aims at reproducing and grounding a more experiential and authentic rendering of the West.

Of course, Daves is most often singled out for his particularly sympathetic attention to so-called Indian-themed material in films such as *Broken Arrow*, *Drum Beat*, and *The Last Wagon*. These films, while retaining many of the elements typical of Native American-centered Westerns (for example, their interracial couplings rarely survive the machinations of the plot or censorship guidelines), are unusual for their detailed representation of the rituals, customs, and living conditions of specific tribes within particular and generally appropriate geographic locations. As numerous critics (as well as the director himself) have noted, Daves came from a family deeply embedded in the settling of the West, and had direct experience of Native American culture after spending three months residing with the Hopi and Navajo in 1926.[4] Daves himself has stated that he was also something of a scholar of the nineteenth-century expansion into the West:

> I have a great library on Americana at home and each film has been the result of a great deal of research. I'm gradually making a whole composite of the west because some of the films like *Broken Arrow*, *Drum Beat* and *The Last Wagon* portrayed Indian themes. Then we gradually move forward in the west through *Cowboy* and *The Hanging Tree* and the bad-man west, which was *3:10 to Yuma*, and gradually up into *Spencer's Mountain* which is a spiritual Western more than a physical one. It's what happened to the sons of the pioneers, so to speak.[5]

Daves' eight Westerns provide a remarkably balanced and nuanced portrait of the West in the second half of the nineteenth century, presenting neither a particularly optimistic nor negative view of race relations, community, or environment.

Between the key years of 1956 and 1958, Daves made three of his best and most significant Westerns at Columbia Pictures with Glenn Ford: *Jubal*, *3:10 to Yuma*, and *Cowboy*. These three films seldom touch on Native American life or characters—they appear very intermittently in *Cowboy* (almost as matter of course), with the inevitable confrontation between them and the cowboys rather deflated by the stampeding of the cattle—and are more concerned with the uncertain development of communities, homesteader or cowboy life, and the friendships between specific characters (a focus on friendship that is often explored between white and Native American characters in the other major series of Daves films). Although they are dotted with action and incident, these films glean from Ford quietness, elusiveness, and a creeping familiarity that is also characteristic of many of the finest moments across Daves' *oeuvre*. This interest in the "familiarity" of documentary detail extends from *Destination Tokyo* (1943), Daves' first film as a director. Although that highly interior film is characterized by its claustrophobic drama and spaces, extended duration, and the intense quietness of the sequences where the submarine enters Japanese waters, it is equally marked by the everyday routines and gestures of underwater existence, Daves' characteristically comprehensive research into submarine life, and specific details of *mise-en-scène*. Daves himself has recognized the important influence of wartime British documentary on this film and the documentary impulse of his subsequent work in the Western.[6]

This chapter reads this collaboration between Ford and Daves as symptomatic of the work of both the actor and director, and their sympathetic, subtle, "benevolent," and relatively unadorned approach to various subjects and character types. In the process, it will help pinpoint some of the key reasons why both of these important but workaday figures have remained relatively underestimated and why they need to be brought to the forefront of a more complex and complete understanding of the variations possible in the "classical" Western, particularly in the late 1950s. It will address the ways in which this trio of films can be examined loosely as a group while also recognizing the striking singularity and "development" of each. Although it will emphasize and highlight the place of Ford in these films, this chapter will also consider these close-to-consecutive films in Daves' career—the equally bold and interesting *The Last Wagon* was made between *Jubal* and *3:10 to Yuma*—in terms of the insights they offer into a broader understanding of the director's work. As such, it will use specific observations about Ford's characterization and representation as a launching pad for an exploration of particular themes and ideas that mark and recur in Daves' often-disparate work.

Although it is relatively common to examine the collaborations between various actors and directors working in the 1950s Western—John Wayne/John Ford and James Stewart/Anthony Mann immediately come to mind—the series of three varied films made by Daves and Ford have only intermittently attracted attention. While at least one of these films, *3:10 to Yuma*, has been championed in terms of Daves' spatially and tonally expressive direction and Ford's morally ambiguous, suggestively violent but effortlessly genial characterization, this quietly extraordinary trio of films have seldom been examined in relation to one another or as part of a body of work. Michael Walker's extensive and highly descriptive essay "The Westerns of Delmer Daves" provides an account of the director's work in the 1950s in relation to specific thematic preoccupations, grouping the films accordingly.[7] Two of the films featuring Ford, *3:10 to Yuma* and *Cowboy*, are paired together as relatively contrastive depictions of homesteader and cowboy life, as well as Daves' most conventional examples of the genre in relation to their representation of character, situation, and event. The third of these films, *Jubal*, is paired with Daves' final Western, *The Hanging Tree*, as a work greatly influenced by the 1950s psychological melodrama and the Method-style performances of particular actors such as Ernest Borgnine and Rod Steiger. The film is marked (or marred, for some) by the contrast between Ford's tight-lipped, buttoned-down persona and the more freewheeling, brooding, and out-of-control performance given by Steiger as the title character's resentful nemesis, Pinky. But this conflict also pinpoints the key allegiances and sensibilities of Daves' work, with Ford's character quickly slotting into and organically occupying the location and environment in a way that is never open to Pinky. But this film is also somewhat distinct from the other two in this "series" in that it provides some kind of backstory for Ford's character, the kind of traumatic event that also fuels and hangs over the protagonists of *The Last Wagon* and *The Hanging Tree*. Daves did make a number of films with other stars—two with Alan Ladd, Gary Cooper, Dennis Morgan, Debra Paget, and John Garfield; four with Troy Donahue during the problematic final stretch of Daves' career in the early 1960s. But it was the three films he made with Ford that provide the best opportunity for examining the ways in which he could work closely with an actor's star persona, collaborate in terms of characterization and emphasis, and develop a complex set of variations upon an established genre and the actors closely associated with it—by the time of *Jubal* Ford had starred in numerous Westerns including *The Man from Colorado* (Henry Levin, 1948), *The Secret of Convict Lake* (Michael Gordon, 1951), *The Man from the Alamo* (Budd Boetticher, 1953), and *The Violent Men* (Rudolph Maté, 1955).

While the three films do draw upon the conventional star persona of Ford, they also represent significant variations upon this "image" and provide an extraordinarily accelerated shift of characterization from the initially inexperienced and wandering cowhand he plays in *Jubal* to the hard-nosed, closed-off patriarch of *Cowboy*. It is illustrative to look at the ways in which Ford is introduced in each of the three films, to see how this mercurial transition in character and performance works. In the opening moments of *Jubal*, Ford's title character, Jubal Troop, stumbles out of the mountains half-frozen. He is then picked up by a rancher, Shep Gordon (played by Ernest Borgnine), who subsequently offers him a job, friendship, and the possibility of becoming part of a community. Ford's character in this film is an initially protean entity whose trust and loyalty is gently thawed by Shep's straightforward, but problematically unsophisticated and jealous, big-heartedness.

Ford's Ben Wade in *3:10 to Yuma* is a much more confident and comfortable character who seems always to command the situation, how events unfold, and the space that surrounds him. He is a character who, at least on the surface of things, wants to do things quietly, intelligently, and professionally, and who is as at home on a horse as he is conducting a hold-up or kicking back on the bed of the bridal suite at a hotel in Contention City. Although his character does develop in some surprising ways, and retains a degree of unpredictability, he always gives the impression of carefully weighing up the options and granting at least lip service to the ethics and pragmatics of every situation. The film opens with images of the parched earth of the drought-stricken landscape, craning up to show the weary movement of a stagecoach as it dustily trails through the soil against a low-hanging, sun-bleached skyline. Frankie Laine's popular title song establishes the characteristic inevitably of the narrative, and the iconic sparseness of the environment and situation ("there's a lonely train called the 3:10 to Yuma"). After the credits, the film fades up to the stagecoach being held up by Wade's gang. The first proper glimpse we are given of Wade is a slow pan to a mid-shot of him on horseback as he gently smirks at the situation unfolding before him.

As the hold-up devolves into a messier encounter than he had envisaged and carefully planned, he exhibits little regret, reflection, or remorse when "forced" to first shoot and kill one of his gang, and then the stagecoach driver who was holding him hostage. Although we never quite forget the hard-edged intent and clinical nature of this murderous act, the film uses Ford's likable and commonly implacable persona as a means for us to become entranced and seduced by his character's congenial, easeful, playful, and effortlessly polite manner. When Ford is onscreen he always arrests our attention, his glinting and smartly darting eyes directing our gaze across the *mise-en-scène*. He is a character and actor we enjoy spending time with. David Thomson has complained, in his short and largely dismissive account of Daves' career, that Ford is unable to bring a real feeling of menace or nastiness to Wade; but as Kent Jones (2013a) has forcefully argued, it is this combination of charm, deeper undercurrents, and a sense of something close to "grace" that makes the character and film soar and resonate emotionally: "goodness and mercy often arrive unannounced in this film, and come as a surprise even to those who bestow them."[8]

Cowboy takes some of these elements of Ford's established and by then

Figure 4.1 Ben Wade in *3:10 to Yuma*.

very familiar persona, as well as the actor's ability to shift between comedy and drama almost effortlessly as a key motivation for the swings in tone and emphasis that mark the director and actor's final collaboration. Ford's Tom Reese is initially introduced as a rambunctious, caricatured, and even comic figure who commands the space around him, shoots cockroaches off the bathroom wall of his hotel room, and expresses a surprising affection for opera. Ford launches into the film as a celebrity whose reputation and legend has well and truly preceded him—we first see him striding into the hotel lobby, flanked by many of his employees, and immediately turning the business of the hotel upside down. Although this is a very self-conscious performance that masks darker and deeper emotions (consider, for example, the later scene in which he holds Lemmon's noticeably smoldering Frank Harris over a blazing campfire), Tom's breezy and flash self-confidence taps into Ford's surface qualities as a congenial, gestural, and subtly expressive actor.

In some ways *Cowboy* is a partial restaging of the central relationship in *Jubal*, with Jack Lemmon now playing the role of the untutored, inexperienced but insistent "cowboy." But the contrast between Lemmon and Ford as actors is usefully illustrative here of the differences in the characters they play across these two films and how they function in the narrative. Lemmon is unceasingly demonstrative and fussy, while Ford "passively" suggests a subterranean set of motivations and even neuroses that never quite rise to the surface. As several commentators have noted, *Jubal* is what is often called a "Freudian Western," and few of the film's complications of character and narrative escape deep-seated motivation explicated by traumatic events occurring in the distant past (Jubal's involves the death of his father while saving his life, and his mother's seeming indifference). In other respects, *Cowboy* is more closely aligned with

3:10 to Yuma in terms of the ways it dramatizes an emerging friendship based on mutual respect and trust. In all three films, Ford emerges as the galvanizing figure of the narrative who must grow and act decisively and ethically at particular moments in time and in relation to the bonds of friendships and comradeship—of *being* together—that have developed across the movie.

Another recurring element of all three films is a focus upon different conceptions and experiences of time. One of the least satisfying aspects of *Cowboy* is its brevity, and one gets the sense that the film and director would be happier to just spend time with the characters as they hang out, perform the tasks of work, and interact with the often meticulously rendered environment. But it is in *3:10 to Yuma*, the central film in the "series" and one of the great Westerns of the 1950s, that this emphasis upon time is most consistently developed and built into the narrative of the film. A key tension of the drama revolves around whether Dan Evans (Van Heflin) will be able to escort Wade to Yuma prison on the scheduled train conveniently announced in the title. Despite this telescoping of time and event, much of the film is made up of scenes where characters snatch a few moments of respite or rest, or experience time in a radically altered fashion (Emmy: "Down here everybody sleeps between one and two"). Plainly, time distends and elongates for those who are hoping the train will reach Contention City before the arrival of Wade's gang. But for Wade, time seems of little consequence as he weighs up the possibilities of the events he commands and their always-possible reversibility.

A more poetic sense of time is communicated in the beautiful seduction scene between Wade and Emmy (Felicia Farr), a barmaid at the Bisbee Saloon (a much more successful pairing of these actors than in *Jubal*). Wade snatches a brief romantic encounter while he is attempting to escape from the posse sent out in the aftermath of the hold-up. In this scene Ford demonstrates his seductive and intimate qualities as an actor, managing to seduce Farr's Emmy while falling back on what appears to be the most clichéd of pick-up lines ("Didn't I see you some place?") and talking about specific prostitutes he once had a great affection for (he had initially flirted with Emmy when he put down the money to pay for the gang's drinks). It is a mark of Ford's charm as an actor that he can make such unpromising encounters feel dreamily and nostalgically romantic. The sex scene that follows, as was typical of the period, is elided by a cut to another scene showing the discovery by the posse of the makeshift grave of the gang member, before returning to the post-coital exit of the couple from a curtained bedroom. As is typical of Daves' Westerns, the downmarket saloon that surrounds them and becomes familiar to us is meticulously rendered and feels lived-in, providing exquisite details of environment such as the grain of the wood of the bar and the placement of Emmy's "bedroom" in a room leading straight off from the saloon (and next to the marshal's office). But the main effect of this brilliantly sketched-in scene is to suggest a sense of real intimacy and connection, a feeling of knowingness that transcends the "reality" of what has just unfolded. The somewhat cryptic dialogue between the pair that concludes this encounter further reinforces this sense of the characters being out of time (or occupying a different conception of it). After their tryst, Emmy exclaims to Ben, "Funny, some men you can see every day for ten years and never notice; some men you see once and they're with you the rest of your life." One suspects that Wade has had this impact on a lot of women—but there is still something genuinely felt and intimate about their stolen connection.

This moment with Emmy is paired with the subsequent supper scene at Dan's home, in which the manacled Wade sits down to a meal with the Evans family on his way to a rendezvous with the train in Contention City. Although *3:10 to Yuma* is not a particularly self-conscious or artificial film—it actually goes out of its way to realistically render and concretize its setting, as I have argued earlier—it does carefully utilize the conventions of the genre and the accepted screen personas of several of its actors. Wade is also caught, at several moments, whistling the film's theme song. It is almost impossible, during this scene set in the Evans' modest home, not to think of George Stevens' *Shane* (1953) and the role that Alan Ladd's title character played for both the community and the family he was billeted with. This is clearly signposted by the dialogue of the children—here, about the genial Wade's notorious reputation as a ruthless killer—and the presence of Van Heflin's struggling father in both films. Similarly, Ford leans upon the insouciant charm, ease, and comfort of his screen persona, while never fully relegating the violent, self-righteous, and even sadistic dimensions that simmer across a film like Fritz Lang's *The Big Heat* (1953). In this scene, Wade also "seduces" Evans' wife, Alice (Leora Dana) and ingratiates himself into the family by complimenting her on her cooking, displaying his careful manners, getting Dan to cut his meat for him, and speaking to Alice of the past while Dan, jealous, looks on. But the menacing calm and contradiction of Wade's character is reinforced in his parting line as he exits the house: "I hope I can send him back to you all right." This *coup de grace* demonstrates Wade's quiet control of what seems to be an adverse situation, but also articulates both his very real menace and the possibility that he actually does want to return her husband to her unscathed. This conclusion is tested and confirmed in the film's surprising and triumphal final moments.

3:10 to Yuma stands out amongst these three films for its strong and nuanced portraits of its female characters. Both Emmy and Alice encounter Wade in the course of their everyday lives. Dan has been pushed into the role of deputy by the difficult circumstances in which he finds himself, and his need to purchase water from his neighbor to help stave off the drought. Alice and Emmy are portraits of women who have been hardened, but also strengthened, by their environment; luminous but unvarnished figures whose hardscrabble lives are inscribed by the work they perform. The rituals of work are another preoccupation of these three films, and help situate their particular attention to time and temporality. A key aspect of *Cowboy* is its depiction of the various facets of frontier life on a cattle drive; while *Jubal* also takes time out to show us the largely diurnal activities of the cowhands (alongside its pointed, unromantic scenes around the campfire at night). A striking example of this occurs early in *Jubal* when we are shown Pinky, an otherwise menacing, scheming, seething, and seemingly out-of-place ball of existential resentment plonked in a bucolic environment—a serpent in Eden, perhaps—saving a young calf after the death of its mother. It is in these moments of quiet that Daves manages to bring something truly striking to the Western genre. It is also in this regard that the choice of Ford to star in these three films has its most significant and potent impact. As Jones has argued:

> [Ford] was never more in his element than he was with Daves. In Ford, as he would Gary Cooper in *The Hanging Tree* (1959), Daves found an actor whose manner of being was closely aligned with his own affinities ... Ford and Cooper in *Jubal* and *The Hanging Tree* are men who have awakened to the revelation of goodness, and whose existences are disturbed and complicated by the desires of other, more impatient souls.[9]

Although Ford's characters in these three films express a consistency of temperament and even development, they do "awaken" to their better natures at important junctures in the narrative.

Ford is also undoubtedly one of the easiest actors to watch in Hollywood cinema. He often takes great pleasure in the moment, or seems content to just occupy a time and place with an economy of gesture, expression, and action (the "manner of being" Jones is describing). Much of the drama (and comedy) in *Cowboy* emerges from Tom's unwillingness to break from the hard-won patterns of a lifetime, as well as his conflict with Jack Lemmon's Frank Harris, a neophyte who must learn the difficult lessons of life on the trail. Yet again, *Cowboy* and *Jubal* provide something of a mirror image of each other. The "father–son" relationship that emerges quickly in *Jubal*, but is spoiled by Pinky's festering resentment and Shep's lack of sophistication and insight, is gradually reinstated across the peripatetic journey that structures *Cowboy*. Remarkably, Ford is able to move convincingly from the wandering cowhand (and much-derided goat-herder) of *Jubal* to the crusty veteran of *Cowboy* across only two years.

Although it is productive to think about these male relationships in terms of the father–son dynamic, they also home in on a particular preoccupation across much of Daves' cinema: friendship. Jones argues for this in relation to a broader understanding of Daves' cinema: "He was drawn to the bonds between people rather than the divisions, to friendship and love rather than discord and vengeance."[10] As Jones has also pointed out, "Daves is an absolute rarity in cinema, an artist of the good."[11] Although I would argue against the singularity and exceptionalism of Jones's reading of Daves' cinema, and its applicability across his still diverse work, this interest in the goodness in people and outcomes does find significant expression across these three films with Ford and how they figure the notion of friendship. In some cases his willingness to pursue the ultimate goodness in his characters can seem surprising, or somewhat out of step with what has occurred previously in the movies.

The final moments of *3:10 to Yuma* hinge on this shift from acquaintanceship to friendship between Dan and Ben, and the almost spiritual coming together of the motifs of bonding, rain/water, movement, and marriage that structure and elevate the film. Ben's friendship, and even familiarity, shifts from his closest confidante in the gang, Charlie Prince (Richard Jaeckel), to Dan during the long sequence in which they are holed up in the bridal suite of the hotel in Contention City. As Dan and Ben become familiar and share the domestic space of the room, Charlie awaits—jilted!—downstairs. In *Cowboy*, it is only when Tom and Frank are finally boxed into a cattle car and have to work together to avoid being trampled that they manage to locate the shared space that enables them to enter Chicago as partners and friends. This shift or grace note is comically reinforced by their subsequent occupation of twin bathtubs in their "shared" hotel suite. It is worth noting that Ben and Dan also end up in such a railroad car, escaping Contention City as they work together to throw themselves across the threshold of the baggage car and into its more contained "domestic" space. The tragedy of *Jubal*—and of the three films, it is certainly the most tortured—is in the betrayal of the friendship between Jubal and Shep. But alongside the more heated pyrotechnics of the film's central friendship is another that is quieter, more enduring, and instantly equanimous between Jubal and Charles Bronson's Reb Haislipp. The ease and compatibility of this friendship is highlighted by the economical and even unstated ways in which the two characters meet and recognize one another during the first encounter with the rawhiders camping out on Shep's land. Although Pinky later recounts the obvious attraction between Jubal and Naomi (Felicia Farr) in the same scene, giving this as a reason for Jubal's softness in dealing with the interlopers, the sequence is much more successful in its expression of the bond between Reb and the title character. I realize that the account I have given here suggests a deepening homosexual subtext across these three films—and there is some validity in that, particularly in the deliberate play on this dimension in that long hotel sequence in *3:10 to Yuma*—yet they are probably better approached in terms of how they explore friendship and homosocial bonding. This emphasis on friendship is highlighted in the mutual seduction between Ben and Emmy in *3:10 to Yuma*; although the two become lovers, their exchanges better express the knowingness that emerges out of friendship.

As both Bertrand Tavernier and Jones have argued, Daves' rendering of landscape, setting, and environment is deeply attentive to the specificities of location and the relationship of characters to their surroundings. *Jubal* was shot between 29 July and 15 September 1955, around Jackson Hole in Wyoming. *3:10 to Yuma* was filmed in winter between 28 November 1956 and 17 January 1957 in such areas of Arizona as Elgin, Wilcox, Old Tucson, and Sedona. *Cowboy* was shot around Santa Fe and various other locations between 14 June and 26 July 1957.[12] Daves was very careful in his selection of settings and locations throughout his career, holding a particular affection for the high country that features in all three Ford films. Whereas a director such as Howard Hawks often seems to spend much of his time trying to get his characters indoors, there is an ease and care with environment—both exterior *and* interior—in Daves' films that illustrates a greater affinity for these landscapes, histories, and stories. In contrast to the more self-consciously composed, though poetically beautiful, landscapes, spaces, and places of John Ford, the lived-in, unforced quality of Daves' environments attests to the "presentness" of what we see before us. As Coursodon has argued:

> Daves's approach to the genre was far from unselective. His westerns eschew legendary figures, epic-scale spectacle, adventure, and action for their own sake, everything that would tend to glamorise and romanticise the West. Rather, they are concerned ... with giving an accurate picture of the conditions of life in the West under various circumstances. Neither do they use genre as a convenient showcase for moral (or political) allegories; the characters' moral problems spring from the very conditions under which they live.[13]

Although Coursodon overstates the naturalism and realism of Daves' still clearly Hollywood Westerns, it is true that they do stand in contrast to the work of many of these other filmmakers, even those widely celebrated for their depictions of the West. In certain respects, Anthony Mann is a more obvious point of comparison with Daves, but his Westerns commonly pit characters against a hostile and unforgiving environment that tests and stages their psychological and physical struggles. Daves' films typically present a clear affinity or connection between character and environment. These locations are seldom used to stage or influence the psychology or situation of a character. Nevertheless, location and character are not indifferent to one another, their relationship producing a sense of "mutual respect."

Of the three films Daves made with Ford, *Cowboy* provides the most stereotypical view of the environment as it dramatizes the harsh conditions and repetitive actions of cowboys on the hard-bitten trail. Although there are scenes that illustrate this harshness and the impersonal nature of place, the relationship between character and environment often seems organic and natural, *part* of it, and some distance from the extreme locations used in a film like Ford's *The Searchers* (1956), where homesteaders are indeed "way out on a limb" trying to farm in Monument Valley. In his wonderful essay on *Jubal*, Jones claims,

> There is not one scene in this film, inside or outside, in which that location [Jackson Hole] is reduced to a mere backdrop, as often happens in westerns. There is a hushed, at times quietly enraptured quality to this western melodrama that seems directly linked to the humbling majesty of the mountains and skies.[14]

Tavernier takes this acceptance of environment even further, arguing more broadly that "Daves does not mythologise Nature but befriends it, the way his characters do, at least those who must live or survive in it."[15] Ford's characters in these films provide something of a "barometer" for this accepting and, to some degree, unshifting relationship to environment. For example, Wade in *3:10 to Yuma* seems as at ease on horseback, or framed by the low landscape of the scrubby desert, as he is sitting down to supper handcuffed, kicking back on an overstuffed bed, or darting into a moving carriage as it heads toward his imprisonment in Yuma. But this film does use landscape and environment in a more symbolic fashion than the other two films. The contrasts between the exclusive interiors of Chicago and the wide outdoors in *Cowboy*, or the boxed-in and oppressive interiors of the cantinas and Shep's home and the unfenced fields and prairies in *Jubal*, are little more than an expedient and simple means of staging the central drama of the narrative. The landscape in *3:10 to Yuma* expresses and stages the central dilemma of community that drives the film. The drought that is gripping the land provides a neat metaphor for the subsistence existence of Dan and his family, the struggle of married life, and the gradual drying up of assistance that Dan is promised, receives, and is finally denied by the townspeople. Part of the wonder of this film is the way that it stages this process of "evaporation" and provides a sympathetic understanding of those characters who reluctantly withdraw their support. The arrival of the rain at the end is both an apt metaphor and a dramatically obvious device illustrating the release of tension. It returns the film to the patterns and cycles of everyday life and the natural world, while also suggesting the spiritual and even divine dimensions of Wade's "conversion." But this transcendence is neatly undercut by the comfort and confidence of Ford's performance combined with the cheeky cocksureness of his final line: "Besides, I've broken out of Yuma before."

But, in conclusion, I do not want to give the impression that the actions and events in these films are not felt, or do not hold deeper and more mysterious implications. Although Ben Wade travels toward Yuma of his own volition—a moment of male bonding celebrated by the large drops of replenishing rain that fall across his and Dan's hat brims and faces as they look out from the baggage car at the now wondrous landscape—his opening act of murder cannot be completely forgotten or compartmentalized. The tryst between Ben and Emmy is also informed by the knowledge that she came to Bisbee for the dry desert air to help her deal with her tuberculosis. Death hangs over all three of these films in a matter-of-fact fashion. One of the most interesting characters in *Cowboy* is an ex-sheriff and gunslinger, Doc Bender, who joins the cattle drive because he has wearied of having to kill those who constantly challenge his mastery. We fear throughout that his presence will result in a confrontation with one of his fellow cowboys. He ends up being a relatively genial, knowing, if rather melancholy figure who decides to leave the group just prior to the end of the drive. But he speaks longingly of catching up with an "acquaintance" in a town they stop outside of: "we were good friends." Reports quickly filter back to the group that he has hanged himself after this friend challenged him to a gunfight and Doc was "forced" to shoot him down. The pointlessness and soul-searching nihilism of this act disturbs the cowboys, who have previously taken in their stride the casual death of one of their number killed during a juvenile game involving a rattlesnake. But Doc's weary and disappointed act and the cowboys' "hysterical" response to it also highlight the developing bonds of the characters and the patterns of friendship that have been staged across the film. In some ways the departure of Doc, signifying the ultimate failure of his own grasp at friendship, leaves open the possibility of the closer bond between Frank and Tom: "I'm tired of burying people." The casual presence of death alongside life also highlights the "complete" nature of Daves' portrait of the West, and the crucial role that Ford plays in negotiating a path through these physical, emotional, and spiritual landscapes, settings, and environments. When looking back on the string of Westerns Daves made in the 1950s, it may be well be the comfortable, congenial, embodied, amiable, friendly but sometimes steely presence of Ford that provides the clearest "symbol" of the director's great contribution to the genre. As Ford's Wade says early in *3:10 to Yuma*: "Where a man lives, that's where he should be buried."

BIBLIOGRAPHY

Capra, Frank, *The Name above the Title* (New York: Macmillan, 1971).
Coursodon, Jean-Pierre, with Pierre Sauvage, *American Directors, Vol. 1* (New York: McGraw-Hill, 1983).

Ford, Peter, *Glenn Ford: A Life* (Madison: The University of Wisconsin Press, 2011).

Jones, Kent, "*Jubal*: Awakened to Goodness," The Criterion Collection (2013a), <http://www.criterion.com/current/posts/2765-jubal-awakened-to-goodness> (last accessed 11 November 2015).

Jones, Kent, "*3:10 to Yuma*: Curious Distances," The Criterion Collection (2013b), <http://www.criterion.com/current/posts/2766-3-10-to-yuma-curious-distances> (last accessed 11 November 2015).

Shipman, David, *The Great Movie Stars: The International Years* (London: Angus & Robertson, 1980).

Tavernier, Bernard, "The Ethical Romantic," *Film Comment*, January–February 2003, <http://www.filmcomment.com/article/delmer-daves-bertrand-tavernier> (last accessed 11 November 2015).

Thomson, David, *The New Biographical Dictionary of Film*, 4th edn (London: Little, Brown, 2002).

Walker, Michael, "The Westerns of Delmer Daves," in Ian Cameron and Douglas Pye (eds.), *The Movie Book of the Western* (London: Studio Vista, 1996), pp. 123–60.

Wicking, Christopher, "Interview with Delmer Daves," *Screen*, 10:4/5 (1969): 55–66.

FILMOGRAPHY

Badlanders, The, director Delmer Daves, featuring Alan Ladd, Ernest Borgnine, Katy Jurado, Claire Kelly (Metro-Goldwyn-Mayer, 1958).

Big Heat, The, director Fritz Lang, featuring Glenn Ford, Gloria Grahame, Jocelyn Brando, Lee Marvin (Columbia Pictures, 1953).

Broken Arrow, director Delmer Daves, featuring Jimmy Stewart, Jeff Chandler, Debra Paget, Basil Ruysdael (20th Century Fox, 1950).

Cowboy, director Delmer Daves, featuring Glenn Ford, Jack Lemmon, Anna Kashfi, Dick York (Columbia Pictures, 1958).

Destination Tokyo, director Delmer Daves, featuring Cary Grant, John Garfield, Alan Hale, John Ridgely (Warner Bros., 1943).

Drum Beat, director Delmer Daves, featuring Alan Ladd, Audrey Dalton, Marisa Pavan, Charles Bronson (Warner Bros., 1954).

Hanging Tree, The, director Delmer Daves, featuring Gary Cooper, Maria Schell, Karl Malden, George C. Scott (Warner Bros., 1959).

Jubal, director Delmer Daves, featuring Glenn Ford, Valerie French, Rod Steiger, Ernest Borgnine (Columbia Pictures, 1956).

Last Wagon, The, director Delmer Daves, featuring Richard Widmark, Felicia Farr, Susan Kohner, Tommy Rettig (20th Century Fox, 1956).

Man from the Alamo, The, director Budd Boetticher, featuring Glenn Ford, Julie Adams, Chill Wills, Hugh O'Brian (Universal-International, 1953).

Man from Colorado, The, director Henry Levin, featuring Glenn Ford, William Holden, Ellen Drew, Ray Collins (Columbia Pictures, 1948).

Pocketful of Miracles, director Frank Capra, featuring Glenn Ford, Bette Davis, Hope Lange, Arthur O'Connell (United Artists, 1961).

Searchers, The, director John Ford, featuring John Wayne, Natalie Wood, Jeffrey Hunter, Vera Miles (Warner Bros., 1956).

Secret of Convict Lake, The, director Michael Gordon, featuring Glenn Ford, Gene Tierney, Ethel Barrymore, Ann Dvorak (20th Century Fox, 1951).

3:10 to Yuma, director Delmer Daves, featuring Glenn Ford, Van Heflin, Felicia Farr, Leora Dana (Columbia Pictures, 1957).

Violent Men, The, director Rudolph Maté, featuring Glenn Ford, Barbara Stanwyck, Edward G. Robinson, Dianne Foster (Columbia Pictures, 1955).

NOTES

1. Capra, *The Name Above the Title*, p. 474.
2. Shipman, *The Great Movie Stars*, p. 184.
3. Coursodon, *American Directors*, p. 84.
4. Wicking, "Interview with Delmer Daves," p. 60.
5. Ibid.
6. Ibid. p. 59.
7. Walker, "The Westerns of Delmer Daves," pp. 123–60.
8. Thomson, *The New Biographical Dictionary of Film*, p. 206; Jones, "*Jubal*: Awakened to Goodness."
9. Jones, "*Jubal*: Awakened to Goodness."
10. Ibid.
11. Ibid.
12. Ford, *Glenn Ford*, pp. 317–18.
13. Coursodon, *American Directors*, p. 84.
14. Jones, "*Jubal*: Awakened to Goodness."
15. Tavernier, "The Ethical Romantic."

CHAPTER 5

Delmer Daves, Authenticity, and Auteur Elements: Celebrating the Ordinary in *Cowboy*

Sue Matheson

Delmer Daves' 1958 Western *Cowboy* opens in a Chicago hotel where Frank Harris (Jack Lemmon) is a clerk who has fallen in love with the daughter of a Mexican cattle baron, Vidal (Donald Randolph). Vidal orders Harris to stay away from the girl (Maria, played by Anna Kashfi), and returns with her to Mexico. In order to follow her there, Harris purchases a partnership in Tom Reece's (Glenn Ford) next cattle drive. Regretting his decision to take a tenderfoot on the trail, Reece attempts to buy Harris out, but Harris holds him to their deal. Life as a cowhand strips away Harris's romantic delusions. In Mexico, he learns that Maria's father has married her off and that she is not interested in leaving her new husband. On the trail, he discovers that the men with whom he is working are not even remotely like the heroes of Western dime novels. As he adjusts to being a "cowboy," Harris becomes first hostile and then callous. Reece attempts to mentor him on the trail, but Harris refuses to listen. After Reece saves his life in a cattle car on the train going back to Chicago, Harris finally grows up. Back in Chicago, Reece, Harris, and the other rambunctious cowboys take over part of the hotel where Harris used to work. In the final shot of the movie, Reece and Harris are enjoying the fruits of their labor, sitting in their bathtubs, drinking whiskey and smoking cigars, laughing, and shooting cockroaches off the bathroom walls.

Advertised as an 'adult' Western, *Cowboy* received mixed reviews upon its release. The review in *Variety* lavished praise on the movie, calling it "one of the fastest, freshest Westerns in a long time" and enthusing that it "has everything a Western should have. Cowboys and Indians, cattle (including a stampede) and cow ponies, barroom brawls and bronco busting, all the classic elements ... seen with a fresh approach that gives it a special stature of its own." Meanwhile, Bosley Crowther in the *New York Times* was much less enthusiastic: "For a movie supposedly intended to give you a realistic idea of the lean and leathery lives of the fellows who drove cattle and trailed herds in the old days, [producer] Julian Blaustein's 'Cowboy' has a surprisingly plump and comfortable look . . . It makes the life of the old cowboy seem quite similar to that of the typical pokes in Hollywood." He concludes his review by asking readers, "Do you remember 'Red River'? Well, 'Cowboy' doesn't even come close."

It must be said in response that, as a realistic treatment of the West, *Cowboy* is not designed to resemble a movie like Howard Hawks' *Red River* (1948). Unlike that film, *Cowboy* does not borrow its materials from frontier lore and legend, just the difficult, dangerous, monotonous, day-to-day work of the trail hand. As its trailer announces, "*Cowboy* is about the *real* West" and is meant to appeal to jaded viewers who are "plumb sick of childish Westerns." Jack Lemmon, who appears in the trailer, emphasizes this, assuring viewers that *Cowboy* is "*adult* in every sense of the word. The issues are *real*, so are the people." *Cowboy* is, as Lemmon notes, "the story of *real* life Frank Harris, adventurer and *real* life cowboy."

Cowboy reflects its director's interest in and extensive knowledge of American history and Western culture. As Daves explained to Christopher Wicking in a 1969 interview for the journal *Screen*, "I have a great library on Americana at home, and each [Western] has been the result of a great deal of research." All of Daves' Westerns display his high regard for his family's pioneering history. Notes the director, "*Broken Arrow* was a dedication to my father and to my father's family. This is all part and parcel of my heritage." He continues:

> I have my grandfather's diaries and he crossed the plains twice with the Mormons, went through the ordeals of being on watch and having Indians attack and all that kind of thing. My father's mother was born in California two months after the covered wagon arrived there and her mother, my great-grandmother was seven months pregnant crossing the Sierra Nevada Mountains in a covered wagon. Out of respect for these people, you can't tell stories of the west and fake it, and that has influenced me in my directing life . . . That's the reason I think in most of my Westerns there is a documentary feeling.[1]

Daves stresses the importance of historical realism in *Cowboy*, stating, "I wanted very much to say: 'This is how the cowboy lived and what he did.' It was really a documentary of the life of a cowboy, based of course on Frank Harris's book, but we took liberties with it, because I think Harris lied about fifty percent of the time in his book."[2]

Given its emphasis on authenticity, it is not surprising that *Cowboy*, like

Broken Arrow, revises the Western's aesthetic, cultural, and social references. As Daves points out to Wicking, *Broken Arrow* "was the father of the so-called adult Western ... I think we ended up with the public understanding the Apaches and all the American Indians as a result of it, because then they reassessed Chief Joseph and all these great leaders ... Since then all films have been affected by it."[3]

Daves located his shooting of *Cowboy* primarily in Santa Fe, New Mexico, because of his attachment to Arizona and respect for his grandfather.

> My grandfather's diary tells how he twice took contracts with the army to be wagon train captain that went from Denver, Colorado down to Santa Fe, so I literally stood where my grandfather had stood in the 1960s and early 1970s, and was inspired by it because I got a great sense of belonging to this country.[4]

Furthermore, his Westerns should be considered as a group because they are meant to form a comprehensive whole:

> [S]ome of the films like *Broken Arrow*, *Drum Beat* and *The Last Wagon* portrayed Indian themes. Then we gradually move forward in the west through *Cowboy* and *The Hanging Tree* and the bad-man west, which was *3:10 to Yuma*, and gradually up into *Spencer's Mountain* which is a spiritual Western more than a physical one. It's what happened to the sons of the pioneers, so to speak.[5]

In this composite, while *Broken Arrow* revises the Western's presentation of Native Americans, *Cowboy* deconstructs the Western hero. This is most apparent during Daves' realistic treatment of the cattle drive. In Westerns, the cattle drive often functions as a rite of male passage: moving cattle down the Chisholm or the Pawnee Trail toughens a tenderfoot into a rugged individualist, and ensures that he becomes a team player. Drives furnish and complicate the plots of movies with their constituent tests of manhood that include the cutting out, roping, and branding of cattle, riding as a nighthawk, and the warding off of outlaws, rustlers, and Indians. The stampede also is a typical trial experienced during the cattle drive.[6]

As Jim Kitses argues throughout his seminal 1969 study *Horizons West*, in the Western, the journey westward is both a physical movement across the landscape and a spiritual quest. Daves' treatment of driving a herd of cattle to market, however, firmly grounds greenhorn Frank Harris's adventure in the category of material gain, not spiritual growth. In *Cowboy*, the issue at hand is secular rather than sacred. The pursuit of wealth motivates both protagonists. Reece takes Harris on as a partner for the cattle drive because he needs money to replace the grubstake that he lost in a poker game. Harris's stated reason for coming to Chicago is "to get into the cattle business, to make a fortune on the trail," and he sees becoming Reece's business partner as a means of achieving that goal. "I have no intention of remaining a hotel clerk all my life," he says.

Similarly, Reece's cowhands are portrayed as hard-nosed capitalists. On the trail, work that results in profit is the cowhand's paramount concern. Thus, the wellbeing of the cattle is privileged over that of the men tending them. With "a herd of cows to worry about," Reece forbids Harris from leaving camp to rescue Charlie from a bar fight: "You go into town, you start trouble, and we'll lose more men. We'll have the whole town right on our hands here." Harris proves a quick study. When he later saves an abandoned newborn calf, the act is not a humane gesture. As he tells Capper, who wanted to leave the calf for the coyotes, "This thing is worth twenty dollars in Chicago." Reece, who overhears the exchange, approvingly says, "I'm glad to see you're learning."

Cowboy repeatedly invokes conventional Western scenarios only to subvert them. Throughout, Daves' treatment of the cattle drive critically examines romantic notions of manhood, male friendship, masculinity, and honor that have come to be associated with the classical Western. Reece's cowhands are not knights of the Plains like the protagonists found in *Red River*. In that film, the cowhands are simple men with sterling characters who live and die by the Wild West's code of honor. In *Cowboy*, by contrast, the hands are, in Harris's words, "the most miserable bunch of men I ever seen saw in my whole life." "I never thought life on the trail would be like this," he says to them. "I thought I would be living with some men, not just a pack of animals."

When not working with cattle, Reece's men accordingly prove themselves to be a collection of disordered and disorderly personalities. After the first supper on the trail, for instance, Paul Curtis's (Richard Jaeckel) idea of fun is to use a stick to throw a "prairie eel" at his comrades. The rough horseplay results in the death of an unnamed trail hand. Tossed about the campfire by Charlie (Dick York) and Curtis, the angry rattlesnake falls around the neck of a bystander who has been ignoring the horseplay and bites the cowboy's neck, injecting its deadly poison into his jugular vein. There is nothing that can be done to save the man. Devoid of empathy, the men ignore their dying comrade, who lies wrapped in a blanket. To pass the time, Curtis teases Joe Capper about having unnatural appetites. "I didn't even know that Indian," Capper says, weakly defending his actions. "Besides, I threw everything away except one haunch." Curtis, neither disgusted nor repulsed by Capper's confession, merely asks, "Which haunch did you keep?" Joe's reply is equally pragmatic: "Well, the left one of course. The right one's the working haunch. They're always tough." No one around the chuck wagon is shocked by the highly unsavory thought that there is a cannibal amongst them. The talk then turns to Charlie, who only thinks of women, and his "dreams of Mexican gals." When Curtis returns to the man he injured, what seems to be a gesture of caring is revealed to be one of pragmatic self-interest: discovering the man has died, Curtis begins to take the boots off the corpse. Shockingly, Reece proves to be as socially challenged as his men when he condones Curtis's stealing from the dead. He quells Harris's objections, saying, "Somebody does something stupid, there's no reason to make more trouble. You don't like what goes on around here, that's just too bad. Nobody said you were gonna like it."

Needless to say, these men do not sing "Shall We Gather at the River" as the unnamed man is buried. There is no religious ceremony at this funeral (another staple of the classical Western), because no one knows "the right words." According to Reece, only the physical fact of the man's death is important. It is unimportant to understand why he died. "All we know is a man's dead," he says. "And that's that." Even the nature of the man's death is considered unimportant. "In the long run I don't think it would have made any difference anyhow," Reece says, officiating over the open grave. Aptly, the cowboy could not be considered a hero in Reece's eulogy. A pragmatist like his men, the trail boss can only say that "he was a good man with cattle. Always did the best he knew how. I hope someone can say the same over me. All right, fill 'er up."

As the cowboys leave their camp the next morning, an extreme low angle shot first appears to award them a heroic status as they pass by in single file. But the snake's-eye point of view reveals the dead man's boots hanging from Curtis's saddle horn and pans 180 degrees as Curtis passes, following the dangling boots and framing the fresh grave in the foreground as Curtis's horse passes by it. As the other horses walk by, the cowboys' backs, like Curtis's, turn on the lonely wooden cross that is fashioned from two sticks. All the men riding by the grave are shrouded by an oppressive, low-hanging black raincloud. Only a few steps past the grave, the cloud dissipates and open sky appears. Riding under a clear sky with their backs turned to the grave, the cowboys seem to have forgotten the dead man at once. As the cinematography indicates, out of sight is out of mind; Daves' trail hands live in the moment, not the past.

Here it should also be noted that being a "rugged individualist" does not elevate the trail hand in *Cowboy*. Reece's men are essentially antisocial. Interested only in themselves, their behavior is unprincipled. For instance, Harris (with his gentlemanly behavior) is warned off helping Charlie by Slim Barrett (Robert "Buzz" Henry), who is leaving a Mexican bar. "Better stay out of there, Harris," Barrett says. "Charlie's inside asking for trouble. You get one of their knives across your belly, you won't be able to hold your guts in with both hands." Returning to camp to recruit help for Charlie, Harris finds the others equally unwilling to help their comrade. Joe Capper's response to Harris's warning that Charlie is about to get his throat cut is, "Oh, that's his

Figure 5.1 "Fill 'er up": the cowhand's funeral.

problem." Curtis also tells Harris, "That's no reason for us getting hurt." Bender will not become involved in the upcoming fight, because he does not like "the odds." Moreover, when Harris asks Reece what he is going to do about Charlie, Reece replies, "I'm going to go to bed. Same as you ... man's old enough to get himself in trouble, man's old enough to get himself out of trouble." In the end, no one goes back to town to help Charlie.

Even the appearance of marauding Apaches does not persuade the trail hands to band together and support one another to ensure their wellbeing and that of the herd. The group instead turns on one of its own in order to survive. Not surprisingly, it is Curtis who counsels his comrades to do the most dishonorable action imaginable. "While they're busy with Harris [who is in an arroyo by himself rounding up forty head] we can get away with the herd," he says. "He's a goner anyway."

By now, it is obvious that the trail hands are misandrists and murderers. Their disordered personalities, marked by poor behavioral controls, are callous and, with the exception of Doc Bender, remorseless. Curtis and Charlie attempt to kill one another because they are tired and working too hard. Joe Capper's undesirable diet becomes a running joke. Watching the Apaches ride by, Curtis comments, "It must make you feel kinda *hungry*, huh, Joe?" For Curtis, Capper, and Charlie, male friendship is simply impossible.

Sadly, Bender, the sheriff-turned-trail-hand, misses his "good friend" Sam Hacker, and attempts to return to town life at the end of the drive, because "a man has to have something besides a gun and a saddle. You just can't make it all by yourself." Shortly after leaving the cowboys, Bender commits suicide, because he was forced to shoot Hacker in self-defense. His "best friend" had pulled a gun on him while the two were drinking in a saloon. "There was nothing else he could do," Charlie tells Reece. "He had to kill the guy." After Hacker dies, Bender "went over to the livery stable and hung himself." The classical Western's concepts of male friendship and honor are so lacking in *Cowboy* that almost everyone seems to be a social misfit. No one in town, especially Charlie, "could figure out why" Bender would want to kill himself.

Closely associated with the figure of the cowboy, another Western icon that Daves uses to deconstruct coming-of-age in the genre is the horse. As Gretchen Bisplinghoff points out:

> The emblem of the horse, a certain kind of horse, represents key elements of the identity of the cowboy, especially the cowboy star. Popular cowboy heroes were double-billed as partners in an inseparable team of horse and man: Tom Mix and Black Jack, Roy Rogers and Trigger, the Lone Ranger and his great horse Silver. These horses all shared the same common characteristics of being fine-blooded, flashy-gaited animals which separated them from the other horses in the films and demonstrated the status of their owners.[7]

Appropriately for a trail boss, Reece rides a fine-blooded, high-headed, and high-stepping chestnut gelding which Ralph Bauer, in *The Horse, the Gun and the Piece of Property*, would recognize as enhancing "the star's qualities as much as the star enhances the horse's."[8] In color, features, and intelligence, no other horse in the movie is the match of Reece's spirited animal. His broad blaze and flashy white boots immediately catch the viewer's eye, making Reece easily identifiable in wide shots. Highly responsive to his rider's commands, this quarter horse displays excellent confirmation and outstanding athletic ability. Quick, smooth-gaited, and able to turn on a dime, he would enhance the horsemanship of any person riding him. It is also evident that Reece values his mount highly. He will not use the horse to attempt to ring a bull when competing against Vidal's son-in-law in Mexico. He tells Mendoza, "I don't want to get him cut up like that other horse." Reece's relationship with his horse, however, is unlike that of Tom Mix and Black Jack, or Roy Rogers and Trigger. Reece does not offer the animal affection. His quarter horse, neither a pet nor a performer, is a professional athlete, a working cattle horse that is cared for accordingly.

In Chicago prior to their departure, Reece specifically includes a lecture on the nature of the horse when educating Harris about the realities of life on the actual trail. According to Reece, Harris is "an idiot" for believing that driving cattle is about "lyin' out there under the stars listenin' to the boys singin' around the campfire and your faithful old horse standin' there grazin' at the grass by your side." He compounds Harris's naivety:

> All that hogwash about [bonding with] horses. The loyalty of the horse, the intelligence of the horse. You know a horse has a brain just about the size of a walnut? They're mean, they're treacherous, and they're stupid. There isn't a horse born with enough sense to move away from a hot fire. No sensible man loves a horse. He tolerates the filthy animal because ridin's better than walkin'.

Thus, when it is time for the cowboys to choose their mounts for the drive, Reece makes a point of introducing Harris, who does not even know how to put on his chaps, to a "filthy animal" with "a brain the size of a Mexican bean." An ugly, long-eared, miserable, raw-boned, roman-nosed, unremarkable bay gelding, Harris's horse is as green at herding cattle as his rider. When the cowboys claim their mounts, Harris is the last man to do so, and he gets what Reece has warned that he will end up with: a horse "that's not fit to ride." Because Harris's horse is not broken, he has to be "eared" to be saddled. When Harris climbs aboard, he does not enjoy more than a second in the saddle before being jettisoned by his mount. Nor does Reece allow Harris to choose another, easier horse to ride. "If you can't ride that horse, you're gonna have to carry him," he says. Indeed, Harris learning to ride his horse becomes a running joke for the trail hands: he disrupts meals, his horse bucking through the chow line with men shouting as they dive for safety. His horse is also so rough-gaited that Harris becomes extremely saddle-sore. After a day of riding the animal, he cannot sit in his saddle properly and must stand in his stirrups. At night, his aching buttocks have to be toughened up with salt water and whiskey by Joe Capper.

As Bisplinghoff observes, the masculine identity of the cowboy in the classic Western is shaped by the power and freedom associated with the horse. In his mastery of the horse—often represented in the archetypal scene of the hero taming a wild stallion—the cowboy claims the horse's powers as his own.[9] Harris, however, acquires neither strength nor freedom from taming his horse. The scars that he acquires should indicate he has undergone male rites of initiation, but these wounds are not ennobling emblems of masculine rituals of torture; they are only saddle sores. At the end of the drive, as the cattle are being loaded onto the train that will take them to the stockyards in Chicago, Reece informs Harris that he has not become a man. "You haven't gotten tough," he tells him. "You've just gotten miserable." Evidently, Harris has much more to learn before he can be considered an adult. In the train on the way back to Chicago, Mendoza kids Reece about his student's progress and

Figure 5.2 Homosocial bonding in *Cowboy*.

reveals the next ordeal through which Harris will have to pass to acquire his manhood: "I have to laugh. You made this fellow tough. Now you don't like what you made. Well, he learned how to handle cows; maybe he will learn how to handle women."

Ironically, it is Reece, not Harris, who is transformed by the experience of the cattle drive. Shot in the leg, Reece, not the neophyte, experiences the initiate's metaphoric death and begins to perform atypical acts. He orders the herd stampeded into an arroyo to save Harris from Apaches even though, as mentioned above, Mendoza points out that "we will never get the cattle back. Not in this country." Furthermore, on the way back to Chicago he saves Harris from being trampled in a cattle car. Reece says that he's "tired of burying people," but he becomes unusually self-sacrificing as he mentors Harris. The film's ending, in which he and Harris rest side by side in matching bathtubs and shoot at cockroaches, suggests both friendship and equality. However, homosocial bonding ultimately proves to be an end in itself, rather than a passage to a higher plane of existence.

In *Cowboy* a bath proves to be a tub of hot water and the eradication of vermin merely pest control. Neither is a purification ritual. Harris's horse and his adventures have not carried him into the untamed frontier of the mythic Wild West. Instead, he and Reece find themselves where they began, having traveled East, not West, back in polite society, preparing to partake of the opera season. As Bertrand Tavernier has noted, in Daves' Westerns "the City and Civilization are not systematically depicted as noxious, corrupting entities, as in, say, Capra."[10] Daves' concern for historical realism over spiritual mysticism results in an implicit critique of the Western.

Another important element of *Cowboy*'s critical examination of the Western is its emphasis on visual authenticity. Daves painstakingly chose legitimate locations in which to make his films, and *Cowboy*, shot in Arizona, is no exception to this rule. "I make every effort to get to [the place where it happened]," he tells Wicking, adding,

> [B]y the way, that doesn't necessarily mean the actual spot . . . I'll show you Texas, but in *Arizona* where it's flat. It has the Texas feeling, but at least we have clouds, at least we have shadows; we haven't dust that just coats everything . . . [It's] the equivalent of the place in Texas. All of my films are done in high desert country, seven or eight thousand feet high. There's something special about the atmosphere. It's clean and clear—I love to shoot in the winter time.[11]

Having lived on the desert and being familiar with the nature of light there, Daves carefully designed *Cowboy* to be a color film full of blacks by design. Being the primary element of composition, shadows, or blacks, define the mood of a shot by providing dramatic contrasts that bring three-dimensional depth and realism to the screen. The solid blacks used during the funeral, which takes place at night, and especially Daves' pan of the cowboys' heavily shadowed faces when Reece asks if anybody knows "the right words," foregrounds and isolates the mourners' individual expressions, transmitting their individual emotions of anger, confusion, fear, and sorrow. Mirroring the darkness of their comrade's resting place, the blacks in these shots situate the living in the blackness of the grave and offer the viewer a comprehensive, poetic image of the human condition: "If it hadn't been a snake that got him, it would've been a steer or a Comanche," Reece says, defusing the tragedy that has occurred while reminding his listeners of the reality of the proximity of death.

Daves effectively reverses this treatment of chiaroscuro shortly after the funeral when using low-key natural lighting to shoot the mission located north of Guadalupe. Meeting Maria for the last time, Harris rides up to the mission that dominates almost half of the screen. Silhouetted as a solid black (with the exception of the bell-tower apertures that reveal the brilliantly backlit cumulus of the calm evening sky), the mission overpowers the tiny silhouette of Maria's horse tied to a hitching rail before it, and the figure of Harris on his horse approaching the rendezvous. The diminished figures of humans and animals transmit the insignificance of the individual and his or her desires in a culture dominated by religion and tradition, long before Harris discovers that Maria has come to the mission to bid him farewell and save her marriage. It is she, not the cowboy, who rides off into the sunset.

In both of these examples, the landscape, the classical Western's most epic ur-form, is reduced and emptied of its usual symbolic references. During the funeral, the natural setting is not visible because the heavy shadows allow only the men's faces to be seen. The blacks prevent the viewer from seeing even the grave. Accordingly, the cowboy's faces become the terrain that the camera explores. At Harris and Maria's rendezvous, the mission's silhouette blocks the viewer's eye from seeing the land in which the scene is set and bookends the frame, making the panoramic view, so familiar in the classical Western, impossible. Daves' camera insists that the primary integers of the West are its man-made religious and social constructs, and not the land itself. As Tavernier points out, "nature in Daves's films is not imparted with the grandeur, the epic theatricality so admired in Ford, who manages to convince us that one could farm and raise cattle in Monument Valley, a thoroughly unrealistic proposition. Daves does not mythologize Nature."[12] Instead of foregrounding nature and thereby printing the West's legend, Daves' use of blacks in *Cowboy* imparts a modern aesthetic and a preoccupation with architectonics to the screen, reminding the viewer of the immediacy of the moment and privileging of the present.

Cowboy's treatment of authentic natural images in a complex cinematic study of locality further deconstructs Western iconography. The most poetic revelation of danger in *Cowboy* occurs when a band of Apaches, intent on killing Harris and taking forty head of cattle, ride by Reece and his men. Climbing a backlit ridge, the Apaches, in single file, guide their horses into the arroyo behind it, disappearing into the point of tension on the upper right of the screen beside the sharply defined black of the small butte that serves to bookend what has become a standard visual composition of the Hollywood Western. This is the type of "beauty shot" that one would expect to find in a classical Western directed by John Ford. Based on Charles Russell's low-angle presentations of Native Americans on the warpath and, later, Russell's luminous color palette for pastoral presentations of Native Americans, Ford's depictions of the Apache in *Stagecoach* (1939) and his Cavalry films solidified the nineteenth century's Romantic view of the "noble savage" in Western film.

Continuing to contrast styles when cutting to the arroyo below, *Cowboy*'s camera then switches abruptly to a documentary presentation of Harris rounding up his cattle. Naturally lit with a flat, realistic feeling to it, there are mid-tones but no blacks in this shot. Daves' next shot cuts back to what has become a classical Western riff. In the next shot, Daves' Indians snake their way through the arroyo according to the principles of *repoussoir* in a nineteenth-century landscape painting. Bracketed by rocky outcroppings framing its edges, the shot's composition directs the viewer's eye from left to right as the horses follow a winding path toward the lower right-hand corner of the screen that is framed by a large piñon pine tree in the immediate foreground which increases the illusion of the arroyo's depth.

Designed to jar the viewer's conceptions of what a Western should look like, Daves' Fordian presentation of the Apache and nineteenth-century landscape composition are intercut with realistic representations of the cowboys that, as noted above, deconstruct any possibility of Reece and his men being considered gallant or heroic. As the camera switches between shots of the trail hands at their camp, the raiding party on the butte, and Harris in the arroyo with the cattle, the cowboys' conversation emphasizes the fact that Reece's men are, like their horses, mean, treacherous, and stupid, as all are willing to sacrifice Harris in order to save the cattle.

Once the cowboys attack the Apaches, shots of the arroyo's *repoussoirs* and Daves' Russell-inspired portrait of a lost, lyrical West quickly vanish. Daves shifts styles, and his indigenes participate in the cowboys' documentary moment. The depiction of the battle between cowboys and Indians is not idealized as a clash of opposing social forces. With the exception of one cowboy who uses a handgun, rifles are used. Harris dismounts from his horse to shoot accurately and uses the piñon trees as cover. Men gallop their horses off horizons to avoid becoming easy targets. Reece shoots horses, disabling their riders. Both cowboys and Indians miss their shots. In the end Harris attempts to help Reece, who is shot in the knee, but it quickly becomes obvious that their skirmish with the Apaches has not resolved their personal antagonism over money.

Daves' juxtaposition of the Romantic and the Real is not restricted to this incident. Other visual ur-forms appear throughout *Cowboy*. An earlier Fordian moment, for example, occurs when Reece and his men cross the border into Mexico. The camera presents the viewer with a dramatic low angle reminiscent of the lone horsemen that one finds in Ford's movies, inspired by Frederic Remington's depictions of the "Wild West." Mendoza spurs his horse up a ridge and pauses beneath the overhang of a hoodoo to take off his hat and wipe the sweat off his brow. Yet the romance of Mexico and the freedom that this shot promises are quickly deflated when Harris arrives at the Vidal ranch and discovers that Maria has been married.

Cowboy also probes a primary integer of the cattle drive itself: the stampede. An act of mass impulse, a stampede occurs when a herd of cattle collectively begins running with no clear direction or purpose, typically eliminating everything in its path. Since they were first committed to celluloid, dramatic images of runaway herds of tightly packed cattle, flanked by daring, hard-riding cowboys, all galloping at top speed across the open prairie, pulverizing anyone or anything that is unable to escape their path, have thrilled and fascinated audiences.

In order to drive the Apaches away from Harris, Reece and his trail hands atypically begin the stampede by firing their rifles into the air to spook the herd of cattle that is milling in an arroyo below them. Mirroring the scene that concludes the stampede found in *Red River*, Reece's tightly packed cattle are first seen contained by the high walls of what appears to be a small, tight canyon. The cattle fill the screen, their bodies, heads, and horns directing the viewer's eye into a golden spiral that ends around the low left-hand point of tension on the screen, and satisfies classical requirements of beauty and completeness of form. When the cowboys on their horses begin shooting their rifles and spill over the side of the arroyo to slide down the canyon's walls into the herd, the stampede begins. In the next shot, the completeness of the herd fragments as the cattle turn and begin to gallop toward the camera.

Unlike Hawks, Daves does not score his stampede. Without music to heighten the dramatic impact of the action, the stampede in *Cowboy* is presented as an authentic event in which only the sound of hooves, the shouts of the trail hands, and an occasional rifle shot are heard. The danger to the men riding with the running cattle is real. In *Cowboy*, there are no rear screen projections of a galloping herd and no movie stars mounted on moving plastic horses and shooting their Colt .45s into the "stampede" safely projected on the screen beside them. Unlike the cattle in *Red River*—which are shown to be contained by the cowboys who ride alongside the herd, flanking the steers to ensure that they are tightly packed and running shoulder-to-shoulder when pouring over the banks of arroyos, up gentle rises, and through the cowboys' camp, pulverizing a chuck wagon—the cattle in *Cowboy*, which begin the stampede as a single group, quickly spread apart, galloping no more than four abreast, fanning out in several directions as the arroyo allows and running up hills, and escape their pursuers.

Like Hawks, Daves cuts away to low-angle shots of the legs and bellies of the running cattle during the stampede to transmit the terrifying power of the stampeding animals, but, in general, he favors the wide shot, giving *Cowboy*'s stampede a documentary look. Once the stampede begins, Reece's men gallop beside the herd, directing and encouraging the cattle to run. Ironically, while doing so, they are riding like Hawks's cowboys, who are depicted as attempting to halt the galloping herd in *Red River*. Although shooting is heard in the background during *Cowboy*'s stampede, it is important to note that no man uses a pistol to encourage the running cattle or shoots into the herd in the attempt to turn the cattle. Only one rider with a pistol is visible during the stampede, and he is engaged in chasing off Apaches, not keeping up with the steers. The cowboys seen riding with rifles in hand are either shooting in the air to make the cattle run, or are engaged in a running gun battle with the Indians. Because of the gun battle, it is not possible to attempt to "head" the herd (turn it in a circle onto itself to stop the stampede). As Harris points out, the runaway steers will stop when they are ready to and not before—and when the stampede is over, Harris is furious, because the cattle have been "scattered all over the territory."

One of the most popular ur-forms used in the classical Western lexicon conveys to the viewer the experience of the Ideal and/or the Sublime emptied of human presence. The West is a place that cannot be fenced in (culturally or naturally) or contained on the screen. In the classical Western, the camera panning to depict the landscape is a recognizably American response to terrain, stressing not only the scale of the view but also its expansiveness. Now considered a standard compositional convention in the Western, Ford's panoramic treatments of the tiny vastness and depth of Monument Valley that trace the passage of a tiny stagecoach on its way to Lordsburg and its accompanying cavalry in *Stagecoach* produced by a high crane shot to exaggerate the enormity of the landscape, introduced a new magnitude of exteriority of the American Sublime to the screen in 1939 that had been previously experienced in the romantic landscapes of painters like Albert Bierstadt, Charles Schreyvogel, Thomas Cole, and Frederic Church, and in the photographs taken by William Henry Jackson, Carleton E. Watkins, and Timothy O'Sulllivan. As Tag Gallagher points out, the effect of Ford's panorama in *Stagecoach* is that of "a consciousness expanding forcibly; an alienated stare at the world's vastness, at an immensity embarrassing our trepidant love."[13]

Unlike Ford, Daves' signature shot in his Westerns is not the pan that creates Western panorama, but the crane shot. "I was a bit of a pioneer with the camera boom (you call it a crane over here) particularly in Westerns and so much so that I built my own," Daves says to Wicking. Furthermore:

> It's a six-wheel-drive truck with the camera crane on it . . . Other booms always had to be on an angle, but our boom goes straight up in the air like a telephone pole, and you can figuratively shoot all round, and almost straight. So this allows me to do my boom shots, almost with a sense of music. The crew tell me I look like Toscanini directing an orchestra . . . In Westerns you are controlled a little by the action. If the action speeds up a little more than you thought you have to create the action, emotionally with the camera at the same time. So the men all watch me when on the boom and I ride the boom right alongside the operating camera man: "Look out, it's happening, now lift." That's very characteristic of many of the shots that I do in the Western films. Sometimes I'll insert moments of beauty into a film that have little to do with the dramatic content, just because it's beautiful and the boom particularly is good for that purpose.[14]

As Graham Clarke points out, landscape photographers choose pristine environments with as little evidence of human settlement as possible, constructing their own Arcadias, ideal images in an ideal land.[15] Jacques Lourcelles argues that Daves' crane shots function to create panoramic effects because they "often have no immediate, logical connection with the plot [and] magnify the emotions which in turn help the spectator commune with the landscape."[16] Unlike Ford's panoramas, which celebrate the sublime emptiness of the West, Daves' documentary impulse saturates the pristine Western landscape with human figures, cattle, chuck wagons, and buildings. In *Cowboy*, the crane shot when Reece and the cowboys arrive to break horses, for example, lifts to include horses and riders in the shot but does not continue to rise to a degree such that, as in Ford's Westerns, the human element is dwarfed by the seemingly limitless landscape beyond. Daves' crane shot instead tilts down, using the tree in the foreground to frame and bookend Reece and the chuck wagons that follow him into camp.

Connecting the men with the animals and the land, more high-angle crane shots are used to enable the viewer to see all of the action in the corral as the cowboys break their horses for riding. In these shots, Daves again carefully limits the scope and expansiveness generally awarded the crane shot by using the corral's fencing to frame and enclose the action. In Daves' Western landscape, there is very little emptiness or opportunity to commune with nature: *Cowboy*'s subject, after all, is neither the Sublime nor the Ideal, but the coherence found in the West between the figures of man, horse, and cattle. Revising what is considered a primary element of the authentic West, Daves carefully steers clear of landscape conventions and codes. In *Cowboy*, the land generally exists without reference to the social or political, signifying a natural rather than a cultural context and serving to create, in part, the documentary feeling he wanted to achieve in *Cowboy*.

Daves' personal vision of the American West, his attention to historical accuracy, and his groundbreaking work with camera placement and lighting to convey the messages of his "adult" Westerns distinguish him as an honest director, a sophisticated commentator, and an auteur filmmaker. Billed as "adult in every sense of the word [and] really the West," *Cowboy* was another important step in Daves' chronicling of the authentic West. In this account of the West, the legend is not fact. As in *Broken Arrow*, Daves' radical documentary approach in *Cowboy* reassesses genre stereotypes, challenges romantic and heroic conventions of the West's mythos, and sets his work with the Western apart from that of the Western's mythmakers. Unlike Howard Hawkes and John Ford, Daves debunks America's cinematic frontier in *Cowboy*, presenting the viewer with a complex vision in which the Real, measured against a cinematic ideal, works to deconstruct the classical Western. In the final analysis, Daves' celebration of the ordinary in *Cowboy* examines and critiques the aggressive, accumulative instincts and antisocial appetites that reside in the American character. *Cowboy* shows that it is possible for men to make a fortune in the cattle business and escape the blessings of civilization by being trail hands, but, as Señor Vidal points out to Frank Harris, it is important to remember that "money is no particular recommendation" of one's character.

BIBLIOGRAPHY

Bisplinghoff, Gretchen, "Travelers and Cowboys: Myths of the Irish West," *VisionQuest: Journeys toward Visual Literacy* (1997): 185–9.
Brauer, Ralph, *The Horse, The Gun and The Piece of Property* (Bowling Green, OH: Bowling Green University Popular Press, 1975).
Clarke, Graham, *The Photograph* (Oxford: Oxford University Press, 1997).
"Cowboy," *Variety*, 11 February 1958, <http://www.varietyultimate.com/archive/issue/DV-02-11-1958-3> (last accessed 11 November 2015).
Crowther, Bosley, "'Cowboy' is Standard Western Saga," *New York Times*, 20 February 1958, <http://www.nytimes.com/movie/review?res=9F0DEEDD133FE53BBC4851DFB46683 83649EDE> (last accessed 11 November 2015).
Gallagher, Tag, *John Ford: The Man and His Films* (Berkeley: University of California Press, 1986).
Kitses, Jim, *Horizons West* (Bloomington: Indiana University Press, 1970).
Tavernier, Bernard, "The Ethical Romantic," *Film Comment*, January–February 2003, <http://www.filmcomment.com/article/delmer-daves-bertrand-tavernier> (last accessed 11 November 2015).
Wicking, Christopher, "Interview with Delmer Daves," *Screen*, 10:4/5 (1969): 55–66.

FILMOGRAPHY

Broken Arrow, director Delmer Daves, featuring Jimmy Stewart, Jeff Chandler, Debra Paget, Basil Ruysdael (20th Century Fox, 1950).
Cowboy, director Delmer Daves, featuring Glenn Ford, Jack Lemmon, Anna Kashfi, Dick York (Columbia Pictures, 1958).
Hanging Tree, The, director Delmer Daves, featuring Gary Cooper, Maria Schell, Karl Malden (Warner Bros., 1959).
Jubal, director Delmer Daves, featuring Glenn Ford, Valerie French, Rod Steiger, Ernest Borgnine (Columbia Pictures, 1956).
Last Wagon, The, director Delmer Daves, featuring Richard Widmark, Felicia Farr, Susan Kohner, Tommy Rettig (20th Century Fox, 1956).
Red River, director Howard Hawkes, featuring John Wayne, Montgomery Clift, Walter Brennan, Joanne Dru (United Artists, 1948).
Stagecoach, director John Ford, featuring John Wayne, Claire Trevor, Andy Devine, John Carradine (United Artists, 1939).
3:10 to Yuma, director Delmer Daves, featuring Glenn Ford, Van Heflin, Felicia Farr, Leora Dana (Columbia Pictures, 1957).
"Trailer," *Cowboy*, <http://www.tcm.com/mediaroom/video/147731/Big-Stampede-The-Original-Trailer-.html> (last accessed 6 August 2014).

NOTES

1. Wicking, "Interview with Delmer Daves," p. 59.
2. Ibid.
3. Ibid.
4. Ibid. p. 60.
5. Ibid.
6. Examples include *The Old Chisholm Trail* (1942), *Cattle Stampede* (1943), *Red River* (1948), *Apache Ambush* (1955), *The Tall Men* (1955), *The Big Land* (1957), *Cattle Empire* (1958), *Gunfighters of Casa Grande* (1964), *The Cowboys* (1972), *The Culpepper Cattle Co.* (1972), and *City Slickers* (1991).
7. Bisplinghoff, "Travelers and Cowboys," p. 185.
8. Brauer, *The Horse, The Gun and The Piece of Property*, p. 36.
9. Bisplinghoff, "Travelers and Cowboys," p. 188.
10. Quoted in Tavernier, "The Ethical Romantic."
11. Wicking, "Interview with Delmer Daves," p. 61.
12. Tavernier, "The Ethical Romantic."
13. Gallagher, *John Ford*, p. 147.
14. Wicking, "Interview with Delmer Daves," p. 64.
15. Clarke, *The Photograph*, p. 65.
16. Quoted in Tavernier, "The Ethical Romantic."

CHAPTER 6

Home and the Range: *Spencer's Mountain* as Revisionist Family Melodrama

Joseph Pomp

Though successful upon its release in 1963, *Spencer's Mountain* has very little, if any, reputation to speak of today. Two main explanations jump to the fore, both encapsulated by a set of polarities between which the film is stranded. On the one hand, it lacks the moral value (or moralizing didacticism, depending one's perspective) of its source novel of the same title by Earl Hamner, Jr.; nor does it flaunt the crowd-pleasing buoyancy of *The Waltons*, the TV series adapted from the same source.[1] Caught between a literary and televisual iteration, Delmer Daves' *Spencer's Mountain* stands out even more conspicuously by taking as its setting the Grand Teton Mountains of Wyoming rather than the backwoods of the Virginian Appalachians of the other two versions. On the other hand, the film seems to have fallen through the cracks by fitting neither within the melodramatic mode with which it is ostensibly aligned, nor within the genres with which film critics generally associate Delmer Daves. Indeed, though *Spencer's Mountain* takes place in a landscape of the great American West that is familiar territory for Daves, it is arguably his only family melodrama.

An overdue re-evaluation of *Spencer's Mountain*, which this chapter seeks to enact, depends upon unsettling these assumptions about both the film's adherence to melodrama and Daves' relationship with that narrative mode. In fact, one of the main reasons why critics may not have canonized Daves as a major auteur in the 1960s is that, despite his reputation primarily as a director of Westerns, he actually did often delve into the melodramatic mode. This was a mode entirely out of fashion amongst auteurists, who preferred the coarse masculinity of a John Ford or Raoul Walsh. This aversion to melodramatic excess in fact continues to be an impediment to Daves' critical appreciation today.[2] Indeed, on a certain level, *Spencer's Mountain* typifies what Christine

Gledhill sees as the reason behind the mode's low critical estimation: "melodrama could offer neither the thematic and evolutionary coherence exhibited by, say, the western, nor sufficient cultural prestige . . . condemned as it was by association with a mass and, above all female, audience."[3] Though it is irrefutable that *Spencer's Mountain* was manufactured for as wide an audience as possible, we shall see how its distance from the Western, both ideologically and narratologically, may not be as great as it might initially seem.

Let us first consider the film's origins. As already mentioned, Delmer Daves transplanted Earl Hamner, Jr.'s novel from the Blue Ridge Mountains of Virginia to the Grand Teton Mountains, in which he had set a Western in 1956. "I have always loved the scenery of the Jackson Hole countryside since I did *Jubal* there 10 years ago with Glenn Ford, and I vowed then to return one day," Daves explained. "The opportunity arose with *Spencer's Mountain*, which I read while still in galley proofs and asked the studio to buy."[4] Enthusiasts of Virginian and Appalachian literature may have been disappointed by the geographical alteration, but we have to consider that Warner Brothers might not have allowed Daves to make the film anywhere but in the West. The backwoods family melodrama was a viable subgenre of Warner melodramas but, by the 1950s, Daves had established a reputation for himself at the studio for his Westerns, and so his decision to move the novel's setting west may have been a strategic one as the studio trusted him to perform well in that terrain.

Drawn largely from his own boyhood experiences as the eldest son of eight children in a small Virginian mountain town, Earl Hamner, Jr.'s novel chronicles the coming of age of one aptly named Clay-Boy Spencer, Jr. The youngest in a clan of "prodigious drinkers, courageous fighters, incomparable lovers" (Daves borrowed this quote in the character notes that precede his screenplay), Clay-Boy grows from just another one of the kids to an academic star in high school. Clay-Boy's teacher encourages him not to stay in the town and work at the local mill, but to pursue a college education. Again, like Clay-Boy, Hamner wound up matriculating at the University of Richmond. While the novel drags a bit (with episodes, readily left out of the film, such as the addition to the family of two newborn twins and the marriage of Clay-Boy's uncle Virgil to a specimen utterly alien to the town of New Dominion, a Jew), on the whole the narrative feels ready-made for a filmic adaptation. Hamner uses many devices of narrative economy familiar to cinema, such as cross-cutting.[5] Indeed, the novel foreshadows the career Hamner would go on to have as a film and television writer and producer. Several key scenes—for example, one in which Clay goes into the university dean's office to challenge their initial rejection of Clay-Boy—are re-staged in the film verbatim.

Perhaps the main reason, though, why Daves saw the potential for a great studio film in the novel is that, despite its timeless, wholesome American values, it loosely fits into the wave of postmodernity and self-satire that had been overtaking Southern literature in the 1960s. This possibly began in 1961, the same year that *Spencer's Mountain* was published, with Walker Percy's *The Moviegoer*.[6] In Hamner's case, this mostly surfaces in the excess of generic details of the American homestead, such as hearty breakfasts overflowing with coffee, bacon, fried eggs, and biscuits. Hamner includes the requisite amount of God-fearing and amen-chanting to appease his church-going readership, but he also takes delight in various comedic episodes in which Clay pokes fun at the church, which amount to a sort of picaresque novella with the novel. Additionally, Daves knew from experience that melodramatic narratives tended to travel well between page and screen. Although many of the Hollywood melodramas held in high regard today were also adapted from novels (*Written on the Wind*, *Some Came Running*, etc.), as were all three of Daves' prior melodramas (*A Summer Place*, *Parrish*, and *Susan Slade*), this was certainly nothing new. "While it would be overreaching to assert that melodrama was somehow more profoundly intertextual than other cultural forms," Ben Singer writes in his study of melodrama in the early twentieth century, "it is fair to say that sensational melodrama was probably unsurpassed in this regard."[7] Small wonder, then, that Hamner's tale of the Spencer family would have a long life across media. In 1970, Hamner wrote *The Homecoming*, a short sequel to the novel, which was adapted by CBS as a TV movie in 1971. The success of that production led to the creation of the series *The Waltons*, which aired from 1972 to 1981, winning the Emmy for outstanding drama series in its first season, and became the second-most-watched show in the U.S.

Daves started writing the first draft of *Spencer's Mountain* aboard a flight to Argentina to attend a film festival on 12 March 1962.[8] Hamner extolled Daves' script, writing to him, "The movie will be a memorable one, and the kind that lives on in memory long after a person has seen it."[9] After twenty-five days of shooting on location in Jackson Hole, Wyoming, followed by eighteen days in the studio, and one day in southern California to film the university campus scenes, principal photography was completed on 21 August 1962, six days ahead of schedule.[10]

Not only was the physical landscape of *Spencer's Mountain* familiar to Daves, but so too was the emotional landscape. We should see the late 1950s and early 1960s as a seamless period of transition for Daves, from his string of later westerns—*Cowboy* (1958), *The Badlanders* (1958), and *The Hanging Tree* (1959) did not shy away from melodrama even as they stayed within the borders of that masculine genre—to full-on melodramas, some of which, namely *A Summer Place* (1959) and *Susan Slade* (1961), we could even categorize as woman's films. Of course, we should not forget that melodrama is the composite of drama and *Melos*, the Greek word for music, and so (as many scholars have noted) just about every Hollywood film could technically be classified as a

Figure 6.1 On location in Jackson Hole, Wyoming.

melodrama. Few would dispute, though, that the classical Westerns, with their yearning, sun-kissed landscapes and dynamic, wailing scores, more often than not veer in the direction of melodrama. If the aspects of melodrama embedded in the Western are clear, then we should note the elements of the Western in *Spencer's Mountain*. The opening moments of the film share so much with that genre that they might lead the viewer to believe, in fact, that he or she is in for a "cowboy picture." The image track opens with a majestic crane shot that pans across the Grand Tetons, with light emanating like a revelation through thick clouds above. The mountains themselves, quite exceptionally for a location alone, are touted in the opening titles. Meanwhile, the sound track bursts off with Max Steiner boldly quoting "America the Beautiful," which returns both as a leitmotif in the incidental music throughout the film and in a rendition by African American stage star Barbara McNair (making her film debut). Whereas the melodrama often expresses the great challenges of American life, *Spencer's Mountain* has at its bedrock the ideology of the Western, namely that the country is a wonder to be savored and defended by the citizens of the U.S. This is just the start to the film's unmooring itself from melodramatic convention. Its departures extend far beyond the realm of audio-visual design.

If, as Thomas Elsaesser writes, "The family melodrama ... more often records the failure of the protagonist to act in a way that could shape the events and influence the emotional environment," then *Spencer's Mountain* poses a categorical challenge to the genre to which many have disdainfully relegated it. Elsaesser goes on to write that melodramatic characters' "progressive self-immolation and disillusionment generally ends in resignation," a condition that is antithetical to Daves' entire worldview and appeal to us as an auteur.[11] It is one of the states of mind, along with cynicism and paranoia, that Kent Jones identifies as refreshingly absent in nearly all of the director's output.[12] Perhaps the chief reason why those qualities haunt post-war film melodramas is that they operate under a patriarchal, heteronormative ideology that enforces authority by instilling fear and oppression. *Spencer's Mountain* conspicuously dismantles film melodrama's so-called "classic realist" paradigm, governed by this same ideology, in a legion of ways. Perhaps the most important consideration is the figure of the father himself. Clay (Henry Fonda) is a freewheeling drunkard who is comfortable enough in his community (after all, the domineering landmark is a mountain named after a man from whom he is directly descended) not to demand much from those around him. He lets his son Clay-Boy do whatever he wants—even apply for a ministerial scholarship to the university, despite all things clerical being anathema to him personally. I would even go so far as to say that the real figure of authority in the Spencer family is the mother, Olivia (Maureen O'Hara), who at one point lays down the law with Clay-Boy. She tells him that he needs to stay around and fulfill his familial duty to help look after his younger siblings and make the best of his situation at home. Since we know that one of the main reasons Clay-Boy wants to leave is to follow his girlfriend, Claris Coleman (Mimsy Farmer), we could read this scene as a warning sign of castration that hints at a more complex Freudian schema to come later in the film. While Clay is mostly unchanged from the novel, Daves deliberately undercuts a patriarchal framework by excluding the book's opening episode, in which Clay-Boy panics about whether he will be able to join the older Spencer men on their annual Thanksgiving hunt despite his mother's forbiddance.

Perhaps Daves' most critical move in putting forward a revision of the family melodrama and its patriarchal underpinnings is a focus on young love. Whereas the standard family melodrama that revolves around a fraught romance places it in the lap of a parent, often a widow (as in the paradigmatic case of *All that Heaven Allows*), *Spencer's Mountain* is driven by the tender love affair between Claris and Clay-Boy. "At the narrative-thematic core of family melodramas is a metaphoric search for the ideal husband/ lover/father who . . . will stabilize the family and integrate it into the larger community," writes Thomas Schatz.[13] Metaphorically or otherwise, everyone in the small town puts their faith not into a grown man but into young Clay-Boy, because he symbolizes the future of the community in his quest for higher education. Also, in his relationship with Claris, who is the daughter of Colonel Coleman—as the owner of the quarry, the wealthiest man in town—Clay-Boy has the potential to bring social prestige and perhaps eventually a small fortune to his family.

As if the emphasis on a son rather than a father were not subversive enough, Daves then pushes the politics of gender by acknowledging the fact that, in the early teenage years, females have had more years of sexual maturity than men have, and largely call the shots. Before we meet Claris, we see how in Clay-Boy's life women are the actors and he is the mostly passive object of their affection. Early in the film, a girl approaches him in front of his house and smiles, "I know you, you're Claris Coleman's fella." She then strokes his leg and says: "You and me could have some fun, you know what I mean?" and then, "Listen, whenever you get the urge to, you just toss some pebbles on my window and I'll come running." When we do meet Claris, she too flaunts her sexual confidence. "They say I'm the dangerous age," Claris explains to Clay-Boy with a flirtatious smile. "Stuck me in a girls' academy." She then flexes her body to demonstrate her prowess at Phys. Ed., but then while fiddling with one of Clay-Boy's shirt buttons says that her favorite subject, about which she could teach him a thing or two, is called Marriage and the Family. Back at the Spencer house, after comparing the way the baby is sitting in the sink to how he must have looked inside Olivia's womb, Claris apologizes, "Well, it's just that I'm terribly enthralled with human reproduction right now!"

Refusing to settle for simply putting forward a female character who is realistically more sexually mature than her male counterpart, Daves also makes Claris more ambitious and directed career-wise. Whereas in the novel Clay-Boy tells Claris he wants to be an archaeologist in Egypt, in the film Claris presents this career option as her decision on what they should be when they enter their adult life together. "Yesterday it was baby doctors!" Clay-Boy responds in bewilderment. She fantasizes about traveling around the world excavating relics, but he brings the daydream back down to earth by saying that there is no need to travel when the family mountain itself has plenty of Native American relics. Claris, urban sophisticate that she is in comparison to his farm-boyishness (she even pejoratively calls him a hillbilly at one point), wears the pants in the relationship on all fronts. Just as he has Claris, instead of Clay-Boy, fantasize out loud about the prospective careers they might share, Daves also puts one of Clay-Boy's other important lines in the book—about their relationship, and how he won't be able to pay for dates at school—into Claris's mouth instead. The resulting scene makes Clay-Boy seem utterly impotent: still unsure whether or not he will be able to afford the college tuition, he does not utter a word in response to Claris's excitement that, as fate would have it, she will be matriculating at the same university. During the same meeting, she makes a challenging advance, perhaps the most surprising of all the sexual suggestions in the film given the period: "Do we have to wait four years?" she prods at Clay-Boy while pecking his ear. "Can't we start practicing now?"

It is worth noting that Claris's sexual maneuvering of Clay-Boy might not be possible if she did not inscribe herself within the Spencer home as much as the baby-in-the-sink scene illustrated. Indeed, as is to be expected in an example of that most Oedipal of film genres, Clay's sex and family lives are intimately interrelated. Clay-Boy's actual loss of virginity comes a few scenes later, only after a moment with his parents that cries out for a psychoanalytic reading. Helping his mother support Clay, suffering from a limp after the tree that killed Zebulon fell on his foot, Clay-Boy tucks his parents into bed and tells them he has decided not to go to college after all. Perhaps this is in recognition both of his duty to the family, and of the true allure of leaving home—that is to say, an ability to copulate at will with Claris. When they raise an eyebrow at his decision, he explains that he "made a promise to God to give it up" if God let Clay survive the tree accident. Staying firmly within Oedipal territory, Daves stages a familiar scenario in which the young man can only fulfill his sexual fantasy once his father dies. Since Clay is still living, Clay-Boy has repressed his desire to embark on a new life of freedom, sexual or otherwise. Of course, the parents assure him that this is one promise he should not feel the need to keep with God, but Olivia reaffirms the Oedipal tension of the scene by rolling over to Clay once they are alone and the lights are out and murmuring, "Thanks for giving me a son like that."

The scene that ensues literalizes the allure of forbidden sexual arrangements. Claris catches a shirtless Clay-Boy toiling on the new house and reels him in for an embrace. Clay-Boy protests, "It's kind of indecent, kissing in broad daylight." "That's what makes it sexy," Claris retorts with a randy smile, before leading him off to a secluded part of the mountain to take their affection further. The mountain scene in *Spencer's Mountain* famously caused quite a stir amongst reviewers, but what strikes the contemporary viewer as much more startling is that Daves cuts away to parallel action wherein Olivia sits down on a hammock in which Clay is reclining and says, "We never did smooch—not before marriage." "Depends on what you mean by smooching," Clay flirts. "Means: *making love*," spells out Olivia. "Not really . . . only around the edges, like you like to let me," Clay adds, while lowering his wife on top of him and tapping her behind. This functions as a consummation of an earlier moment of tension between the spouses, when Clay makes some off-handed remark with a creative use of the word "butt," and, after Olivia chastises him, he spanks her back, which sends the Spencer kids looking on into a frenzy, chanting, "Daddy spanked Mama!"

The sexual suggestiveness of *Spencer's Mountain* did not make it to the screen without contention in the early 1960s. Upon reviewing the screenplay, one Geoffrey M. Shurlock (presumably of the Production Code office) wrote to Jack Warner, saying, "We feel that the sex affair between Clay-boy and Claris is unacceptable. Furthermore, we believe some of Claris' dialogue is unacceptable blunt [sic] and sex suggestive. The sequence dealing with the mating of the bull and the cow, likewise ... in its present condition, is excessive."[14] Warner Brothers, meanwhile, seems to have been eager to capitalize on the burgeoning 60s zeitgeist of sexual liberation and feminism. Just a few months before releasing *Spencer's Mountain*, Warner Brothers put out *The Chapman Report* (George Cukor, 1962), based on a novel by Irving Wallace (itself inspired by the Kinsey reports) about four women's various sexual anxieties. Additionally, the studio's next picture to feature Henry Fonda was *Sex and the Single Girl* (Richard Quine, 1964), a romantic comedy based on the 1962 feminist handbook by Helen Gurley Brown. Daves' participation in this wave of sex-positive, youth-driven, and lighthearted films affirms not just his continued relevance beyond the period typically considered his prime, but also the significance of his revisionist melodrama. Whereas Sirk and Minnelli, evoking the repressiveness of the 1950s, underscored the tragedy of the family melodrama, Daves was hip to the loosening up of the 1960s and appropriately infused the genre with comedy.

Having demonstrated how the sexual politics of *Spencer's Mountain* goes against the conventions of the family melodrama and links it to the romantic comedies of the 1960s, I want to return to the subject of the physical landscape of the film to clarify its relationship to both the Western and the standard domestic melodrama. Martin Lefebvre explains that, in contradistinction to setting, "landscape, at least in the visual arts, is *space freed from eventhood*."[15] Indeed, what distinguishes the landscape of the titular mountain from the valley upon which the plot unfurls is its autonomy. Spencer's Mountain remains all but untouched to the viewer, towering majestically in the background. I hesitate to use that banal word "background" here, because of the one-dimensionality it brings to mind in relation to the cinema; the French equivalent, *fond*, brings much more weight, with its secondary meanings of "depth," "core," and (in the context of cooking) "base." Sergei Eisenstein noted that landscape is "the freest element of film ... and the most flexible in conveying moods, emotional states, and spiritual experiences."[16] Although Daves does not spend a great deal of *Spencer's Mountain* focusing his lens on the Grand Teton Mountains themselves, his decision to return to them for this film confirms Eisenstein's point about a landscape's ability to conjure up deep emotions. The mountain range articulates a tone and feeling that cannot be put into words, but which nonetheless is obviously a key component of Daves' melodramatic mode, exhibited not just in *Spencer's Mountain* but also in his Westerns set on similar, or the very same, terrain (in the case of *Jubal*). The clearest indication that this landscape bolsters the poetics of melodrama can best be derived from comparing it to the most iconic setting for an American Western: Monument Valley. For John Ford and others (but for Ford in particular), that jagged landscape on Navajo desert land clearly symbolizes the frontier: barren, acrid, and isolated, fit only for the most resilient of men. Wyoming, by contrast, is lush and inviting, with rivers, fields, and snow-capped mountains. It is perfectly suited to the nuclear family unit.

The heterogeneity of this topography strongly differentiates *Spencer's Mountain* not just from the Westerns framed by monochrome desert-scapes, but also from the family melodramas bound by the home. To be sure, the spatial limitation of the domestic melodrama provided directors with a visual challenge that, when met with the tools of Technicolor and CinemaScope, resulted in some of the most impressive accomplishments of post-war Hollywood (think for instance of *Written on the Wind* and Nicholas Ray's *Bigger than Life*). The confines of the domestic space reinscribed the familial and sexual tensions of the 1950s from which *Spencer's Mountain* so clearly seeks to divorce itself. The family's outdoorsy lifestyle enables Clay-Boy's freedom to study in peace and quiet at the library that he and his teacher Miss Parker set up. It also allows him the freedom to sneak off with Claris, as in the case of the infamous mountain scene described above. While the Spencers of course have a home to call their own, they and Daves alike are more interested in the construction of a new one. I would in fact argue that the visual climax of the film is when Clay decides that the whole project is holding the family's real progress back, and torches it. Clay's dream is no longer the one that matters. His project has become to help his son fulfill his own goals as much as possible.

That the goal is such a generic one as gaining college admission, of course, betrays the fact that fierce individualism has no place in Daves' cinematic universe. A further telling sign of this is Daves' reworking of a scene in the novel in which Olivia asks Clay for money to buy Clay-Boy a high school graduation ring. In the novel, Olivia fires back at Clay's protest, "You want our son to be different?" As a way to establish that Clay is perfectly fine with his son straying from the pack, and also knowing that he is destined for greatness, Clay declares, "You're A-1 right . . . others ain't gonna amount to a hill of beans!"[17] By comparison, in the film, Olivia tells Clay, "I want him to have one . . . it's a kind of sign, a sign that he's special." Clay responds with a surprising nonchalance, "All our kids is special." Although the film places disproportionate focus on Clay-Boy, this line encapsulates the nonhierarchical, democratic spirit that characterizes it as a quintessentially Delmer Daves film. Critics such as Bertrand Tavernier have noted that Daves' dedication to community stands as a productive alternative to the clubhouse snobbery that auteurists ascribe to Hawks, and the fierce independence of Ford's protagonists.[18]

Another marker of Daves' egalitarianism is his avoidance at all costs of any form of cynicism or snobbery—particularly impressive given his pedigree as a Stanford graduate. He knows as well as we do that Clay and Olivia are not the smartest people in the world, but he doesn't care; it is people's humanity and good intentions, of which the Spencers have plenty to go around, that interest and inspire him. These principles drive the poignant moment that Daves adds after Clay and Olivia have signed off on Clay-Boy's college application. Olivia tells her son to look at the inscription inside his college ring: "Victory with honor." "It's one of them mottos," Clay looks on at Clay-Boy with tears welling up in eyes. "Mother picked it out of a book," he adds with a slightly embarrassed, toothy grin. Indeed, the cynical viewer may be revolted by this scene, or the one in which the teacher, Miss Parker, presents Clay-Boy with a placard, "THE WORLD STEPS ASIDE TO LET ANY MAN PASS IF HE KNOWS WHERE HE IS GOING." These feel-good gestures add up to a sort of yard-sale aesthetic. "This stuff is nice," we might say to ourselves. "But do we want anything to do with it?"

These moments of bric-a-brac kitsch are only intensified when matters of religion appear. I imagine the cynical atheist walking out of the theater when, after Clay-Boy receives the rejection letter, Olivia hypothesizes that maybe God wanted to keep her son out of college, on account of their sin of pride about his high-school accomplishments. Indeed, although the film does away with a lot of the Baptist flavor of the novel, it retains an underlying affirmation of religion. Clay goes from being a self-proclaimed heathen to a proud regular at the Baptist church on Sundays. Moreover, when family and friends line up to send the boy off to college at the end of the film, his grandmother instructs him, "Don't take up any fancy ways, boy. Trust in God and go to church." To which Mr. Goodson, the preacher concurs, "Amen." But this is a major part of small-town American life, and Daves would be amiss to cast it off completely, pushing the boundaries as he already is with his probing of teenage sexuality. Even in the Hamner novel, though, nothing is wholly sacred. The priestly and the profane are in fact tightly interwoven. In both novel and film, the cow and the bull that trigger Clay's speech to his son about the birds and the bees have nice biblical names, Chance and Methuselah, as does the grandfather, Zebulon.

The film only reached wide release in the late spring of 1963, but it began screening as early as February in anticipation of becoming an Easter tentpole. The *Hollywood Reporter* review noted, "The screenplay is a good one . . . It is honest and straightforward, although a sex episode involving the young, would-be scholar does not seem in key. The scene in which the young man finds there are to be no consequences of this act is a trite scene and could be cut for benefit."[19] Film critic Judith Crist went even further, so notoriously in fact that the following quote was cited in several of her obituaries: "That for sheer prurience and perverted morality disguised as piety [the film] makes the nudie shows at the Rialto look like Walt Disney productions."[20] Ironically, it appears that these coastal critics fell on the conservative end of the film's spectrum of reception. The National Screen Council awarded it a Blue Ribbon Award for excellence in family entertainment.[21] While the film does not seem to have

Figure 6.2 In a sea of Jackson, Wyoming locals: Daves in the tie and cardigan (back left-of-center) and James MacArthur, who plays Clay-Boy (middle right-of-center).

maintained much of a reputation since its release, even amongst Delmer Daves enthusiasts, the story of the Spencer family (or the Waltons, as they were re-named for CBS) remains dear to many Americans. I had the strange but enlightening experience of stumbling upon a copy of the first season of *The Waltons* at a Cortez, Colorado outpost of that evil empire founded by whom other than Sam Walton, and, upon explaining to my companion that I was watching it for research on the novel and film that came before it, being interrupted by the cashier: "Ah, yes, Earl Hamner!"

Spencer's Mountain may be denigrated as a sappy progenitor to a TV series of pure kitsch, but television adopted melodrama on a grand scale by the mid-1970s, and so it is less a mark against the films than a historical coincidence that *Spencer's Mountain* and *Peyton Place* (Mark Robson, 1957) were subjected to second lives on the tube. Also, if the melodrama seems more excessive than in other films of Delmer Daves, there may be an explanation that would further confirm the earnestness of the work. Daves' son hypothesized that Delmer had turned to family melodrama after *The Hanging Tree* out of a concern for his own father's declining health.[22] He wanted to pay tribute to that greatest of American institutions. This anecdotal evidence could account for the graveyard scenes in the film, which, admittedly, feel tacked on. Daves adds a family cemetery to the side of the mountain upon which Zebulon gets fatally trampled by an oak tree he is helping his son to chop down, and foreshadows this episode with a scene randomly placed into the early moments of the film, in which Zebulon potters around, dusting off his father Hannibal Spencer's tombstone.

I must admit that one difficulty *Spencer's Mountain* poses to the viewer comes in Henry Fonda's tentative line-readings, which sound as if he is simultaneously asking himself why he agreed to take the part. It helps to bear in mind the irony that what Fonda thought was such trite and conservative material (he apparently declared the screenplay "old-fashioned corn—it will set movies back twenty-five years"[23]) now appears, as I have attempted to show, quite progressive in terms of Hollywood gender politics, and strikingly original for a family melodrama.

BIBLIOGRAPHY

Elsaesser, Thomas, "Tales of Sound and Fury: Observations on the Family Melodrama," in Christine Gledhill (ed.), *Home is Where the Heart Is: Studies in Melodrama and the Woman's Film* (London: British Film Institute, 1987), pp. 43–69.

Gledhill, Christine, "Introduction," in Christine Gledhill (ed.), *Home is Where the Heart Is: Studies in Melodrama and the Woman's Film* (London: British Film Institute, 1987), pp. 1–4.

Hamner, Earl Jr., *Spencer's Mountain* (New York: Dial Press, 1961).

Jones, Kent, "*Jubal*: Awakened to Goodness," The Criterion Collection (2013a), <http://www.criterion.com/current/posts/2765-jubal-awakened-to-goodness> (last accessed 11 November 2015).

Kreyling, Michael, *Inventing Southern Literature* (Jackson: University Press of Mississippi, 1998).

Landazuri, Margarita, "Spencer's Mountain," <http://www.tcm.com/tcmdb/title/16112/Spencer-s-Mountain/articles.html> (last accessed 11 November 2015).

Lefebvre, Martin, "Between Setting and Landscape in the Cinema," in Martin Lefebvre (ed.), *Landscape and Film* (New York: Routledge, 2006), pp. 19–60.

Pinkerton, Nick, "Bombast #93," 7 May 2013, <http://blog.sundancenow.com/weekly-columns/bombast-93> (last accessed 11 November 2015).

Schatz, Thomas, "The Family Melodrama," in Marcia Landy (ed.), *Imitations of Life: a Reader on Film and Television Melodrama* (Detroit, MI: Wayne State University Press, 1991), pp. 148–67.

Singer, Ben, *Melodrama and Modernity: Early Sensational Cinema and its Contexts* (New York: Columbia University Press, 2001).

Tavernier, Bernard, "The Ethical Romantic," *Film Comment*, January–February 2003, <http://www.filmcomment.com/article/delmer-daves-bertrand-tavernier> (last accessed 11 November 2015).

FILMOGRAPHY

All that Heaven Allows, director Douglas Sirk, featuring Jane Wyman, Rock Hudson, Agnes Moorehead, Conrad Nagel (Universal Studios, 1955).
Badlanders, The, director Delmer Daves, featuring Alan Ladd, Ernest Borgnine, Katy Jurado, Claire Kelly (Metro-Goldwyn-Mayer, 1958).
Bigger than Life, director Nicholas Ray, featuring James Mason, Barbara Rush, Walter Matthau, Robert F. Simon (20th Century Fox, 1956).
Chapman Report, The, director George Cukor, featuring Shelley Winters, Jane Fonda, Claire Bloom (Warner Bros., 1962).
Cowboy, director Delmer Daves, featuring Glenn Ford, Jack Lemmon, Anna Kashfi, Dick York (Columbia Pictures, 1958).
Hanging Tree, The, director Delmer Daves, featuring Gary Cooper, Maria Schell, Karl Malden, George C. Scott (Warner Bros., 1959).
Jubal, director Delmer Daves, featuring Glenn Ford, Valerie French, Rod Steiger, Ernest Borgnine (Columbia Pictures, 1956).
Parrish, director Delmer Daves, featuring Troy Donahue, Claudette Colbert, Karl Malden, Dean Jagger (Warner Bros., 1961).
Sex and the Single Girl, director Richard Quine, featuring Tony Curtis, Natalie Wood, Henry Fonda, Lauren Bacall (Warner Bros., 1964).
Some Came Running, director Vincente Minnelli, featuring Frank Sinatra, Dean Martin, Shirley MacLaine, Martha Hyer (Metro-Goldwyn-Mayer, 1958).
Spencer's Mountain, director Delmer Daves, featuring Henry Fonda, Maureen O'Hara (Warner Bros., 1963).
Summer Place, A, director Delmer Daves, featuring Richard Egan, Dorothy McGuire, Troy Donahue, Sandra Dee (Warner Bros., 1959).
Susan Slade, director Delmer Daves, featuring Troy Donahue, Connie Stevens, Dorothy McGuire, Lloyd Nolan (Warner Bros., 1961).
Written on the Wind, director Douglas Sirk, featuring Rock Hudson, Lauren Bacall, Robert Stack, Dorothy Malone (Universal Pictures, 1956).

NOTES

1. Hamner, *Spencer's Mountain*.
2. Jonathan Rosenbaum, for instance, mentioned in a recent blog post ("The Delmer Daves Problem," 1 June 2013) that *Jubal*'s melodramatic excess ruined the picture for him: <http://www.jonathanrosenbaum.net/2013/06/the-delmer-daves-problem/> (last accessed 11 November 2015).
3. Gledhill, "Introduction," p. 6.
4. 10 May 1962. Delmer Daves Papers, Special Collections, Stanford University Libraries, box 64, folder 9.
5. See, for instance, pp. 147–8 of the novel.
6. See Kreyling, *Inventing Southern Literature*.
7. Singer, *Melodrama and Modernity*, pp. 263–4.
8. Delmer Daves Papers, box 63, folder 3.
9. Ibid. 10 May 1962.
10. Delmer Daves Papers, box 64, folder 9; box 66, folder 3.

11. Elsaesser, "Tales of Sound and Fury," p. 55.
12. "In his cinema, there is no pure malignance, only misguided jealousy, ambition and envy. Resignation, cynicism, and paranoia—among the most common characteristics of postwar American movies—are almost entirely absent" (Jones, "*Jubal*: Awakened to Goodness.")
13. Schatz, "The Family Melodrama," p. 160.
14. Delmer Daves Papers, "Letter to J. L. Warner, 9 May 1962."
15. Lefebvre, "Between Setting and Landscape in the Cinema," p. 22.
16. Sergei M. Eisenstein, *Nonindifferent Nature*, trans. Herbert Marshall (Cambridge: Cambridge University Press, 1987), p. 217; quoted in Martin Lefebvre's introduction to *Landscape and Film*, p. xii.
17. Hamner, *Spencer's Mountain*, p. 23.
18. See Tavernier's "The Ethical Romantic."
19. Anon., review of *Spencer's Mountain*, *The Hollywood Reporter*, 19 February 1963, p. 3.
20. Judith Crist, review of *Spencer's Mountain*, *New York Herald Tribune*, May 1963.
21. Delmer Daves Papers, "Letter from Ben Shlyen, Box Office, Kansas City, MO to Daves, 8/14/63," box 66, folder 14.
22. Pinkerton, "Bombast #93."
23. Landazuri, "*Spencer's Mountain*."

CHAPTER 7

Delmer Daves' *3:10 to Yuma*: Aesthetics, Reception, and Cultural Significance

Fran Pheasant-Kelly

In 2012, the BAFTA-nominated film *3:10 to Yuma* (1957) was selected by the Library of Congress for preservation. According to Librarian of Congress James Billington, this choice was made in light of its "enduring importance to American culture."[1] While Delmer Daves' work has long been acclaimed for its direction and visuals, this more recent accolade, together with the release of a critically commended remake in 2007 (directed by James Mangold and starring Russell Crowe and Christian Bale), has rekindled scholarly interest in the earlier film. Much of this current research concentrates on the beleaguered masculinity of its protagonist, a theme not only relevant to the post-war contexts of the first production, but also appropriate to the post-9/11 zeitgeist of the remake.[2] Consequently, several enquiries focus on a comparison between the two films, and their relationship to the original short story by Elmore Leonard on which they are based.[3] Alternatively, psychoanalytic perspectives inform analysis whilst others adopt a generic approach, centering on Daves' Westerns as a discrete body of work.[4] Contemporary analyses also emphasize the aesthetic qualities of Daves' films, with Bertrand Tavernier designating some of his Westerns as "masterpieces."[5] Aside from their dramatic visual orchestration, the cultural significance of Daves' Westerns lies in their realistic depiction of the harshness of frontier existence, offering a more historically accurate portrayal of life than is typically articulated by the Western. In addition, they present more progressive images of women than is usual for the genre, and also provide sympathetic and more authentic representations of Native Americans (as opposed to the stereotypical depictions that had hitherto populated the genre).[6]

While there are indications that deviation from certain of these generic tropes caused negative responses to Daves' Westerns in Britain, critical reception of *3:10 to Yuma* at the time of its release is in fact consistently positive. Descriptions of it ranged from "very good" to "one of the most perfect small-scale works of the fifties" and, a decade later, as "the most perfect of Westerns."[7] James Powers labels it as "the best western since *Gunfight at the OK Corral*," while an anonymous review in *Film Daily* describes the direction as "excellent" and photography as "fine" with reference to Charles Lawton's "atmospheric black and white photography," and "competent performances" by cast members.[8] Likewise, *Monthly Film Bulletin*'s anonymous reviewer suggests that "what gives the film its edge . . . is its sharp direction and firm characterisation of the two main antagonists, very capably played by Van Heflin and Glenn Ford. The latter, in particular, gives one of his least-mannered and most effective performances for some time."[9] *Variety* contends that "Ford's switch-casting, as the quietly sinister gang leader, is authoritative, impressive and successful . . . and Heflin measures up fully and convincingly to the rewarding role of the proud and troubled rancher."[10] Vincent Canby too comments particularly on performance and characterization, as well as the film's generic format, noting that "it falls in a position halfway between action drama and the more pretentious off-beat Western of ideas."[11] He also remarks on the film's visual style, suggesting that "Delmer Daves seems to have directed it with an eye for startling and/or moody camera angles rather than for telling its story in sharp terms of visual movement."[12] For Richard Whitehall, Daves' film is a

> miraculous balance of a number of disparate elements, mixing action (the opening stagecoach robbery is played on lateral movement from left to right of screen), irony (the shot which alerts Wade's gang to his presence is loosed off by Dan protecting Wade from a murderous attack), and allegory (the final rainstorm), with a wonderfully visual use of shadows for dramatic effect (the shadow of a hanging man), for romantic feeling (the heavily shadowed bar interiors for the beautifully yearning and nostalgic scenes between Felicia Farr as Emmy . . . and Ben Wade), and for atmosphere.[13]

(Reportedly, Howard Hawks criticized the film, but his account revealed a marked misinterpretation of it.[14]) Recent critical reviews of the film continued in a similar vein, with, for example, Tavernier describing "the stunning originality of Daves' style, handling of dramatic structure, and approach to genre, which set him apart from his contemporaries."[15] For Philip French, both *3:10 to Yuma* and *Broken Arrow* are Daves' best films.[16] Contemporary reviews of *3:10 to Yuma* are, however, somewhat polarized in their views regarding comparison between the original and the 2007 remake, with some suggesting that the remake surpasses Daves' version, whilst others maintain that it "lacks the purity of the original," which "is the finest of the psychological westerns."[17] French also comments on the ending of Daves' version, which was dismissed by critics of the time, and interprets this as an integration of the mythic Grail legend.[18] Conversely, Carol MacCurdy describes the ending as uneven in that it "demonstrates the script's conflicting aims in terms of wanting to follow Leonard's bravura ending and homage to male bonding, as well as satisfy a 1950s' audience's expectations for moral clarity."[19]

Even as scholars and critics, both contemporary to the film and those writing more recently, comment favorably on the casting, characterization, generic hybridization, and narrative strength of *3:10 to Yuma*, detailed discussion of its visual style to date has been limited, with the focus remaining on the aforementioned qualities.[20] This is surprising given that cinematographer Charles Lawton's interpretation is often described as atmospheric, striking or skillful.[21] Specifically, such stylization involves a propensity for extreme camera angles, rising crane shots, shadows, and doubling effects, aspects that often endow the film with a noir sensibility. At the same time, if, under Daves' direction, Lawton's rendering of the landscape addresses the harsh reality of sustained drought and consequent impoverishment that this causes, it also contrives sublime and poetic images. Accordingly, this chapter examines the aesthetics of *3:10 to Yuma*, engaging theoretically and critically with works pertaining to the Western as appropriate. Whilst acknowledging the film as one of several Westerns directed by Daves, the focus will remain on *3:10 to Yuma*, examining its distinctive textual aspects and their cultural resonances.

3:10 TO YUMA

The film revolves around the fortunes of Dan Evans (Van Heflin), an impoverished rancher whose land and cattle are affected by drought, and who is unable to afford access to water. His failure to intervene during a hold-up of the Butterfield stagecoach, and the subsequent murder of its driver, causes his wife to appear critical of him, and further undermines his masculine identity. An opportunity arises for Evans to reverse his fortunes by delivering Ben Wade (Glenn Ford), the notorious outlaw responsible for the hold-up, to the train bound for Yuma Prison. Evans accepts the task not only to earn money to pay for water supplies to his ranch, but also to prove his masculinity to his wife and two sons. Ultimately, the latter aspiration assumes priority as he refuses a significant bribe from Wade, and even an offer of payment from stagecoach owner Butterfield (Robert Emhardt), regardless of whether he completes the task or not. This indicates that his quest does not solely relate to money, but rather is a way to re-affirm his status as husband and father. Evans also expresses a moral obligation to Alex Potter (Henry Jones), who is killed whilst supporting him in his quest to bring Wade to justice. In capturing and delivering Wade to the train bound for Yuma, Evans not only earns the respect of both his sons and wife, but also garners admiration from Wade. The latter character, too, subsequently displays qualities of redemption and compassion as, in the end, he boards the train voluntarily to prevent Evans being killed by the other gang members. Culturally, the film therefore departs from the genre's standard cowboy-versus-Native-American scenario, and focuses instead on the internal psychological constitution of the two protagonists. At the same time, the enhanced capacity of women in comparison to other Westerns of the period challenges the established gender roles of the genre, while the film primarily illuminates the struggles against poverty facing the rancher. The latter is an aspect often effaced in the mythologizing of the West: as David Murdoch explains, lack of water was a major difficulty facing ranchers and farmers, with severe drought in the 1880s leading to agricultural catastrophe in the 1890s.[22] Accordingly, as conveyed in the film, "[b]y the 1890s, those who controlled water rights dominated the Western economy. . . All in all, pioneers in the West had entered a very high-risk game: in addition to extremes of heat and cold, the devastating effects of hail, insect plagues and drought, they were at the mercy of market forces."[23] The problem of drought is made central to the film's narrative organization, with Evans' inability to afford irrigation rights presented as a failure of his patriarchal identity. The issue of a threatened masculinity not only relates to the austerity of life depicted in the film's fictional realm but also heralded a real-world perception of a crisis in masculinity at the time of the film's release.[24] In sum, if Daves' film recounts a story of recovered masculinity, its reputation is founded on a departure from the formulaic tropes of the Western, as well as its arresting visual approach, the latter employing a distinctive repertoire of cinematographic techniques.

AESTHETICS AND CULTURAL SIGNIFICANCE

According to Michael Walker, "*3:10 to Yuma* is . . . one of [Daves'] most stylish films, with shot after shot strikingly composed."[25] Its characteristic visual features include the deployment of leading diagonals, and generally balanced and often symmetrical composition; the consistent use of naturalistic side- and high-contrast lighting; extremes of tonality and contrast; shadows and doubling effects; extreme camera perspectives and rising crane shots; consistent deep focus; and interactions between cinematography and *mise-en-scène* that effect a dynamism and energy across the frame and invest the landscape with narrative and historical significance. Certainly, as Wallington contends, "Landscape is never a backcloth, always integral to the action."[26] And as Tavernier suggests, "all these locales are pregnant with meaning (more

Figure 7.1 Opening of *3:10 to Yuma*.

poetic than symbolic), filmed with a lyrical, emotional power but devoid of the picturesque."[27] Tavernier further remarks that, as well as crane shots, Daves' use of "lateral tracking shots, which show his extraordinary mastery of space— are movements of *integration*: of character within community, landscape and setting—and of emotional entrenchment."[28] The expansive tonal range of Daves' visuals, spanning from deep blacks through to pure whites, is an aspect allegedly drawn from Mathew Brady's black and white photographs, upon which the film relies.[29]

One might propose that Daves' use of sharply focused visuals and wide depth of field also draws on Brady's techniques. Indeed, as Daves' only monochrome Western, the film establishes a typically striking impact in its opening sequence. A minimalist image, divided into scorched plain and sky, is punctuated by a diagonal trail of horses' hoof-prints imprinted into the arid earth (the effect of drought on the land was achieved with the use of red filters throughout), leading the eye from the lower left of the frame diagonally upwards to the right of the image.[30] From the extreme upper left, just visible on the horizon, a stagecoach comes into view, appearing black against the desert, while the broad tonality of the image extends through to encompass white clouds.

As the carriage travels across the horizon, the camera simultaneously rises, shifting the earth–sky boundary downward to take further account of the clouds. Initially only distantly discernible, the coach speeds from left to right across the plain (and the frame) before the camera then slowly descends just as the coach turns. It subsequently travels directly toward the camera along the extreme lower right of the composition, becoming more prominent as it approaches closer and leaving clouds of billowing dust in its wake (visually indicating the parched environment). Thereafter, the coach diverts diagonally right to left toward the lower left corner of the frame, corresponding to the tracks that originally led the viewer's eye into the image. As it does so, the camera continues to shift downwards, and the stagecoach increasingly dominates, and eventually fills, the frame. The combined effect of moving coach, rising dust clouds, and shifting camera perspective (and horizon) is to create both a sublime landscape and dynamic image, establishing several of the artistic tropes that permeate the rest of the film. A sense of movement within the frame continues as the camera tilts down (in subjective viewpoint from the coach driver's perspective) to view, first, the black shadows of the galloping horses, and then pans across to take account of the horses themselves. The reins oscillate as the coach driver drives the horses onwards, and further promote the dynamism of the scene. Much of this energy arises out of Daves' proclivity for the rising crane shot, a tendency that pervades all of his films, although, according to Walker, "it was on this movie that Daves began to use the crane shot more overtly."[31] Daves uses a Chapman crane and, in conversation with Derek Todd, commented that

> To my mind there's nothing more arresting than a crane's eye view of the characters in relation to their background and events in their lives... By combining the eye of the camera with the crane you give the audience the unique experience of relating human relationships with the infinity of space that surrounds each human being.[32]

As Daves continues to explain, "[the crane shot] also has the great quality of retaining and enlarging viewpoints with a fluidity and grace that eliminate any abrupt cutting that could minimise a vital story point."[33] Indeed, Daves goes on to discuss the use of the crane shot, particularly in the Western, when typically "a very big close shot of an actor [sees him] looking at something. The camera moves from this huge close-up to infinity and shows you what he has seen, a hundred miles of desert."[34] Daves enlists spontaneity and pacing in his use of the crane shot that he likens to the expression of music and emotion, a tactic that perhaps accounts for the fluidity and kinesis of his films, and clearly manifests in the opening scenes of *3:10 to Yuma*.[35]

The lower-left-to-right diagonal traversing across the frame is a trait that the film consistently adopts, and is immediately evident thereafter as first, cattle stream down diagonally right to left across the frame, followed by a sequence in which Charlie Prince (Richard Jaeckel), Wade's sidekick, also rides in the same direction (thereby introducing one of the film's villains). The cattle scene again displays a full tonal range, ranging from deep blacks in the cattle's coats through to the bleached white sand of the desert hills, while the use of deep focus renders sharp both the foreground trees and the background hills. Just as Prince pulls up his horse and directs his gaze out toward the left of the frame, with the cattle concurrently herding diagonally from upper right to lower left, a parallel edit discloses the Butterfield coach also traveling right to left, following the same trajectory as the cattle. Subsequently, the camera intercuts between the herding cattle and the traveling coach, graphically matching their respective tracks, before a cut to close-up of the horses pulling the coach suddenly brings the viewer closer to the action. This suddenness of close-up is a repeated element in *3:10 to Yuma* and is achieved either, simply, by a cut to close-up, or, more usually, through a crane shot that typically swings round to the left and descends as the subject approaches, leading to the aforementioned right-to-left diagonal action and the subject to dominate the frame. At the same time, the sequence (like others) displays a propensity for low-angle perspectives, with the cut to close-up concurrently adopting a low-angle viewpoint of the stagecoach driver. This sequence is followed by a scene that is partially obliterated by dust clouds, which generate a striking visual effect whilst simultaneously further illustrating the barrenness of the land. As the dust clears, the camera pans across the gang members on horseback, the tenor of the extra-diegetic music indicating a mounting sense of threat. The camera then rests on Ben Wade, who is framed more closely than the rest of the gang, suggesting that he is the gang-leader. At this point, Dan Evans and his two sons ride into view, their movement too following an upper-right-to-lower-left pattern and, again, they are viewed from a low angle. Such low-angle perspectives mostly occur in an omniscient capacity, rather than from the viewpoint of any of the characters. In other words, the style of cinematography, especially the angle of framing, does not always serve a narrative purpose, or exist to encourage identification with any particular character.

While an early low-angle shot of Dan Evans on horseback as he talks to his wife, Alice (Leora Dana), may cause one to suppose his dominance in relation to her, and a high angle of her might correspondingly indicate her inferior position (as suggested by Fehrle), otherwise, a low-angle perspective is merely an expression of Daves' aesthetic sensibilities.[36] For instance, in a scene during which the marshal (Ford Rainey) summons his men and asks for two volunteers to escort Wade to Contention, a low-angle shot, omnisciently instigated, is directed up toward the surrounding semi-circle of men, so they appear to be set against a darkened sky. Subsequently, a high-angle shot looks down on the men, once more tightly framing them and emphasizing their semi-circular formation. The composition of the image appears quite precise in that the hats of the three cowboys situated toward the lower right of the frame seem to recede in size the closer they are to the center top of the frame, recreating a consistent preoccupation of Daves' visuals: the diagonal across the frame (and echoing previous scenes). To balance the symmetry of the composition, a series of barrels then forms an equivalent diagonal on the opposite side, arising from

Figure 7.2 Inside the Contention Hotel in *3:10 to Yuma*.

the lower left of the frame. It also ascends toward the center top of the frame, so that the topmost barrel coincides with the position of the aforementioned topmost cowboy's hat, thereby creating what Wallington describes as a "rigorous geometry and formalism of . . . framing."[37]

The lower-left-to-upper-right-leading diagonal is not restricted to landscape images, but is prominent in interior scenes too. For instance, just after Wade, Evans, and Butterfield have ascended the staircase in the Contention Hotel and walked across its first-floor gallery (a camera close-up resting ominously on a chandelier, later to be the site of Alex Potter's hanging), Wade, followed by Evans and then Butterfield, repeats the hat-receding format described above. Here the stair banister echoes the diagonal (the scene thus features the typical threesome so prevalent in the film).

Also noticeable in this sequence is the heightened use of shadows. Indeed, what is absent from contemporaneous analyses and reviews is mention of an inclination toward noir tropes. Although more recent studies regularly comment on the use of shadows, other noir aspects permeate the film and become more prominent as it progresses, these features being consistent with the film's psychological dimensions, Evans' beleaguered masculinity, and, ultimately, Wade's potential incarceration. To achieve these shadowy results, Todd recounts that "[Daves] goes out scouting his locations with a watch and compass to calculate just where the photogenic shadows he wants will fall."[38]

If outdoor shots appear naturally illuminated, indoor scenes—for example, the sequence during which Ben Wade is captured—almost invariably entail naturalistic side-lighting. In conversation with Christopher Wicking, Daves describes how this effect was a product of the raking sunlight, the intention clearly being to incorporate light and shadow.[39] Light is itself used in an almost painterly fashion for aesthetic impact—illustrated when Wade, accompanied by Potter and Evans, travels overnight on horseback to Contention. As they catch the sunrise, the light strikes first Potter's hat, followed by Wade's, then that of Evans, each brightly illuminated and the only objects discernible in the semi-darkness.

An obvious outcome of this preoccupation with side-lighting is the tendency to noir stylistics. As Simon Petch notes in his psychoanalytic interpretation of the film, "such poetic interplay of shadow and reflection creates an intriguingly patterned drama of reflective and distortive surfaces, a drama in which human figures mean more that they know, in which surfaces hint at hidden depths."[40] The use of side-lighting typically affords the visuals a broad tonal range, on occasion producing extremes of contrast. For Diana Young, this differential, whereby the film is "shot in stark, high contrast black and white," is reflective of the binary nature of the conflict between law and lawlessness since "[t]he images are clearly demarcated against an often empty and bleached-looking landscape."[41]

The significant use of shadows is first evident when Wade and his gang stop at a bar in Bisbee, with pronounced shadows cast both across the walls, and across each character's face. After the rest of the gang has departed, Wade returns to see Emmy (Felicia Farr), the barmaid, and this time, shadows are even more pronounced. Wade stands to the far left of the frame, his shadow casts across the entire width of the image, before he approaches Emmy, whereupon the camera cuts to medium shot. A two-shot of them together, Emmy's face fully illuminated (and Wade's half in shadow), then cuts to close-up. "You know you look kinda skinny," Wade tells her. "I feel skinny," replies Emmy and the camera then zooms in just as Wade says "I don't mind a girl being skinny just so she has blue eyes to make up for it. You got blue eyes?" The camera then cuts to an extreme close-up, Emmy's eyes cast downward as she tells him they are brown before then looking up meaningfully at Wade. The combined effect of the camera slowly moving in to frame the two more closely and their increasingly intimate conversation creates a moment of closeness. This culminates in Emmy's exquisitely poignant upward glance at Wade and their passionate embrace, thereby creating a scene that owes entirely to Daves' direction, since it was absent in the original story.[42]

Indeed, women play crucial roles in all of Daves' Westerns (with the possible exception of *Drum Beat*), leading Wallington to comment that Daves is "something of a feminist, and women are usually responsible for man's comprehension of himself."[43] Even if female characters appear to assume the stereotypes of "virgin" and "whore" in *3:10 to Yuma*, conveyed by Alice and Emmy respectively, both women are nonetheless represented as independent and resourceful, and account for more screen time and detailed characterization than films of the genre usually afford women. As Douglas Pye argues:

> [i]t is generally accepted that the Western's representation of women is . . . massively skewed . . . The whole history of the Western is . . . bound up with reducing Native Americans and women to functions in a symbolic world centring on White male characters and embodying White male visions of national and gender identity.[44]

In this respect, Daves, who is described as a "documentarian of the Western film" and who himself states that "I will never subordinate mere fact to dramatic use," nuances the representation of women.[45] Indeed, despite the fact that the film is set in the late nineteenth century and that Daves clearly strives for a more historical portrait of life at the frontier, the female characters appear to be a reflection of contemporaneous, shifting gender norms. Challenges to masculinity at that time, occurring as a result of what Fehrle observes as women becoming more centralized in the workplace and beginning to reject their traditional roles, are presented in the film initially as Alice's interrogation of Evans' lack of response to the attack on the Butterfield stage.[46] As Fehrle also notes, "[Evans] finds himself in a situation in which he cannot live up to the expectations of his sons and fulfil the demands of a 1950s hegemonic masculinity: to be a 'real man' . . . he would have to engage the outlaws."[47] Moreover, while *3:10 to Yuma* is not explicit in its reference to the erotic encounter between Wade and Emmy, their relationship is certainly made clear. As Tavernier notes, such implied eroticism circumvented the Hays Code that was in place at that time.[48] Tavernier also contends that the way in which their exchange is presented has a distinctive quality in its treatment of women: "Beautifully staged and photographed, such scenes are unique in a genre that usually gives short shrift to female characters."[49] As he further remarks, "more often than not, women are the driving force, or the filmmaker's mouthpiece: they challenge the film's heroes, educate them in matters of the heart, without any hypocrisy or Puritanism."[50]

Aside from the encounter between Emmy and Wade, shadows are equally noticeable in the hotel room at Contention when Evans guards Wade in a bridal suite. Wade's silhouette is cast against the wall behind him, even though we learn that the time is approaching midday. This apparent discrepancy arises because of Daves' preference for distended shadows, revealed when he explains how he shot *3:10 to Yuma* in winter, partly for the clear photographic conditions (shooting at seven or eight thousand feet is another preference, for similar reasons), but also for the long morning shadows.[51] Significantly, Evans' shadow is cast against Wade, potentially implying either Evans' (soon to be realized) influence on Wade, or overlap in their characters in relation to moral values which, in fact, turns out to be the case since Evans seems tempted by bribes from Wade. However, Daves' discussion with Wicking further reveals that the significance of the shadows lies not merely in a suggestion of moral ambiguity in his characters, but more in their indication of the hardships of their everyday lives:

> Buddy Lawton, the cameraman, and I got together at the beginning and created a black and white image of the whole. I told Buddy I wanted to make a film without filling in shadows. I said I'd lived on the desert and I know what a drought is like. I said: 'We're not going to fill any of these shadows.'[52]

Shadows are deployed particularly effectively to convey the hanging of Alex Potter from the central stair chandelier in the Contention Hotel. While this approach may have been to satisfy censors at that time, it nonetheless heightens the dramatic and ominous effect of the interplay between light and dark. As Butterfield re-enters the bridal suite to inform Evans of Potter's death, the tight framing of the two men pulls out to include Wade, the positioning of the three men again carefully orchestrated to create a leading diagonal from the left lower corner of the frame. The image is replete with shadows of each man cast against the adjacent man, perhaps suggesting that one can influence the other, but also promoting a sense of claustrophobia. Together with dramatic extra-diegetic music, the confines of the room heighten the film's noir sensibilities. Equally, the use of close-ups, extreme close-ups, and extreme camera angles, together with the intermittently exaggerated sound of the ticking clock, accentuate the intense atmosphere that each man seems to feel as the time approaches ten past three. Such intensity is signaled by Evans' behavior in the form of angry outbursts, these being mediated through extreme low- and high-angled camera positions and more rapid editing.

Certainly, another favored camera shot is the close-up, with groups of either Wade's gang or the marshal's men often filmed in a tightly framed composition. In one such scene, the marshal from Bisbee rides out to rescue the survivors of the Butterfield stage hold-up. We see him and his two men on their horses, positioned so that the latter recede away from the camera, their hats positioned to create a diagonal that is organized to create an effect of diminishing perspective (much like the semi-circular grouping described previously). In fact, as noted earlier, Daves seems to favor groups of three (for instance, Alice and her two sons). Otherwise, characters often appear in two-shots, with the same confined framing and close-up camerawork deployed. This stylistic trait perhaps reflects Daves' endorsement of community, for, as Tavernier notes, Daves refuses "to promote and extol individualism ... favouring characters who are integrated into a community ... No Daves character makes it on his own, whether negotiating a peace treaty or getting an outlaw onto the train in Yuma."[53]

If the use of close-up favors characters, then Daves also incorporates a range of panoramic long shots and crane shots to achieve landscape images, typically constructed with maximum depth of field, full tonal range, and figures presented as miniaturized in the foreground of the frame. Mostly set against arid mountains, the images thus strive toward sublime, rather than picturesque effect, mobilized by the land's combination of starkness and beauty. One such scene features Wade's gang traveling to Bisbee, the setting comprising mountains that rise up in the background and the men riding diagonally right to left, just as the camera descends and sweeps right to left from a crane shot to follow their line of travel. The sequence again displays the movement enabled by Daves' use of the crane. An especially striking vista materializes when Evans, Potter, and Wade arrive at Contention, the sequence filmed in the early morning with exposure set to create a high key effect. As Butterfield joins the three men, a panoramic shot that positions the men to the far right of the frame affords a low-level perspective of the town at dawn, the horizon also extremely low, so that the men appear to be superimposed against the sky (another stylistic trait of Daves), and the scene predominantly entailing a cloudscape. This propensity for landscape images, presented to sublime effect (and therefore largely filmed in a static or slow mode), belies the film's average shot length of 6.4 seconds, which is quite short for pre-1960 films.[54]

Daves deploys the same high-key strategy when filming Alice's journey to Contention, a sequence that further suggests women as being independent and more prominent in the narrative than other Westerns of the time. Alice travels alone and is not intimidated by the prospect of encountering the gang at Contention. En route she meets a group of the town's women whose concerns are focused on Dan, their collective framing (which echoes the groupings of male characters noted earlier) again implying a supportive community of individuals who depart from Western female stereotypes. As Alice travels onward, the lyricism and high-key notes of the landscape seem to correlate with the luminosity associated with her, her white hood clearly having Madonna-like connotations. Here, Daves utilizes his preferred image composition involving the traverse of her carriage from the left upper frame through to center, toward the spectator then away to a diagonal leading toward the lower left of the frame, before the coach appears full-frame. Full tonality is evident, with a backdrop of dark mountains, and sun-bleached grasses traversing the midsection of the scene. A fence arises from the lower left of the composition, further denoting Daves' preference for leading diagonals.

Conversely, during the funeral of the coach-driver killed by Wade, the townscape of Bisbee assumes a dark and somber mood, the crude crosses of the makeshift cemetery starkly interspersed with thin upright desert cacti, as if the land itself is reflecting the frame of mind of its inhabitants. Falconer also comments on the stylization of the town's *mise-en-scène*, drawing attention to the strange emptiness of Bisbee and Contention, where both "are characterised by an extreme sparseness of population."[55] While it is noted in the short story, Falconer suggests that Daves' film elaborates more fully on the emptiness, and while narratively explained by Wade as the townsfolk "getting out of the heat" (metaphorically to avoid the impending gunfight), this barren quality arguably reflects the town's state of mourning.[56] In a similar vein, the darkened, gloomy interior of the Evans' farmstead echoes their dire financial circumstances. In other words, settings consistently mirror the disposition, personality, and situation of the characters.

A feature rarely mentioned in scholarly articles or reviews of Daves' films is his propensity for utilizing buildings and architecture as framing devices. This technique is used consistently in *3:10 to Yuma*, symbolically harnessing, for instance, Evans' wife to the homestead. Even so, the wooden beams of the farm's porch also frame Dan, and, rather than being solely tied to gender, as suggested by Fehrle, this mode of framing arguably implies entrapment, another typical noir trait.[57] This possibility is more strongly intimated as the sequence progresses, with Dan and Alice's discussion thereafter positioning Dan so that the vertical wooden bars supporting the porch are behind him, while their shadows fall on an adjacent wall, thus appearing to enclose him on the opposite side too. At the same time, the couple discuss their desperate financial situation and the effects of drought on their cattle. Overall, therefore, as suggested by both Tavernier and Wallington, settings and landscape do not function merely as backdrops for action but are integral to the expression of characters, their lives, and their emotions. In fact, the combined effect of Daves' stylistic decisions on the way that home, landscape, and characters are represented is to demythologize representations of frontier life and indicate the bleak realities of the characters' existence and the land as inhospitable and difficult.

The implication is that such portrayals offer a more authentic experience of life on the frontier—an approach that varies from many 1950s Westerns which, paradoxically, elevate the genre's archetypal conflicts to a mythical plane, as evident, for example, in *Shane* (George Stevens, 1953). Underlying these depictions is the fact that in 1926 Daves lived with the Hopi and Navajo Indians for three months, which significantly influenced the way that he represented Native Americans in his other Westerns, especially *Broken Arrow* (1950).[58] As Whitehall notes, "[Daves] felt strongly about the misrepresentation of the American Indian."[59] He goes on to add that Daves deviates from formulaic depictions of frontier-chasing cowboys to address the realities of a hostile environment. Here, the hero "is a man fighting, and more important, *working* to keep a toe-hold in a hostile land. Few directors have caught so exactly the flavor of bleak, wooden constructions and sterile dust of the shack towns of the desert or have tried to set their characters as firmly as part of a *working* community."[60]

CONCLUSION

In summary, it is fair to suggest that a range of aesthetic features that indicate Daves as an exemplary filmmaker distinguishes *3:10 to Yuma*. A propensity for rising crane shots, leading diagonals, broad tonality, wide depth of field, framing devices, and kinetic cinematography endow the film with a dynamism that reflects the characters' inner psychology as well as their external experiences. At the same time, certain qualities—notably the psychological dimensions of its beleaguered male protagonists, together with the use of high-contrast lighting, extreme camera angles, and pronounced shadows and associated doubling effects (which imply ambiguous identities)—imbue the film with a noir sensibility. In a related way, depictions of landscape and townscape, which range from the lyrical to the sublime and somber, enable the mediation of the mood of an entire town, or the aspirational characteristics of an individual. In presenting the frontier setting as austere and sublime, and exploring its damaging effects on characters' lives, the film serves to dismantle certain mythic aspects of the genre. Whereas Daves' other Westerns purposely steer away from stereotypical representations of Native Americans, *3:10 to Yuma* instead focuses on uncovering the true nature of a rancher's impoverished life. At the same time, it nuances the portrayal of women so that they move beyond being merely "functions in a symbolic world centring on White male characters."[61] The aesthetic accomplishment of *3:10 to Yuma* is indicated by its many plaudits, both in contemporaneous critical reviews and recent scholarship, whilst its preservation by the Library of Congress in 2012 acknowledges the merits of a film that mediates meaningful cultural and historical messages through its distinctive visual style.

BIBLIOGRAPHY

Anon., "*3:10 to Yuma*," *Film Daily*, 112:27 (1957a): 7.
Anon., "*3:10 to Yuma*," *Monthly Film Bulletin*, 24:284 (1957b): 116.
Anon., "*3:10 to Yuma*," *Variety*, 14 August 1957c: 6.
Anon., "Delmer Daves," *Film Comment*, 6:4 (1970): 89–90.
Anon., "Into the Western," *Irish Times*, 26 February 2011.
Baker, Bob, "Delmer Daves," *Film Dope*, 9 (1976): 37–8.
Benshoff, Harry, and Sean Griffin, *America on Film: Representing Race, Class, Gender, and Sexuality at the Movies* (Malden and Oxford: Wiley-Blackwell, 2009).

Bordwell, David, *The Way Hollywood Tells It: Story and Style in Modern Movies* (Berkeley and London: University of California Press, 2006).
Canby, Vincent, "*3:10 to Yuma*," *Motion Picture Herald*, 208:6 (1957): 481.
Daves, Delmer, "Closing the Gap," *Action*, 5:2 (1970): 25–6.
Falconer, Peter, "*3:10* Again: A Remade Western and the Problem of Authenticity," in Rachel Carroll (ed.), *Adaptation in Contemporary Culture: Textual Infidelities* (London and New York: Continuum, 2009), pp. 62–71.
Fehrle, Johannes, "(Re)Making Men in the 1950s and 2000s: Delmer Daves and James Mangold's *3:10 to Yuma*," in Rudiger Heinze and Lucy Kramer (eds.), *Remakes and Remaking: Concepts, Media, Practices* (Wetzlar: Transcript Verlag, 2015), pp. 57–80.
French, Philip, "TV Film of the Week: *Cowboy*," *Observer*, 12 March 2000a.
French, Philip, "TV Film of the Week: *3:10 to Yuma*," *Observer*, 2 July 2000b.
French, Philip, "Films of the Day: *3:10 to Yuma*," *Observer*, 23 March 2008.
French, Philip, "Film Choice: *3:10 to Yuma*," *Observer*, 31 January 2010.
King, Susan, "National Registry Selects 25 Films for Preservation," *Los Angeles Times*, 12 December 2012, <http://articles.latimes.com/2012/dec/19/entertainment/la-et-mn-national-film-registry-20121217> (last accessed 11 November 2015).
Kitses, Jim, *Horizons West: Directing the Western from John Ford to Clint Eastwood* (London: British Film Institute, 2004).
Leonard, Elmore, *Three-Ten to Yuma and Other Stories* (New York: Harper, 2006).
MacCurdy, Carol, "Masculinity in *3:10 to Yuma*," *Quarterly Review of Film and Video*, 26 (2009): 280–92.
Manchel, Frank, "Cultural Confusion: A Look Back at Delmer Daves' *Broken Arrow*," *Film and History*, 23:1–4 (1993): 58–69.
Murdoch, David, *The American West: The Invention of a Myth* (Cardiff: Welsh Academic Press, 2001).
Nachbar, Jack, "The Western," *Journal of Popular Film and Television*, 30:4 (2003): 178–9.
Newman, Kim, *Wild West Movies* (London: Bloomsbury, 1990).
Nichols, Mary, "Revisiting Heroism and Community in Contemporary Westerns: *No Country for Old Men* and *3:10 to Yuma*," *Perspectives on Political Science*, 37:4 (2008): 207–20.
Peek, Wendy, "The Romance of Competence: Rethinking Masculinity in the Western," *Journal of Popular Film and Television*, 30:4 (2003): 206–19.
Petch, Simon, "Return to Yuma," *Film Criticism*, 32:2 (2007): 48–69.
Pinkerton, Nick, "Films By Delmer Daves," *Sight and Sound* 23:7 (2013): 97.
Powers, James, "*3:10 to Yuma*: First-Rate Western with Strong Cast," *The Hollywood Reporter*, 8 August 1957.
Pye, Douglas, "Introduction: Criticism and the Western," in Ian Cameron and Douglas Pye (eds.), *The Movie Book of the Western* (London: Studio Vista, 1996), pp. 9–21.
Tavernier, Bernard, "The Ethical Romantic," *Film Comment*, January–February 2003, <http://www.filmcomment.com/article/delmer-daves-bertrand-tavernier> (last accessed 11 November 2015).
Todd, Derek, "Delmer Daves tells Derek Todd about his Crush on Cranes and . . ." *Kinematograph Weekly*, 2964 (1964): 24.
Walker, Michael, "The Westerns of Delmer Daves," in Ian Cameron and Douglas Pye (eds.), *The Movie Book of the Western* (London: Studio Vista, 1996), pp. 123–60.
Wallington, Mike, "Author and Genre: The Films of Delmer Daves," *Cinema*, 4 (1969): 6–9.
Whitehall, Richard, "On the *3:10 to Yuma*," *Films and Filming*, 9:7 (1963a): 51–4.
Whitehall, Richard, "A Summer Place," *Films and Filming*, 9:8 (1963b): 48–51.
Wicking, Christopher, "Interview with Delmer Daves," *Screen*, 10:4/5 (1969): 55–66.

Young, Diane, "Law and the Foucauldian Wild West in Michael Cimino's *Heaven's Gate*," *Law, Culture and the Humanities*, 7:2 (2010): 310–26.

FILMOGRAPHY

Broken Arrow, director Delmer Daves, featuring James Stewart, Jeff Chandler, Debra Paget, Basil Ruysdael (20th Century Fox, 1950).
Drum Beat, director Delmer Daves, featuring Alan Ladd, Audrey Dalton, Marisa Pavan (Warner Bros., 1954).
Gunfight at the OK Corral, director John Sturges, featuring Burt Lancaster, Kirk Douglas, Rhonda Fleming, Jo Van Fleet (Paramount Pictures, 1957).
3:10 to Yuma, director Delmer Daves, featuring Glenn Ford, Van Heflin, Felicia Farr, Leora Dana (Columbia Pictures, 1957).
3:10 to Yuma, director James Mangold, featuring Russell Crowe, Christian Bale, Ben Foster, Gretchen Mol (Lionsgate Films, 2007).

NOTES

1. James Billington quoted in King, "National Registry Selects 25 Films for Preservation."
2. MacCurdy, "Masculinity in *3:10 to Yuma*"; Nichols, "Revisiting Heroism"; Peek, "The Romance of Competence."
3. Falconer, "*3:10* Again"; Fehrle, "(Re)Making Men."
4. Petch, "Return to Yuma"; Walker, "The Westerns of Delmer Daves."
5. Tavernier, "The Ethical Romantic."
6. Manchel, "Cultural Confusion"; Walker, "The Westerns of Delmer Daves." Of the ten Westerns that he directed or co-wrote, four involve Native Americans, while, of the remainder, *3:10 to Yuma* and *Cowboy* focus on relationships between two men. *3:10 to Yuma* explores the tensions between its male characters and reflects on their respective masculinities, articulating these via explorations of internal psychological conflicts.
7. Whitehall, "On the 3:10 to Yuma," p. 51; Canby, "*3:10 to Yuma*"; Whitehall, "A Summer Place," p. 50; Wallington, "Author and Genre," p. 9.
8. Powers, "*3:10 to Yuma*: First-Rate Western with Strong Cast"; Anon, "*3:10 to Yuma*" (1957a).
9. Anon, "*3:10 to Yuma*" (1957b).
10. Anon, "*3:10 to Yuma*" (1957c).
11. Canby, "*3:10 to Yuma*.".
12. Ibid.
13. Whitehall, "*A Summer Place*," p. 50.
14. Tavernier, "*The Ethical Romantic*," p. 47.
15. Ibid. p. 42.
16. French, "TV Film of the Week: Cowboy.".
17. Anon, "Into the Western"; French, "Films of the Day: *3:10 to Yuma*"; French, "Film Choice: *3:10 to Yuma*."
18. Anon, "*3:10 to Yuma*" (1957c); French, "TV Film of the Week: *3:10 to Yuma*."
19. MacCurdy, "Masculinity in *3:10 to Yuma*," p. 282.
20. Baker, "Delmer Daves," p. 38.

21. Anon, "*3:10 to Yuma*" (1957c); Whitehall, "A Summer Place," p. 50.
22. Murdoch, *The American West*, p. 7.
23. Ibid.
24. This crisis arose following the Second World War when tensions arising from the increasingly prominent role of women, many of whom chose to eschew their traditional pre-war domestic roles of being solely wives and mothers, manifested in visual culture. In addition, Benshoff and Griffin report that many men "felt emasculated by the era's corporate culture" (p. 275).
25. Walker, "The Westerns of Delmer Daves," p. 142.
26. Wallington, "Author and Genre," p. 9.
27. Tavernier, "The Ethical Romantic," pp. 42–4.
28. Ibid. p. 44 (emphasis in original).
29. Wallington, "Author and Genre," p. 8.
30. Daves, "Closing the Gap," p. 26.
31. Walker, "Westerns of Delmer Daves," p. 142.
32. Daves quoted in Todd, "Delmer Daves tells."
33. Ibid.
34. Ibid.
35. Daves quoted in Wicking, "Interview with Delmer Daves," p. 65.
36. Fehrle, "(Re)Making Men," p. 63.
37. Wallington, "Author and Genre," p. 9.
38. Todd, "Delmer Daves tells," p. 24
39. Daves quoted in Wicking, "Interview with Delmer Daves," p. 65.
40. Petch, "Return to Yuma," p. 49.
41. Young, "Law and the Foucauldian Wild West," p. 312.
42. Pinkerton, "Films By Delmer Daves."
43. Wallington, "Author and Genre," p. 7.
44. Pye, "Introduction," p. 9.
45. Whitehall, "On the 3:10 to Yuma," p. 51. Daves quoted in Wicking, "Interview with Delmer Daves," p. 60.
46. Fehrle, "(Re)Making Men," p. 66.
47. Ibid., p. 61.
48. Tavernier, "The Ethical Romantic," p. 48.
49. Ibid.
50. Ibid.
51. Daves in Wicking, "Interview with Delmer Daves," p. 64.
52. Ibid.
53. Tavernier, "The Ethical Romantic," p. 46.
54. Bordwell, *The Way Hollywood Tells It*, p. 121.
55. Falconer, "*3:10 Again*," p. 65.
56. Ibid.
57. Fehrle, "(Re)Making Men," p. 63.
58. Baker, "Delmer Daves," p. 37.
59. Whitehall, "A Summer Place," p. 48.
60. Whitehall, "On the 3:10 to Yuma," p. 51 (emphasis in original).
61. Pye, "Introduction," p. 9.

CHAPTER 8

Changing Societies: *The Red House*, *The Hanging Tree*, *Spencer's Mountain*, and Post-war America

Fernando Gabriel Pagnoni Berns

A dramatic clash of different cultures, broadly conceived, animates many of Delmer Daves' films. In some cases, this clash takes the form of complex racial negotiations, as in Westerns like *Broken Arrow* (1950), *Drum Beat* (1954), and *The Last Wagon* (1956). In others, the clash is between nations, as in *Never Let Me Go* (1953) and *Kings Go Forth* (1958). Still others emphasize differences of class, as in *A Summer Place* (1959) and most of Daves' subsequent melodramas. These conflicts seldom have clear winners and losers, and instead often end with some form of negotiation or reconciliation between the opposed forces. In this way, Daves' films can be seen as dramatizing social progress: the passage from one social stage to another that supplants, in an act of improvement, the preceding one.

This chapter explores how Daves manages these complicated transformations as they take place within characters and their communities. I examine three films as representative of Daves' concern with the rational, evolutionary passage from one social state to another. These are *The Red House* (1947), *The Hanging Tree* (1959), and *Spencer's Mountain* (1963). Drawn from three different decades, with each representing a different genre—mystery, the Western, and family melodrama, respectively—these films demonstrate that Daves' interest in social progress was not a philosophy that the director explored only at one point in his career, or within one particular genre, but was a sustained, consistent authorial concern over the course of his lengthy filmmaking career.

Daves clearly believed in the possibility of social improvement rooted in the idea that, in a healthy community, every social stage will be, indeed, *should be*, better than the immediately preceding one. This outlook is an outgrowth of the belief, common in post-war American culture, that social transformation could be achieved through the rational application of the critical and ethical values of equality and justice to contemporary problems.[1] The idea of a gradualist, ever-progressing, and increasingly better society, represented in Daves' cinema, reflected the desire of moviegoers in America and elsewhere to become "better selves" in the post-war period.

THE RED HOUSE: THE ENTRANCE INTO SOCIABILITY

The popularization of psychoanalysis in the United States in the years leading up to and following the Second World War had a profound impact on American society and culture, especially in the ways in which parents understood their relationships with their children. Whereas the passage from child to adult was once predicated on physical factors or material conditions, like the ability to subsist independently or begin one's own family, now the change was seen as chiefly psychological. According to Sigmund Freud, the definitive event in a child's psychological development is overcoming the Oedipal complex, that is to say the sexual desire for the parent of the opposite sex and concomitant sense of rivalry with the parent of the same sex. Only by learning to repress his or her libido and project desire onto substitute subjects does the child become a "sociable," independent entity.[2] These ideas (and others) strongly influenced American filmmaking in the post-war era, and *The Red House* is no exception. In this film, the change from one social state to the next is conceptualized psychoanalytically.

The film stars Edward G. Robinson as Pete Morgan, a middle-aged farmer with a wooden leg who lives with his sister Ellen (Judith Anderson) and their niece Meg (Allene Roberts) on an isolated farm surrounded by the Ox Head woods. Meg's parents died in a mysterious accident when she was only two years old, and she has lived with the Morgans ever since. Known to those in the nearby town as "the mysterious Morgans," Pete and Ellen make a concerted effort to maintain not only their distance from civilization but a veil of secrecy over their past. The walls they have erected start to crack with the arrival at the farm of Nath Storm (Lon McCallister), a classmate who Meg has asked to help Pete out around the farm. Curious about the surrounding woods, which Meg has been forbidden from venturing into, and which Pete warns Nath never to enter, the teenager sets in motion a chain of events that reveal troubling secrets about the death of Meg's parents and about a mysterious red house in the Ox Head woods.

The film opens with a voiceover that states, "Dense forest once covered all Finey Ridge," but now "modern highways had penetrated the darkness and had brought up the light." There are two features to highlight in this simple statement. First, Daves establishes at the story's outset a duality between a primitive age and a "modern" one which has brought forth rational civilization.

Second, there is the equating of the old, uncivilized ways with darkness and mystery, and the modern times of highways with light. This implies enlightenment, in concordance with the developing faith in the progressive forces that permeated post-war America.[3] The highway, a symbol of carefully planned, nation-unifying collective action, brings with it the light that burns away dark shadows and superstition. The exception, however, is Ox Head Forest, still dark with "whirling paths" and "trails that reach nowhere," except for the path leading to the Morgan farm, "the one of which everybody has heard but little knew." Thus, the film's narration leaves civilization behind and introduces the audience to a sort of fairy tale in which the obscurantism of lore still exists.[4] To reach the Morgans, people must pass through queer paths and dark forests; in other words, leave the lights of modern society behind and enter the shadows that surround the mysterious family.

The darkness in which the Morgans live is a metaphor of the state in which Meg is kept. Though she is a mature teenager, Pete attempts to keep her in a childlike state by limiting both her contact with the outside world and her knowledge of her own past. The familial order that Pete tenuously maintains is threatened by the arrival of Nath, who both awakens Meg's romantic and sexual feelings and disobeys Pete's commands to stay out of the Ox Head woods. Nath and Meg set in motion a chain of events that leads to the revelation of a dark family secret: Pete killed Meg's parents in the red house. He was desperately in love with Meg's mother and, during a heated argument, killed her by accident. He then killed Meg's father and buried them both in the house, and with them the secret of his crime. The red house and Meg are thus both sites of Pete's repression of sexuality and past iniquity. If the house is kept isolated and out of view, Pete's secret will be remain hidden. Furthermore, to keep the past buried and repressed, sexuality should be kept at bay, outside the Morgans' family. Meg is deprived of her prerogative of a natural, progressive maturation and kept in a child-like state, far from womanhood, to preserve a false state of undisturbed, passive innocence. Pete lives in a state of perpetual denial, and his sister has also given up any possibility of romance to be transformed, together with her brother, into the keeper of the secret, a sort of asexual "wife" to Pete.

Rachel Devlin explains that "in the early 1940s, the father began to be portrayed as the most important witness to his daughter's transformations at adolescence."[5] The 1940s and 1950s have widely been envisioned as the historical moment when teenagers dramatically and self-consciously separated themselves from adults, including their parents, by means of their sexualization. Before the Second World War, daughters lived with their parents and gained access to sexuality (i.e., became women) only *within marriage*. In the post-war period, as children gained greater degrees of independence, girls now became sexualized women *within the home*, with the approval of the father figure, and

Figure 8.1 Nath dines with the "mysterious Morgans" in *The Red House*.

thus, as Devlin notes, "the paternal role was actually enhanced rather than diminished."[6] In the case of *The Red House*, the bonds that Pete casts upon his adopted daughter prevent her from growing into a healthy state of femininity. Meg is kept as an asexual child to prevent her entrance into society. She unknowingly carries with her the crime committed by her surrogate family. She cannot gain access to the outside world because she would awaken curiosity, and thus would threaten to expose the family's secret.

Pete, Meg, and Nath form the classical triangle of father, daughter, and suitor, which also explains the hostility on the part of the father toward the suitor.[7] In the 1950s, "paternal authority was officially on the wane, if not extinct, in the United States."[8] What power men did hold over their daughters was reconfigured in terms of erotic bonds between father and daughter. The eroticization of the father–adolescent daughter relationship reformulated paternal power by establishing that girls' psychological health was inescapably dependent upon a good, unrebellious relationship with their fathers.[9] This obedient state is what Meg begins to problematize with Nath coming to the farm, and the subsequent arousal of her sexual feelings.

Simona Argentieri argues that the Oedipus complex, as a stage in human psychological evolution, is overcome when basic differences such as "female" and "male" are learned and exhibited.[10] In this respect, a key scene takes place when Meg, Nath, and Meg's (saucy) girlfriend Tibby (Julie London) search for the red house hidden in the middle of the forest. Tibby is a sexually active girl who is always teasing Nath and flirting with the town's "bad boy," Teller (Rory Calhoun). Tibby despises Meg's shyness, and is eager to abandon the search for the red house to go swimming with Nath. Tibby's clothing in this scene is very feminine: she wears a skirt with a blouse that delineates her breasts. Her outfit is a stark contrast to Meg's looser, "masculine" shirt and baggy pair of pants. While Tibby's sexuality is blooming, Meg is trapped in a non-sexual state.[11]

The idea of incest as a way of being "frozen in time" permeates the narrative.[12] Meg is not only kept in a pre-sexual state, but Pete begins to see in her a resemblance to his lost love, to the point that he starts to call Meg "Geny" (short for Genevieve, the name of Meg's mother). Ellen is fearful about what kind of relationship Pete wishes to keep with Meg. In one scene, Ellen even asks Meg if Pete has touched her, implying that she fears he may have made sexual advances toward her. Ellen herself is not free of the specter of incest, either. She is Pete's sister but, as noted above, she acts more as a wife, with Pete as her "husband" and Meg their "daughter." Interestingly, though, it is not only the Morgans who are uncomfortable with the idea of social integration. Nath's mother, the still-young widow Mrs. Storm (Ona Munson), lives alone with her son, and this is despite his stated desire that she accept the proposal of marriage made by an old beau. Mrs. Storm argues that she has to take care of Nath, but eventually gives in and remarries, (re-)embracing her role as a proper wife, but relinquishing her role as mother to Nath, who is on the precipice of manhood. After the wedding, Nath salutes his mother with a kiss on the lips that, even though both keep their mouths shut, "still raises eyebrows."[13] It must be pointed out that Nath's mother has no role of significance within the story. She only appears twice—in one scene speaking with her son, and another after the marriage—without in either occasion advancing the plot at all. So, why is she there?

Clearly, Daves wanted to have *another* family to serve as an example of people within that little town who refuse to accede to a healthy stage of sociability, preferring instead to live in a family relationship that borders on incestuous. While Nath's mother has none of Pete's dark secrets, the parallel helps to reinforce the connection between Nath and Meg. Only by breaking their respective Oedipal "arrangements" can the adolescents access a better stage that implies maturity and a life of their own. The dark fairy tale that Daves is telling ends when both Nath and Meg emerge from their parents' shadows to live under society's law. As in any Freudian tragedy, *The Red House* ends with the death of both surrogate parents, thereby freeing Meg to take her place as proper bride to Nath. The last shot of *The Red House* shows Nath and Meg in a happy embrace. She now will be, we can assume, the perfect wife, a role sanctioned within society. She has passed from father's rule to husband's rule.

THE HANGING TREE: THE PATH TO A MODERN SOCIETY

The plot of *The Hanging Tree* (1959) is the passage of two periods in U.S. history. It starts with "the death-ridden mercantile-based old America" cemented on lynching and basic desires (including the lustful objectification of women).[14] From this it moves to a modern, capitalist community where women can work with men as equals, while leaving behind a society in a "quasi state of nature."[15] *The Hanging Tree* is not only the title of the film, it is also a symbol of a community that is slowly constructed as a metaphor of America in the post-war era. The film asks for improvement in different aspects of society as a path to reach the state of a new, superior community.

The film opens with the arrival of hundreds of settlers looking for a place to build a new community. The first line of dialogue comes from one of the newcomers as he passes under the tree: "Every new mining camp's got to have its hanging tree." This way, the importance of the hanging tree as a cornerstone for the constitution of the community is doubly marked. The tree is the film's title, and even though the tree is not mentioned again until the end of the film, symbolically its presence looms over the narrative. Even if the hanging tree was not really used as much in the old West as fiction would have us believe, it stands in the popular imaginary as a potent symbol of punishment in those old days.[16] Daves foregrounds this sign as a mirror of a post-war America still struggling to do away once and for all with the barbaric practice of lynching.[17]

That the settlers have chosen this particular site because of the hanging tree indicates that this society has as a primal issue the practice of justice, and that justice is understood as lynching. This particular town, then, will be configured around a communal system of punishment and justice: members who commit some kind of action considered criminal will be executed by their fellow citizens, as there is no sheriff in the place.

Among the arriving settlers are Dr. Joseph Frail (Gary Cooper), who comes running away from his dark past, and Rune (Ben Piazza), a young man who tries to steal some gold nuggets from the miners. He is discovered by gold miner Frenchy Plante (Karl Malden), who shoots and injures the boy. Rune flees a mob that wants to hang him and ends up in the care of Frail, who tends to his wounds and feeds him in exchange for labor. This arrangement does not go smoothly. Rune, at first, mistrusts Frail and feels that the doctor is taking advantage of his superior position. Frail can denounce him if he wishes to, and so he exerts power upon Rune. But this action can be read in two ways: as blackmail, as Rune understands it, or as a sort of restorative justice.

Restorative justice is a relatively new concept in judicial ethics and proposes an alternative to the systems of punishment widely known as "retributive justice," in which a citizen who breaks the law must pay "an eye for an eye." In the restorative justice scenario, some felonies can be rectified not with imprisonment (which is always seen as punishment rather than reparation), but instead with a series of acts that can work as reparation for the misdeed committed.[18] In the late 1950s, Burrhus Frederick Skinner, an innovator in educational psychology, offered one of his most lasting contributions to educational psychology: the idea that positive reinforcement, or rewarding performance of a desired behavior, is more effective in shaping human behavior than punishment.[19] Rune is an adolescent, and his relationship with Frail can be seen as reflecting these post-war developments in teenage behavior that favor guidance rather than punishment. Old practices such as lynching are displaced in favor of educational guidance.

Joseph Frail is a very complex character. He cures Rune and obliges him to work in exchange for his safety. This can be seen, as already mentioned, as an act closer to restorative justice or, as Rune argues, as an act of servitude close to slavery. This contention is important because it either brings Frail closer to, or takes him away from, the current state of the newly founded town. If Rune is Frail's "property," as it can be argued, then the doctor represents an earlier stage of social evolution. His philosophy is that of ownership, the classical ideology of slaveholding America. If, instead, we read the scenario as an opportunity for Rune to make amends for his wrongdoing, then Frail's treatment of him represents a more modern stage in the evolution toward restorative justice. But Frail's position can also be seen in a third way: as that of the ultimate capitalist who objectifies human beings as property, which is an idea that underlies the human relationships within the narrative of *The Hanging Tree*.

How, then, should Frail's actions be best understood? The answer may lie in a small action that he performs. Part of the power that he has over Rune derives from the bullet he extracts from the boy, which would prove that the thief shot by Frenchy and Frail's helper are one and the same. But even though the bullet is the only evidence Frail has to keep Rune "prisoner," Frail tosses it away after the surgical operation, thus relinquishing any real power that he could have had over the young man. If Frail was interested in keeping Rune as his property, he would surely have kept the bullet as a means of blackmailing the boy. Clearly the doctor's purpose is to give the young man a fresh start as a doctor's assistant, even though doing so means that Frail must exert some coercion.

Frail seems to be the "new citizen" of the late 1950s, who needs to find some substitute for older, rejected values through a transformative change of renewed solidarity and justice.[20] As a seeker of a new, improved social state, he looks with disgust at old forms of justice that the town advocates, like lynching, preferring his personal and more sophisticated form of justice—one in which Rune can be of greater benefit to society than as simply a victim of lynching for the perverse satisfaction of bored citizens.

Joseph Frail sees the town from an "elevated" perspective, often in a literal sense. One of the film's first scenes presents him on a hill looking down upon the new arrivals to the community, with the camera sharing his point of view from above. Thus, audiences too can see how the different sites and places that constitute a town are occupied and formed. With the progressive arrival of different social actors, from the people in charge of food to the prostitutes, who also came to fulfill their function within the community. The first building fully completed is the restaurant, the ultimate site for reunion and social life in the old West.

Frail's modern system of ethics contrasts strongly with that of the Bibleman in town, George Grubb (George C. Scott). He is a drunkard who preaches the Bible in exchange for money and warns others about the methods that the doctor, the "butcher" as he calls him, uses to cure people. Grubb believes that people should save their souls first and their bodies second. This character at first seems positioned to have an important role within the story, but as the narration progresses, his presence and influence becomes more and more limited. It can be argued that Grubb's character augments the social dichotomy at the heart of the film: one side dominated by religion, obscurantism, and fear of God, and the other, as represented by Frail, centered in reason, science, and secularism.[21] Once again, we can see how Frail represents a new philosophical perspective that surpasses the dominant ethical paradigm of the town rooted in the hanging tree.

Frail oscillates constantly between many positions within the community. He is the doctor, but also "the best shooter" among the townspeople, and also a capitalist. In many scenes he is shown playing cards in the restaurant, always winning his hand. He even wins an entire property during one of the games. The good doctor's economic power is foregrounded through the film many times. In the opening scenes, he buys his house with gold coins, and he supports both himself and Rune even though it has been previously established that the doctor does not always charge patients, especially poor ones, for his medical services.

The film's action takes place in Montana in 1873, during the peak of the gold rush. Those were years in which people, most of them young, lived only for today, occupied as they were in "chasing a will-o'-the-wisp" of riches.[22] The truth was that many families saw their prospects shattered and livelihoods ruined after many months of fruitlessly pursuing an unreachable dream of sudden wealth. Frail, in turn, is more interested in gaining and accumulating capital as a more secure way of building his future. Again, this displays all the complexities of his character. He is not interested in dreams of gold, and he offers his medical services free of charge to those who cannot pay. At the same time, he also has a strong sense of capitalism and accumulation that resonates strongly in a camp of miners ruined by a useless searching for gold. Still, Rune is told that the doctor has had many opportunities to get rich in the past, but has passed on all of them. This implies that Frail is a sensate capitalist in a world of dreamers, but also a man who privileges the lives of those who live in the community with him. Frail embodies capitalism without the ingenuities of the old gold rush, and without the savage individualism of future neoliberal thinking.

The story comes to its peak when a group of robbers assaults Elizabeth Mahler (Maria Schell), a European girl traveling with her father in search of land to buy. During the fight, her father is killed and, after fleeing the scene, she becomes lost in the mountains. Elizabeth is found days later, sunburned almost to death and temporarily blinded, so she must remain in the care of the doctor and Rune. Soon enough, Frail falls in love with the girl, even though he has no desire in built a family.

Frenchy is the one who actually finds Elizabeth and, from that moment on, he believes that a relationship of owner and property thereby holds between them. Since he has saved the girl's life, the man feels that she is beholden to him as some sort of commodity. Frail senses this too, and take pains to ensure that Frenchy is always kept away from Elizabeth. But after Elizabeth recovers, a truce between Frail, Elizabeth, and Frenchy emerges as the three start a relationship based on business and equality. Together they buy a plot of land to excavate for gold. The whole sequence after the deal is closed shows how Frenchy (and, by extension, the town that he represents) comes to understand women and business. After deciding the percentages owned by each of the partners, Frenchy insists on closing the deal with a handshake as a legitimate institutional method. In turn, Elizabeth will consider the deal closed only after the approbation of a lawyer who certifies that everything is legal—and only then, in Elizabeth's words, will "we shake hands. Agreed?" Elizabeth, like Frail, prefigures a new society, with new roles for women. For her, a business deal is closed only in front of a notary, and not with handshakes or verbal promises taken on faith. A new era of business is beginning, in which women step into the public sphere. On the first day of the new venture, Frenchy suggests that Elizabeth should rest under the shadow of a tree while both men work, a suggestion that she rejects. She is ready to work alongside the men. Thus, the film mirrors what Erin Hatton highlights as "the deep cultural ambivalence about white, middle-class women working" in the post-war era, a situation that, according to her, resulted in "a new and growing sector of the economy that stood in stark contrast to the then-prevalent asset model of work."[23]

In the film's final sequence, the three partners strike gold and the entire town decides to celebrate. Unfortunately, this celebration quickly descends into alcohol-fueled anarchy and with it, the layers of community and civility start to fall apart. After months of working alongside Elizabeth and treating her as his business partner, an intoxicated Frenchy reverts to his old idea of ownership. Arriving at Elizabeth's home, he tries to rape her, but Frail comes to her rescue and, in the ensuing struggle, Frail is forced to shoot Frenchy. Unfortunately, their gunfight becomes protracted, and plays out in plain sight of everybody in town. It ends with Frail kicking Frenchy's lifeless body over a cliff edge. "Inspired" by Grubb's enthusiastic extolling, the townspeople, who need little encouragement, demand the death of the doctor and immediately set out to hang him. In this way the entire community regresses to a previous stage of social development which dictates an eye for and eye, and blood for blood.

The doctor is taken to the hanging tree that had opened the film, to be executed. Here, and as a way of conclusion, transpires an event that prefigures both the coming of a new era in which lynching is understood as a barbaric practice, but also the coming of corrupt justice. Elizabeth and Rune buy Frail's freedom with money. The hypocrisy of the townspeople is manifested in the last line of the film. "She wants to buy her guy," says one of the townsfolk. However, keen as they are to hang the doctor, they ultimately seem more keen for money, and they free him in exchange for gold. Elizabeth and Frail, now free, embrace, and the film ends.[24]

Frail, Frenchy, and Elizabeth are complex characters—especially Frenchy, whose character arc sees him transform from comic relief to villain, to hero, to villain again. Each character embodies the contradictions inherent in the passage from an uncivil social stage represented by a community organized around the need for a hanging tree, to a modern society in which women work alongside men, restorative justice replaces punishment, and capitalism start to shape the everyday. In this respect, it is interesting to consider Mark Eifler's observation that, during the gold rush, and in their transition from would-be gold miners to settled businessmen, the population needed,

> to shift not only goals and expectations but behaviors and attitudes as well. It is typical to think of such confrontations in the West as being between those who sought a wild, irresponsible freedom and those who sought to establish a civil and settled community. The mistake in this stereotype, however, is to suppose that these represent two different groups of people. In reality the lines between these groups ran not between them but *within* them, and those lines were usually blurred, shifting and contradictory at best.[25]

Figure 8.2 Frail is saved from hanging by Elizabeth and Rune in *The Hanging Tree*.

Indeed, the film does not present two stages of community as separate and mutually exclusive spheres, but rather as overlapping, as the same community slowly and uneasily shifts from one paradigm to the next—a shift that, as we see, involves both progression and regression. The many contradictions that come with this passage are manifest in the main characters of *The Hanging Tree*.

SPENCER'S MOUNTAIN: FROM MANUAL LABOR TO INTELLECTUAL WORK

Spencer's Mountain dramatizes, through a simple and sentimental story, the passage of a society based on physical labor to one based on intellectual labor, represented by the many sacrifices that family patriarch Clay Spencer (Henry Fonda) makes so that his son may attend university. Higher education, then, is understood as an evolutionary step within society.

Spencer's Mountain is based on the novel of the same name by Earl Hamner, Jr. (which also inspired the television series *The Waltons*). As Mike Chopra-Grant has noted, the film adaptation makes a significant change from its source: the novel takes place during the Great Depression, while the film's action is framed in the 1950s. By updating the historical period, Daves constructs a contemporary fable. If *The Hanging Tree* works around the passage of a society to a more civilized state, here the passage is twofold: one, "the moment of passage from youth to manhood," and the other (which this chapter will discuss), the dawn of an age that promises the possibility of reaching a new status for everyone, even lower classes, through higher education.[26]

The film tells the story of the Spencer family, made up of quarry employee Clay Spencer, his wife Olivia (Maureen O'Hara), and their nine children. Living on a cows-and-chickens estate in the shadow of Wyoming's Grand Tetons, the family is struggling to make ends meet. Clay, in addition to his work at the mine, endeavors to build the couple's dream home in the hills while also trying to get his book-learning eldest son Clay-boy (James MacArthur), who harbors a potent desire to escape his sheltered mountain life, into college.

The film opens with Clay's voiceover explaining how the family had come to live in the wild state of Wyoming. The saga began with Clay's great-grandfather, who had made a name for himself in the territory. In fact, the narration explains, the mountain carries the surname of the family and many features of the landscape, such as the river, feature names given by the family through the years. The Spencers, while not rich, at least have made a strong name for themselves based on achievement.

Clay Spencer still lives in the house constructed by his great-grandfather, indicating a continuation of the family lineage. The order of things is soon interrupted by two key elements that symbolize the social change that Daves is dramatizing: a ring, and a mechanical table saw. Olivia asks for money from the family's savings to buy a ring as a gift for Clay-boy's graduation. Clay tells her they haven't the money. Unbeknownst to her, however, that money has already been spent as the first installment for the table saw, which replaces the family's old tools and makes their work a little easier.

Work on the mountainside is hard and strenuous. The whole family wakes up very early each day and works until dark. Clay mentions that he has been carving the foundations of the new family house, but winter after winter, the foundations are covered with soil. Two implications can be gleaned from this. First, the family has been following a routine that has not provided for more than their daily survival. The hope of a better future within the mountains seems to collapse, like the foundations of the dream house, year after year.[27] Second, the untamed forces of nature continually oppose the family's ambitions, yet they remain where they are. Clay also talks about old times, when the Spencers had suffered through famine and extreme poverty, indicating that the family's current state of affairs is in some way better. However, since the family does not even have enough money to buy a ring for Clay-boy, it is clear that they have yet to prosper economically despite all their combined effort over the years.

Unlike Frail in *The Hanging Tree*, Clay Spencer is not a character rife with contradictions. Nevertheless, as a man living in changing times, he is not free of at least some ambiguity symptomatic of his time. Clay is a man who privileges family values and orthodoxy, yet he is also the only one from the old generation to shun organized religion. He rejects Sunday mass and visits to church, in spite of his family's constant admonishments. Within this internal tension resonates the stronger shift in the film, that of the passage from an uneducated family who survive through manual labor to the prospect of a new family supported by intellectual undertakings. The successful entrance of Clay-boy into an institution of higher education marks the fact that the upper class's monopoly on learning has been broken. Learning and knowledge in the modern age were no longer restricted to elites, as had been the case for previous generations. Learning was now accessible for all, but with that accessibility came new challenges.[28]

The film is framed by the 1950s, the 1960s, and the interrelation of classes and races for the first time in schools. It is not by chance that during Clay-boy's middle-school graduation ceremony, the girl in charge of opening the ceremony with a song is black (Barbara McNair). It was in 1954—less than a decade before the film was made—that the United States Supreme Court outlawed racial segregation in public schools. This led some to fear the loss of "separate spheres" and the integration of sexes and races in the classroom, which, by the mid-twentieth century, was a "conduit for the expression of mobility aspirations."[29] Maybe because of this, Daves chose to place the story within a contemporary setting. In the 1960s, "the civil rights movements and its central objective of integration dominated American politics and policy as no other social movement in twentieth-century America ever has," and, in this light, *Spencer's Mountain* works as a metaphor for a changing society.[30]

The speech that Clay-boy's teacher, Miss Parker (Virginia Gregg), delivers on graduation day resonates profoundly. She speaks of the transcendence of physical places through knowledge and the union of men and women by means of books and learning. Her address speaks to Clay-boy and his desire to transcend the valley in which he and his family had lived for years, but also speaks, outside *Spencer's Mountain*, of the union of classes and races in schools as necessary to achieve a better world, a better America. Still, doubts linger, especially in the older generation. Even if the Spencers agree to Clay-boy attending university, there is a clash between higher education and the simple and hard-working life in the valley. Clay-boy can access academia, but even so, Clay and Olivia have doubts about their oldest son's future—doubts about how much use higher education can be for a "valley boy." Clay also fears that his son will fail at the university. He extols the virtues of higher education and "men of career," but he also thinks that only the elite can really achieve this goal.[31]

The new illuminated citizen is not only represented in Clay-boy. Claris Coleman (Mimsy Farmer), Clay-boy's girlfriend and the daughter of Clay's boss, horrifies the Spencers when she reveals that not only has she learned about human reproduction at school, but is "enthralled" by the formerly taboo subject. Claris, too, is a citizen of a new era, a better era, in which sexuality can be openly discussed within the family and in schools.[32] We must take into account that the 1960s was a decade in which sexual education in schools faced strong opposition by conservative organizations which, in some cases, were winning the battle against progressive forces.[33]

Clay-boy's departure for university follows a symbolic and sad event: the death of Grandpa Zebulon Spencer (Donald Crisp). As they are working in the valley, a tree cut by Clay falls upon Grandpa, killing him. The death of the oldest Spencer marks the beginning of a new era for the family into which Clay-boy, as the first to attend university, will lead them. The funerary rite at Grandpa's burial works as an inverted mirror to Clay-boy's passage into a new life, one granted by Clay's hard work to send his son to university even though he is not entirely convinced of the utility of this passage.

It has been argued that, in the wake of the Second World War, labor unions "helped shape public policy, as did the American Legion, a vast, national voluntary association made up of veterans that garnered support for the G.I. Bill, a legislative victory that opened up the world of higher education to those denied it before."[34] In *Spencer's Mountain*, Clay mirrors those older generations of laborers who broke their backs to accumulate enough money to grant their children access to higher education, as well as the lower-class workers who expanded higher education opportunities and enabled the employment possibilities that followed.

The scene that best encapsulates the message of the film is that of Clay waiting in the room next to the office of the dean who has rejected Clay-boy's college application. Clay has come to the building to ask why his son has not been admitted to the university. Waiting to be received by the dean, he glances at the various portraits of the institution's teachers, scholars, and directors adorning the walls. While doing so, he murmurs to himself, "They look smart, but I wonder if any of them ever did an honest day's work." This simple statement expresses Clay's real philosophy. Despite his earnest desire to see his offspring gain access to higher education, Clay does not really consider intellectual work as "real" work. He still separates manual labor from intellectual work, the former being "honest" and the second being reserved for an elite with no real desire to work. This line of thought is just another contradiction in a man who is trying to adapt to changing times even as he remains emotionally and ideologically attached to older ways of thinking. He will do everything to give his son the chance of a better life, even when he himself does not really believe in the value of that life. He is, like Doctor Frail, a hinge between two elements of a changing society, and as a result he is rife with contradictions and ambiguities.

CONCLUSION

Following the end of the Second World War, many Americans felt a profound a sense of disorientation as they tried to rebuild their lives and return to normalcy. After the horror of concentration camps and atomic bombs, Americans believed themselves ready to help make a better world, one that would leave behind its violent ways and embrace peace. As *The Red House*, *The Hanging Tree*, and *Spencer's Mountain* demonstrate, for Delmer Daves history involved a progressive change from one social state to another, as successive generations stood ready to embrace the possibilities of a new era. Yet Daves' films are sensitive to the contradictions and compromises involved in social progress. Some, like the Morgans, might choose to live in darkness, but eventually a new generation will find its own path to improvement through a long voyage, as Clay-boy mentions during the last scene of *Spencer's Mountain*.

Daves was preoccupied with the transition taking place in America in the post-war years, and with the possibilities that this era would usher in a better world, one in which democracy, together with the economic growth and prosperity that follows it, would shine a light that would scare away the shadows of incivility. In *The Hanging Tree*, audiences witness the transformation of a society that must leave behind its old ways, embodied in primitive forms of punishment such as lynching, and embrace new standards of justice. In this new society, women work alongside men as equals, intellectual work is just as "honest" as manual labor, and education is within the reach of all who are willing to work for it, regardless of class, gender, or race. Yet this change also requires that the older generation lets go, if not of their own beliefs, then at least of the hold those beliefs have on their children. If the paternal figures—those in charge of promoting the changes and the passage from one social stage to another—cut off the possibilities of freedom of the new generations, little can be done. The older generation, whether healthy like the Spencers or unhealthy like the Morgans, must let go of their offspring so that they may start to find their way to a better world. Whether or not, in reality, the next social stage truly marked an improvement, it is apparent that Daves believed so, and this certainty helped him to mold some of his better films.

BIBLIOGRAPHY

Argentieri, Simona, "Incest Yesterday and Today: from Conflict to Ambiguity," in Giovanna Ambrosio (ed.), *On Incest: Psychoanalytic Perspectives* (London: Karnac, 2005).

Balogh, Brian, "Introduction," in Brian Balogh (ed.), *Integrating the Sixties: The Origins, Structures, and Legitimacy of Public Policy in a Turbulent Decade* (University Park, PA: Pennsylvania State Press, 1996), pp. 1–33.

Bansak, Edmund, *Fearing the Dark: The Val Lewton Career* (Jefferson, NC: McFarland, 2003).
Berg, Manfred, "Lynching and the Ambivalence of Modernity" in Thomas Welskopp (ed.), *Fractured Modernity: America Confronts Modern Times, 1890s to 1940s* (München: R. Oldenbourg Verlag, 2012), pp. 153–68.
Breines, Wini, "Postwar White Girls' Dark Others," in Joel Foreman (ed.), *The Other Fifties: Interrogating Midcentury American Icons* (Champaign, IL: University of Illinois Press, 1997), pp. 53–77.
Carlisle, Rodney (ed.), *Postwar America: 1950 to 1969* (New York: Infobase, 2009).
Chopra-Gant, Mike, *The Waltons: Nostalgia and Myth in Seventies America* (New York: I. B. Tauris, 2013).
Costello, Donald, "From Counterculture to Anticulture," *The Review of Politics*, 34:4 (1972): 187–93.
Devlin, Rachel, *Relative Intimacy: Fathers, Adolescent Daughters, and Postwar American Culture* (London: The University of North Carolina Press, 2005).
Eifler, Mark, *Gold Rush Capitalists: Greed and Growth in Sacramento* (Albuquerque: University of New Mexico Press, 2002).
Fass, Paula, *Outside In: Minorities and the Transformation of American Education* (New York: Oxford University Press, 1989).
Ford, Jane, *Patriarchy and Incest from Shakespeare to Joyce* (Orlando: University Press of Florida, 1998).
Haney, David Paul, *The Americanization of Social Science: Intellectuals and Public Responsibility in the Postwar United States* (Philadelphia: Temple University Press, 2008).
Hatton, Erin, *The Temp Economy: From Kelly Girls to Permatemps in Postwar America* (Philadelphia: Temple University Press, 2011).
Hess, Kären Matison, and Christine Hess Orthmann, *Introduction to Law Enforcement and Criminal Justice* (New York: Delmar, 2012).
Horlik, Allan, *Patricians, Professors, and Public Schools: The Origins of Modern Educational Thought in America* (New York: Brill, 1994).
Irvine, Janice, *Talk about Sex: The Battles over Sex Education in the United States* (Oakland: University of California Press, 2004).
Mattson, Kevin, *When America Was Great: The Fighting Faith of Postwar Liberalism* (New York: Routledge, 2004).
Moore, Susan, and Doreen Rosenthal, *Sexuality in Adolescence* (New York: Routledge, 1995).
Stadter, Michael, "Time-Near and Time-Far: the Changing Shape of Time in Trauma and Psychotherapy," in Michael Stadter and David E. Scharff (eds.), *Dimensions of Psychotherapy, Dimensions of Experience: Time, Space, Number and State of Mind* (New York: Routledge, 2005), pp. 25–38.
Tórrez, Robert, *Myth of the Hanging Tree: Stories of Crime and Punishment in Territorial New Mexico* (Albuquerque: University of New Mexico Press, 2008).
Udall, Stewart, *The Forgotten Founders: Rethinking the History of the Old West* (Washington, DC: Island Press, 2002).
Zinn, Howard, *Postwar America, 1945–1971* (Cambridge, MA: South End Press, 2002).

FILMOGRAPHY

Hanging Tree, The, director Delmer Daves, featuring Gary Cooper, Maria Schell, Karl Malden (Warner Bros., 1959).

Red House, The, director Delmer Daves, featuring Edward G. Robinson, Lon McCallister (United Artists, 1947).

Spencer's Mountain, director Delmer Daves, featuring Henry Fonda, Maureen O'Hara (Warner Bros., 1963).

NOTES

1. Carlisle, *Postwar America* (New York: Infobase, 2009), p. 157.
2. Moore and Rosenthal, *Sexuality in Adolescence*, p. 25.
3. Haney, *Americanization of Social Science*, p. 2.
4. Bansak, *Fearing the Dark*, p. 383.
5. Devlin, *Relative Intimacy*, p. 2.
6. Ibid. p. 6.
7. Ford, *Patriarchy and Incest*, p. 16.
8. Devlin, *Relative Intimacy*, p. 9.
9. Ibid. p. 10.
10. Argentieri, "Incest Yesterday and Today," p. 27.
11. During a conversation between Tibby and Nath, the former explains her plans for the future: economic progress living both together, far from the little town. Nath, in turn, does not expect more in life than to manage a little farm within the town. We must remember that Daves establishes the little town as a place of stagnation, embodied in the Morgans' denial as Tibby enters the stage of adulthood. Then, Tibby's ambitions and sexuality mark her as a restless modern woman who is eager to pass to a superior stage, one metaphorized in the highways mentioned in the opening of the film.
12. Stadter, "Time-Near and Time-Far," p. 33.
13. Bansak, *Fearing the Dark*, p. 385.
14. Costello, "From Counterculture to Anticulture," p. 189.
15. Berg, "Lynching and the Ambivalence of Modernity," p. 158.
16. Tórrez, *Myth of the Hanging Tree*, p. 2.
17. Zinn, *Postwar America*, p. 121.
18. Hess and Orthmann, *Introduction to Law Enforcement and Criminal Justice*, p. 67.
19. Carlisle, *Postwar America*, p. 120.
20. Haney, *Americanization of Social Science*, p. 94.
21. This contrast is marked, furthermore, by hypocrisy. While Grubb is a man who embraces vice (he drinks heavily) and sin (he envies/hates Frail), the doctor, the one that embodies materialism in a double way (he takes care of the bodily in exchange of money) cures the poorest people in the town for free. Daves wants to be clear in his point that the prior stage of obscurantism was stained with hypocrisy.
22. Udall, *The Forgotten Founders*, p. 129.
23. Hatton, *The Temp Economy*, p. 7.
24. Curiously, they do not share a kiss. There has been always something queer about their relationship and the place that Rune occupies in this love triangle. The lack of a final kiss maintains the tension, allowing us to speculate that the story has not ended yet: this is the end of an era, but the beginning of a brand new day.
25. Eifler, *Gold Rush Capitalists*, pp. 188–9.
26. Chopra-Gant, *The Waltons*, p. 23.
27. Olivia reproaches her husband that he has never finished the house he has promised her

since their first year of marriage. Despite their daily hard work, the projects of the Spencers seem to go nowhere.
28. Horlik, *Patricians, Professors, and Public Schools*, p. 205.
29. Fass, *Outside In*, p. 224.
30. Balogh, "Introduction," p. 2.
31. When the family reads the letter notifying the rejection of Clay-boy's scholarship, everyone but the boy takes this fact almost naturally. Obviously, the family does not believe that much in education for low-class citizens. For the family, higher education is still only a dream.
32. She is a modern girl also in her sexual advancements toward Clay-boy, who is much more timid in his sexual innuendo.
33. Irvine, *Talk about Sex*, p. 12.
34. Mattson, *When America was Great*, p. 99.

CHAPTER 9

Partial Rehabilitation: *Task Force* and the Case of Billy Mitchell

Andrew Howe

William "Billy" Mitchell was an early military aviator whose 1925 court-martial caught the imagination of the American public. Born into a family of wealth and political influence, Mitchell nonetheless joined the military at the age of eighteen, distinguishing himself first during the Spanish–American War and, twenty years later, during the First World War, where he rose to the rank of Chief of the Air Service for the U.S. Army. During the early 1920s, Mitchell tirelessly advocated for the primacy of aviation in America's post-war military plans. He argued that airplanes would quickly become the primary military instruments of warfare, and that the nation would best be served by investing heavily in the design and manufacture of specialized aircraft. In order to demonstrate his ideas, he organized a series of high-profile tests and exhibitions, becoming a media darling and nationally famous in the process. He also made numerous enemies, particularly in the Navy, and was eventually court-martialed in what, at the time, was considered to be one of the most noteworthy trials in American history. He was forced out of the Armed Services and died, embittered, a few years prior to the start of the Second World War, a conflict that would prove nearly all of his theories to be sound and his prognostications correct.

Although in no way explicitly acknowledged, the central character in *Task Force* (1949), a film written and directed by Delmer Daves, espouses nearly all of Mitchell's core theories. This chapter examines the film's fictionalized treatment of a real-life figure, exploring the manner in which Mitchell is valorized—in that the film's central character advances the General's strategic arguments—while simultaneously being erased from history. As *Task Force* carries the narrative into the Second World War it showcases a heroic figure instead of a tragic one, situating the character at the crossroads of developing philosophies and missed opportunities in American interwar imperialism. Daves the director will also be examined, particularly for the cinematic qualities that suggest it is time to critically re-examine some of his forgotten films, such as *Task Force*. Finally, Daves' treatment will be put in context with other aviation films from the same era, most notably Otto Preminger's *The Court Martial of Billy Mitchell* (1955), which, coming six years later, was able to openly examine the controversial figure.

Three men are key to this discussion: Billy Mitchell, Delmer Daves, and Gary Cooper, the latter having played the lead role in both *Task Force* and *The Court Martial of Billy Mitchell*. It is interesting to note that each of these figures, in their respective arenas, cultivated a sense of rugged individualism, although with Daves and Cooper this distinction was more about their artistic work than their public personae.[1] It is also interesting to note the role of ego in the formation (and in the case of Mitchell, destruction) of their careers. Whereas Daves and Cooper were generally viewed as being people with whom it was easy to work, allowing their genius to flourish over a longer period, it was the visionary Mitchell whose ego was too strong for his era and whose career ended precipitously due to forces beyond his control. In this regard, *Task Force* is an interesting case study in that it simultaneously demonstrates the ability of art and artists to channel their egos into portrayals of the past, while reflecting the arguments of a non-artist who was excoriated for his passion. History is filled with individuals who were just a bit too far ahead of their time, whose words, while celebrated at some later date, doomed them in their present. This, in essence, is the story of Billy Mitchell, although it is not the story that Daves tells.

In *Task Force*, the director makes the narrative more palatable for viewers who, living in the wake of the Second World War, expected a tale of triumph. Gary Cooper's character is given a different name, Jonathan L. Scott, and service, the U.S. Navy; but most importantly, his arguments for air power during the early 1920s come at the *beginning* of his career, allowing the character to recover from the punishment he faces for stepping out of line and embarrassing his superiors. As Mitchell's actions came when he was a well-established, high-ranking officer, he could not be so easily rehabilitated. The *deus ex machina* of creating a character in Scott who, despite serving as a mouthpiece for Mitchell's ideas, is quite a bit younger than the General was, allows the narrative to extend through the end of the Second World War and the triumph of air power. In this regard, it is as if Daves is allowing Mitchell, vicariously and via the power of cinema, to live to see his genius recognized.

Before embarking on a close analysis of the film, certain aspects of the aviator's career, and how it has been interpreted over time, warrant scrutiny. The son of a U.S. Senator, Mitchell made his name in the First World War, during which he successfully coordinated over 1,500 aircraft—at that

Figure 9.1 Advertisement for *Task Force* (*Daily Variety*, 28 September 1949, p. 14).

point an unconscionable number—during the Battle of Saint-Mihiel.² He ended the war, at the age of thirty-nine, as the Chief of the Air Service for the U.S. Army.³ The qualities that had distinguished him during the war—aggressiveness, determination, outspokenness—conspired to get him into trouble during peacetime. Mitchell began a crusade to reform the nation's air service, making a series of predictions as to where the U.S. would eventually need to go, not only in their armed services but also in other areas impacted by aeronautics. That the items on the following list were bound to happen may seem obvious today, but it is important to note that most of these predictions were considered fanciful at the time. They are as follows: the use of airplanes in fighting forest fires and ensuring border integrity; the widespread use of airplanes for everyday transportation, including between continents; the use of paratroopers in battle; armor-piercing technologies; the creation of an Air Force separate from the Army; the Joint Chiefs-of-Staff system; space travel; and the primacy of air over naval power as the future of both offensive and defensive warfare.⁴ Most of these predictions were, again, considered radical at the time, but it was the last one that in particular struck a nerve, resulting in Mitchell's censure and eventual court-martial. Following the First World War, he relentlessly attacked the Navy for its adherence to a "Dreadnought first" policy, one that gave primacy in strategic funding and planning to battleships over aircraft carriers. Mitchell knew that the aircraft carrier would be the future of naval warfare, predicting in disconcertingly precise detail how and when Japan would attack Pearl Harbor. Adding insult to injury, he arranged to have his planes sink a large German battleship that had been captured at the end of the First World War. Witnessing the test were military leaders from both services, members of the U.S. Congress, journalists, and representatives from twenty foreign nations, ironically including the Empire of Japan.⁵

This successful test humiliated the Navy, although it did convince them to begin guardedly dedicating more of their resources to naval aviation.⁶ The months following this test saw Mitchell at his zenith, as footage of the sinking played on newsreels shown prior to Hollywood films screened in cinemas across the country.⁷ Billy Mitchell was a star, not with the political and military establishments with which he needed to work, but instead with the press and the public. Instead of following up on this success with a more moderate approach, he became more and more strident in his calls for air power, alienating both his superiors and subordinate pro-aviation officers, who began to realize that he was turning into a pariah. According to H. Paul Jeffers, "He was described as arrogantly ambitious, conceited, disrespectful of superior officers, and dismissive of army rules and regulations."⁸ James J. Cooke also notes that Mitchell was "incapable of giving credit to others, and at times he could be unfeeling when his subordinates were in dire circumstances."⁹ Slowly but surely, Mitchell alienated what few allies he had left. Thrust to the side, he purposefully made some comments so outrageous that he knew a court-martial would be inevitable. During a hastily called press conference following the death of a friend and fellow officer in a dirigible accident, Mitchell referred to the administration of the Armed Forces as incompetent, criminal, and "almost treasonable" in their negligence.[10] These comments served their purpose, getting him into trouble but also giving him the stage he so desperately sought. Over the course of his seven-week court-martial, Mitchell was able to air his grievances with the Armed Forces and demonstrate the viability of air power, although in the end he was found guilty and suspended from the service.[11] The trial not only embarrassed the Armed Forces and called attention to America's lack of air power, it also had a direct impact upon several military careers. Mitchell's disciple Henry "Hap" Arnold, who testified on his behalf, would take over the crusade and eventually build the Army Air Corps into a potent fighting force, becoming the highest-ranking Air officer in the process.[12] General Douglas MacArthur, on the other hand, served on the jury of officers deciding Mitchell's fate. MacArthur later claimed to have been one of the few who dissented from the guilty verdict, and noted that "a senior officer should not be silenced for being at variance with his superiors in rank and with accepted doctrine."[13]

A brief analysis of Mitchell's historiography is quite revealing, both in when these biographies and critical works were published and in what phrasing was used to frame the aviator, either in the book's title or in the preface. For instance, despite the media frenzy that surrounded the trial, and the public interest in the future of aviation during the mid-1920s, the first book-length work focusing exclusively on Mitchell did not appear until 1942, with the publication of Emile Gauvreau and Lester Cohen's *Billy Mitchell: Founder of Our Air Force and Prophet without Honor*.[14] The book is noteworthy in its timing, coming out in September of 1942, two years following the Battle of Britain and nearly a year after the Japanese attack on Pearl Harbor. The fact that the Pacific War began when aircraft carriers of the Japanese Navy attacked the Hawaiian naval installation—in conditions predicted with incredible accuracy by Mitchell, who also predicted Japan's attacks upon the Philippine Islands and the Aleutians in Alaska—appears throughout the book as a sort of crucible, a painful moment that nonetheless served to resuscitate Mitchell's reputation.[15] The book also publicizes its agenda in the after-title. Not only is Mitchell the legitimate founder of the Air Force, according to Gauvreau, he is also a "prophet." The phrase "without honor" refers not to Mitchell's outsized ego or combative tactics, but instead to the fact that honor was withheld from him by the military establishment, the representatives of which were focused more on protecting their own careers than on discerning the best way forward for the national defense. After referencing a series of damning letters written following the First World War between Josephus Daniels, Secretary of the

Navy, and Newton D. Baker, Secretary of War, which highlighted America's lack of military preparedness, Gauvreau does not shrink from calling out the interwar American military apparatus:

> [T]he determination of the War and Navy departments to prevent officers from telling the truth to the Congress of the condition of national defense. The letters are important, as in them were shown, full-grown, the blindness, obstinacy and stupidity which were to afflict the Army and Navy bureaucracy and to be reflected in its scoffing and tragic viewpoint of the Air Arm until Pearl Harbor.[16]

In the blink of an eye, the Imperial Japanese Navy demonstrated the folly of America's interwar defensive strategy, most notably their investment in battleships instead of aircraft and aircraft carriers. With six of the latter, Admiral Isoroku Yamamoto demonstrated that naval aircraft could be projected with power halfway across the largest ocean on the planet. Ironically, it was Yamamoto who set into motion the events by which Billy Mitchell would eventually return to grace.

Gauvreau freely admits to having been an acquaintance and supporter of Mitchell's during the 1920s, and the book is framed around a conversation the author had with James V. Martin, "father of half the basic patents for things that fly."[17] Also treated poorly by the Armed Forces for refusing to continue building DH planes, known colloquially as "flaming coffins" by the pilots who flew them, it is no surprise that Martin agrees with Gauvreau about Mitchell's status as a prophet.[18] It is also no surprise that this study compounds a lack of critical distance from its subject with mid-war, patriotic jingoism such as in the following passage: "Billy Mitchell was a great American because he never forgot that the United States was a new thing when it was invented. This country is a great invention, a history of inventions, and the blood of inventors has been its seed."[19] Later studies would follow, ones that despite their greater critical distance or academic rigor still signaled their specific agendas. Despite the changing times, Billy Mitchell has remained quite topical, due in part to the continued ascendancy of air power in both warfare and transportation but also to the sense of injustice that has continued to adhere to his case. It is particularly interesting to note that these books exist in three clusters, which temporally match up to the three major military conflicts in which the United States would become embroiled following the Second World War. The next two books solely dedicated to Mitchell both appeared during the Korean War, in 1952 and 1953 respectively. The former, Roger Burlingame's *General Billy Mitchell: Champion of Air Defense*, laments Mitchell's "crucifixion" and denotes the aviator as "the American herald of a world revolution."[20] The latter, written by Mitchell's sister Ruth Mitchell, is no less laudatory, comparing the aviator to Robert E. Lee in that each was condemned for doing their duty.[21] After a decade's hiatus, three studies appeared between 1964 and 1969, coinciding with some of the heaviest fighting, and aerial bombing, of the Vietnam War.[22] Among these works was the first published by an academic press: Alfred F. Hurley's *Billy Mitchell: Crusader for Air Power*. The next wave of books came during a three-year period (2002–5) that marked the beginnings of American military conflicts in Afghanistan and Iraq.[23] Two of these studies, James Cooke's *Billy Mitchell* and Douglas Waller's *A Question of Loyalty*, appear the most balanced. They measure Mitchell's genius and the ways in which his vision was prescient against the realities of the political landscape faced by his superiors and the fact that numerous other voices promoting air power existed, some of which were ultimately more productive in fostering an evolution rather than attempting to force revolution.[24]

Although Mitchell's rehabilitation as a visionary began with Pearl Harbor, and was solidified due to the critical importance of aerial combat in the Second World War, it took a while before he was once again publicly celebrated as a popular hero—not until Otto Preminger's *The Court Martial of Billy Mitchell*. I would argue, however, that Delmer Daves gave Mitchell a partial rehabilitation with *Task Force*. As a director, Daves has long been saddled with the reputation that, other than his later Westerns and a few other films, he largely peddled in formulaic, low-to-middlebrow fare. In his Linnaean classification of world cinematic directors through 1968, Andrew Sarris relegates Delmer Daves to the chapter entitled "Lightly Likable." The entirety of the narrative entry for Daves reads as follows:

> If you have no kind thoughts for the authoritative absurdities of *Dark Passage*, *The Red House*, *A Summer Place*, *Rome Adventure* and *Youngblood Hawke*, read no further. Delmer Daves is the property of those who can enjoy stylistic conviction in an intellectual vacuum. The movies of Delmer Daves are fun of a very special kind. Call it Camp or call it Corn. The director does not so much transcend his material as mingle with it.[25]

Certainly, many would argue that Daves does not belong in the same league as some of the cinematic luminaries whose careers also spanned the period from the 1920s through the 1960s. However, even if we concede that *Broken Arrow* (1950) and *3:10 to Yuma* (1957) do not compare favorably to John Ford's *The Searchers* (1956) and *The Man Who Shot Liberty Valance* (1962), this does not mean that Daves did not make important contributions to the classical Western. Similarly, just because he lacks a formally experimental masterpiece such as Alfred Hitchcock's *Rear Window* (1954), this does not make Daves' flawed *Dark Passage* (1947) any less important than the equally flawed, yet nevertheless celebrated, *Lifeboat* (1944) and *Rope* (1948).

Such criticisms have largely followed Daves in the scant attention that has been paid to him, much of it following James Mangold's 2007 remake of *3:10 to Yuma*. Jay Boyer's essay on the director in the *American Screenwriters* version of the *Dictionary of Literary Biography* continues Sarris' earlier criticisms:

> If his scripts seem old-fashioned or overwritten, it is because they are first of all narratives that often depend on their own peculiar internal definitions. They seek an emotional response before an intellectual one. And if these faults contribute sometimes to the film's failures as cinematic art, these absurdities of plot or character are also responsible for taking us out of our own lives and problems for a time.[26]

Again, Daves' films are noted for being escapist fare and for not being very intellectual in their expectations from the audience, although in this context it is Daves the writer who is being served. Regardless, either way Daves, when he is not being ignored, is viewed as a lesser vessel during a period marked by some of the most celebrated directors to ever practice the craft. Some of these critiques are fair. *Dark Passage* is an anomaly in Daves' canon as, generally, the director did take the safest route, courting audience popularity through his use of formula. Perhaps this is why Daves, despite choosing a storyline and character for *Task Force* that so closely matched the ideas of Billy Mitchell, fictionalized the story. Making the protagonist quite a bit younger, placing him within the Navy, and allowing the story to run through the events of the Second World War allowed the story to have a happy ending—that is to say, for the specter of Billy Mitchell to attach to the film and for the aviator's ideas to be validated without the risk of having to portray the complex and controversial flyer. Just because Daves takes the safer passage, however, does not mean the film is not notable for its aesthetic or political properties. *Task Force* begins at the end, with Admiral Jonathan L. Scott's retirement following the Second World War. Before going ashore, where as he reminisces with a friend the story unfolds in a single flashback, "Scotty," as he is known, gives a farewell speech:

> Gentlemen, it is difficult to say goodbye. Some of you were serving with me when none of us had ever seen an aircraft carrier. Since that time, we have seen a lot of ocean, and we have seen a lot of sky. Today, as I become a part of the past, you are becoming part of the future. I wish with all my heart that I could share that future with you. I will. But from the beach.

With just a few minor alterations, changing the service from Navy to Army, this speech could very well have been given by Billy Mitchell following his court-martial.

Generally, both Scotty and the film take a dim view of a military bureaucracy steeped in blind tradition and unable to fully understand or value new military concepts. In the very first scene, as Scotty remembers his journey, his immediate boss following the end of the First World War breaks the bad news to Scotty and his fellow fliers:

> The disarmament conference is over. They've sunk the fleet. The Missouri, the South Dakota, the Maine. The Virginia, the Nebraska, the Georgia. Thirty capital ships. More ships sunk with the stroke of a pen than have been sunk in our entire history. I've asked you pilots to assemble here because in the event of an attack on the United States the navy air defense is in your hands.

To this, Scotty cheekily responds "All fifteen of us?" Much as was the case with Mitchell, Scotty spends his career lamenting the fact that those who make the decisions are those who have never been inside an airplane. And much like Mitchell, blessed with a quick wit but cursed by a sharp tongue and lack of judgment, Scotty has a hard time keeping his thoughts to himself. Scotty is witty and charismatic but also polarizing, also having a difficult time keeping his public crusade from interfering with his private life (as did Mitchell, who was divorced by his first wife and subsequently lost custody of his children). Finally, Scotty receives a post in Washington, D.C., where his immediate superiors hope that he can diplomatically argue for air power with the entrenched military establishment. At a dinner attended by the Washington elite, Scotty quickly becomes embroiled in a heated discussion about air power, insulting a key newspaper magnate and the Japanese delegation, including its naval attaché (implied to be Yamamoto later in the film). It is ironic that, during the course of this conversation, one of the men references Billy Mitchell's claim to be able to sink a battleship—the only time that the aviator is mentioned in the film. However, Scotty's multiple clashes with his superiors, with journalists, and even with politicians are reminiscent of Mitchell, as is the public insult of Japan. As Scotty's immediate superior, also an advocate for air power, summarizes the situation:

> I brought you here tonight to charm the big shots, to sell aviation. And in 12 minutes by the clock you've antagonized Japan, told off a powerful publisher, and got the boot from the Chief of Naval Operations. You've been a great help, you're turned yourself into a one-man leper colony.

Much like Mitchell, Scotty finds himself punished for his relentless assault upon the long-standing ideas cherished by his superiors. However, unlike Mitchell, who died in 1936, salvation does exist for Scotty in the form of the

Second World War and the build-up to that conflict, when the Navy begins investing in aircraft carriers. Whereas the waves that Mitchell caused occurred while he was at the top of the game—where he could not simply be ignored, and thus had to be emasculated—as a much younger officer, Scotty is merely demoted until his ideas eventually come into vogue, or at least begin to acquire traction. Much as Mitchell was sent to Fort Sam Houston in San Antonio in an early attempt to keep him quiet, Daves has Scotty banished to the Panama Canal Zone. That Daves does not include the worst elements of Mitchell's personality—such as his relentless self-promotion—bespeaks the director's desire to keep the hero unambiguously heroic. Perhaps the film's only major historic misstep in charting the Navy's antipathy to air power comes during the part of the film where Scotty is stationed at the Naval Academy in Annapolis, teaching midshipmen about naval air strategy. After a lecture, his boss comes into the classroom, reminding him, "You are not here to sell aviation, Scott. Your mission is merely to familiarize the midshipmen with the potentialities and limitations of air power." The film makes clear that this scene occurs following the beginning of the Second World War in Europe, but before American military involvement after Pearl Harbor. Historically, although many Americans continued to espouse the position of non-interventionism, by this period air power was considered by many as key to victory and just about all the world powers had radically increased aircraft production.[27] At this point in the film, Scotty despairs and considers leaving military service, much as Mitchell did during his time at Fort Sam Houston. In one scene an old friend, long since having left the Navy to work for private industry, attempts to recruit Scotty to work at an aeronautic design and manufacturing company. In his recruitment pitch, the friend describes the type of man they are looking for in a description that could very well refer to Mitchell himself: "We don't want a yes man. We want a man who's nuts about aviation. Aggressive."

Two more scenes warrant analysis, for very different reasons. Following the Battle of Midway, Scotty, who has been serving as the Air Operations Officer on the U.S.S. *Yorktown*, recuperates at home with his wife Mary (Jane Wyatt). Despite the crushing blow dealt to Japan, in large part due to the success of two aircraft carriers he helped design, Scotty is morose, telling his wife that due to his age and rank the Navy will never let him fly in combat. Instead, he will continue to be used solely in an administrative capacity. Realizing that he will never live his dream, much like Mitchell never lived to see his vision fulfilled, Mary makes the following statement: "They'll always look up to you, dear. To lead them. Inspire them." This quote could very well pertain to Billy Mitchell and the young officers he inspired, ones like Hap Arnold and Carl "Tooey" Spaatz, who contributed in no small way to the U.S. war effort. The final scene of *Task Force*, prior to the bookend return to the present and Scotty's retirement, involves the aftermath of Scotty's experiences during the

Battle of Okinawa, when a kamikaze breaks through the defenses of the aircraft carrier he now captains, the U.S.S. *Clipper*, to set the ship ablaze. Despite appeals to reason, Scotty steadfastly refuses to give the signal to abandon ship, and the scene then cuts to a shot of the Statue of Liberty framed by the rusted and twisted metal of the ship Scotty was able to save. Overlaid is narration about the end of the war, and we next cut back to Scotty's retirement, which, although unstated, does not appear to be voluntary. Although the implied logistics of this scene are ludicrous (a damaged aircraft carrier would have been taken to Subic Bay in the Philippines or Pearl Harbor or even San Diego, not halfway around the world), Daves can be forgiven due to the complexity of the statement he is making. Scotty has had his day and made his mark. He gave the entirety of his adult life to the preservation of freedom, as symbolized by the Statue of Liberty. However, Scotty has also outlived his usefulness, and is now akin to the twisted scrap metal that frames that Lady Liberty. In much the same way as it was for Billy Mitchell, and as it also was for many soldiers struggling to readjust in a post-war environment, it is time for Scotty to go gently into that good night.

Although by no means a great film or even Daves' best, *Task Force* benefits from strong writing and steady directing. The film contains just the right amounts of action, humor, and tragedy. In one sequence involving Scotty's air group performing their first carrier landings, tension, humor, tragedy, and pathos are interwoven by the director with a deft touch. After making a rough landing on his third attempt, Scotty is attended to by the other members of his squadron. With his plane busted up and his aviator goggles comically askew on his face, he assures his men, "Nothing to it! Simple as winging a ten-thousand-foot dive into a rain barrel!" Danger is undercut by humor, which is then undercut by tragedy in the next scene, when Scotty's friend is killed during an even rougher landing. The third and final scene in the sequence introduces a great deal of pathos as Scotty, for once at a loss for words, nevertheless informs his friend's wife of the tragedy. A later scene suggests that, as a writer, and despite the conservative dictates of the Hays Code, Daves was just as adept as Alfred Hitchcock and Nicholas Ray at working sexuality into a scene. Recovering in the hospital after crash-landing into the ocean, Scotty is visited by two friends. They give him a pair of steel roller skates and a copy of Ernest Hemingway's *A Farewell to Arms*. One of the friends describes the book, perhaps not so coincidentally aping Hemingway's minimalist style: "It's very soothing. It's about love . . . and war . . . and love . . . and stuff." He then goes on to describe the girl who recommended the book, and who helped him wrap it: "I held her string while she tied the knot!" At this moment, Scotty's wife enters the room, and the friend beats a hasty retreat, although not before this statement: "I'm going to make knots back to the gal who ties them. I'm going to show her an inside running hitch!" Even Hitchcock would have been hard-pressed to construct such an elegant multi-entendre, bringing together knot-tying, sex, marriage, and the naval unit for speed! Daves may not belong in the so-called pantheon of Hollywood directorial greats, but sequences such as these demonstrate his skill and ease in working within different emotive narrative structures.

As with many war films released at the time, *Task Force* did well, but has largely been lost among the clutter of other war films released during that period. The number of films focusing upon military aviation released during and following the war indicates not only an obsession with air power, but also an acknowledgement of its importance in the allied victory. Indeed, such films as *A Yank in the RAF* (1941) indicate that Hollywood's obsession with the air war extended back even prior to American involvement in the Second World War. Other popular aviation films released during the war included *Air Force* (1943), *Bombardier* (1943), *Thirty Seconds over Tokyo* (1944), and *Wing and a Prayer* (1944). In addition to being just another one of many air war films, *Task Force* suffers from being sandwiched in between two, I would argue, superior films about the air war in the Second World War. Both *Command Decision* (1948) and *Twelve O'Clock High* (1949) focused upon the European Theater and the Army-Air Corps. The main thing that distinguishes *Task Force* from all of these other films is the fact that it is constructed and even narrated like a biography. Two Hollywood biopics featuring real-life aviators were released later: *The Court Martial of Billy Mitchell* and *Wings of Eagles* (1957), the latter being John Ford's cinematic tribute to his friend Frank "Spig" Wead. Additionally, a British film chronicling the career of aviator Douglas Bader, called *Reach for the Sky* (1956), was released during this period. Surprisingly, Otto Preminger's Billy Mitchell biopic *The Court Martial of Billy Mitchell* has never been linked to *Task Force*, despite the latter's obvious touchstones to the life of the controversial flyer and the fact that Gary Cooper starred in both. Although it did well at the box office, Preminger's film was mired in controversy. Mitchell's supporters felt as if Cooper was too laconic, and Mitchell's detractors felt that the aviator was presented in the film as being far nobler and more self-sacrificing than he was in reality. An army lawyer tasked with reading the script compared the one-sided depiction of the court scenes to a "Star Chamber proceeding," making references to the clandestine, corrupt English courts of the seventeenth century.[28] According to Douglas Waller, "Even the Mitchell family hated the movie. The taciturn and sedate Cooper was totally miscast as Mitchell. The family thought it should have been someone with more overt spunk, like Jimmy Cagney."[29]

Before Charles Lindbergh and Amelia Earhart seared themselves permanently into the American consciousness, Billy Mitchell was the most important aviator during a decade when air pioneers were celebrated for their skill and daring. His trial came at the end of a four-year period that, arguably, saw four of the half dozen most notable trials in American history (Sacco and Vanzetti, Leopold and Loeb, and the Scopes Monkey Trial being the other three). Much as with the Scopes and Sacco and Vanzetti trials, the Mitchell affair was rooted in fear. However, unlike societal anxieties regarding the teaching of Darwinian evolutionary theory, or the intersection of immigration and labor radicalism, the fear in Mitchell's case was restricted to an institutional niche filled with military officers who, much like the strategists of the First World War, looked more to the past than the future in finding their solutions. As Bruce Franklin points out, two of the three true military aviation pioneers—Mitchell and the Italian General Giulio Douhet—ended up being court-martialed. Furthermore, he argued that one reason why Great Britain began the Second World War at somewhat of a competitive advantage is that they chose to *listen* to their visionary Air Marshal Sir Hugh Trenchard.[30] Of these, only Mitchell was enshrined in film, twice, both times by Gary Cooper. *Task Force* is an underappreciated film, lost in the white noise of other, admittedly superior war films, and overshadowed by its director's admittedly superior efforts in the Western genre. In its existence as the first cinematic attempt to demonstrate the growth of air power despite massive resistance, and thus its rehabilitation of Billy Mitchell (partial, in that Scotty stands in for the aviator), *Task Force* deserves a second look. As such, the film perhaps stands as the quintessential Daves film, since he himself was an underappreciated director.

BIBLIOGRAPHY

Boyer, Jay, "Delmer Daves," in Robert E. Morseberger (ed.), *Dictionary of Literary Biography: American Screenwriters* (Detroit, MI: Gale, 1984), pp. 76–82.

Burlingame, Roger, *General Billy Mitchell: Champion of Air Defense* (Westport, CT: Greenwood, 1952).

'By the Numbers', National World War II Museum. <www.nationalww2museum.org/learn/education/for-students/ww2-history/ww2-by-the-numbers/wartime-production.html> (last accessed 11 November 2015).

Cooke, James J., *Billy Mitchell* (Boulder, CO: Lynne Rienner, 2002).

Davis, Burke, *The Billy Mitchell Story* (New York: Random House, 1967).

Davis, Burke, *The Billy Mitchell Affair* (Philadelphia: Chilton, 1969).

Franklin, H. Bruce, *War Stars: The Superweapon and the American Imagination* (Amherst: Massachusetts University Press, 2008).

Gauvreau, Emile, and Lester Cohen, *Billy Mitchell: Founder of Our Air Force and Prophet Without Honor* (New York: E. P. Dutton, 1942).

Glines, Carroll V., "Air Power Visionary Billy Mitchell," *Aviation History* 8:1 (1997): 38–44.

Hurley, Alfred F., *Billy Mitchell: Crusader for Air Power* (Bloomington: Indiana University Press, 1964).

Jeffers, H. Paul, *Billy Mitchell: The Life, Times, and Battles of America's Prophet of Air Power* (St. Paul: Zenith, 2005).

MacDougall, Robert, *Leaders in Dangerous Times: Douglas MacArthur and Dwight D. Eisenhower* (Bloomington: Trafford, 2013).
Mitchell, Ruth, *My Brother Bill: The Life of General "Billy" Mitchell* (New York: Harcourt, 1953).
Sarris, Andrew, *The American Cinema: Directors and Directions, 1929–1968* (New York: Da Capo, 1968).
Waller, Douglas, *A Question of Loyalty: Gen. Billy Mitchell and the Court-Martial That Gripped the Nation* (New York: HarperCollins, 2004).

FILMOGRAPHY

Air Force, director Howard Hawks, featuring John Garfield, John Ridgley, Gig Young, Harry Carey (Warner Bros., 1943).
Bombardier, director Richard Wallace, featuring Pat O'Brien, Randolph Scott, Anne Shirley, Eddie Albert (RKO Pictures, 1943).
Broken Arrow, director Delmer Daves, featuring Jimmy Stewart, Jeff Chandler, Debra Paget, Basil Ruysdael (20th Century Fox, 1950).
Command Decision, director Sam Wood, featuring Clark Gable, Walter Pidgeon, Van Johnson, Brian Donlevy (Metro-Goldwyn-Mayer, 1948).
Court Martial of Billy Mitchell, The, director Otto Preminger, featuring Gary Cooper, Charles Bickford, Ralph Bellamy, Rod Steiger (Warner Bros., 1955).
Dark Passage, director Delmer Daves, featuring Humphrey Bogart, Lauren Bacall, Bruce Bennett, Agnes Moorehead (Warner Bros., 1947).
Man Who Shot Liberty Valance, The, director John Ford, featuring John Wayne, Jimmy Stewart, Vera Miles, Lee Marvin (Paramount Pictures, 1962).
Reach for the Sky, director Lewis Gilbert, featuring Kenneth More, Muriel Pavlow, Lyndon Brook, Lee Patterson (The Rank Organization, 1956).
Rear Window, director Alfred Hitchcock, featuring Jimmy Stewart, Grace Kelley, Wendell Corey, Thelma Ritter (Paramount Pictures, 1954).
Rope, director Alfred Hitchcock, featuring Jimmy Stewart, John Dall, Farley Granger, Edith Evanson (Warner Bros., 1948).
Searchers, The, director John Ford, featuring John Wayne, Natalie Wood, Jeffrey Hunter, Vera Miles (Warner Bros., 1956).
Task Force, director Delmer Daves, featuring Gary Cooper, Jane Wyatt, Wayne Morris, Walter Brennan (Warner Bros., 1949).
Thirty Seconds over Tokyo, director Mervyn LeRoy, featuring Van Johnson, Robert Walker, Spencer Tracy, Tim Murdock (Metro-Goldwyn-Mayer, 1944).
3:10 to Yuma, director Delmer Daves, featuring Glenn Ford, Van Heflin, Felicia Farr, Leora Dana (Columbia Pictures, 1957).
3:10 to Yuma, director James Mangold, featuring Russell Crowe, Christian Bale, Ben Foster, Gretchen Mol (Lionsgate Films, 2007).
Twelve o'Clock High, director Henry King, featuring Gregory Peck, Hugh Marlowe, Gary Merrill, Millard Mitchell (20th Century Fox, 1949).
Wing and a Prayer, director Henry Hathaway, featuring Don Ameche, Dana Andrews, William Eythe, Charles Bickford (20th Century Fox, 1944).
Wings of Eagles, The, director John Ford, featuring John Wayne, Dan Dailey, Maureen O'Hara, Ward Bond (Metro-Goldwyn-Mayer, 1957).

Yank in the R.A.F., A, director Henry King, featuring, Tyrone Power, Betty Grable, John Sutton, Reginald Gardiner (20th Century Fox, 1941).

NOTES

1. Cooper was often tapped to play characters who act according to their own codes of conduct rather than what is expected of them. Examples of these include *Mr. Deeds Goes to Town* (1936), *Sergeant York* (1941), and *The Fountainhead* (1949). Daves' Westerns—including *Broken Arrow* (1950) and *3:10 to Yuma* (1957)—similarly explored characters beholden to their own personal codes of conduct.
2. Cooke, *Billy Mitchell*, pp. 87–94.
3. Ibid. p. 100.
4. Waller, *A Question of Loyalty*, p. 359; Glines, "Air Power Visionary Billy Mitchell," pp. 39–40.
5. Franklin, *War Stars*, p. 99.
6. Davis, *The Billy Mitchell Affair*, p. 117.
7. Franklin, *War Stars*, p. 94.
8. Jeffers, *Billy Mitchell*, p. 13.
9. Cooke, *Billy Mitchell*, p. xi.
10. Ibid. p. 178.
11. Ibid. p. 217.
12. Waller, *A Question of Loyalty*, p. 359.
13. MacDougall, *Leaders in Dangerous Times*, p. 49.
14. Gauvreau and Cohen, *Billy Mitchell*.
15. Glines, "Air Power Visionary Billy Mitchell," pp. 41–4.
16. Gauvreau and Cohen, *Billy Mitchell*, pp. 44–5.
17. Ibid. p. 11.
18. Ibid. p. 12.
19. Ibid. p. 15.
20. Burlingame, *General Billy Mitchell*, p. vi.
21. Mitchell, *My Brother Bill*, p. 9.
22. Davis's *The Billy Mitchell Affair* is referenced above. Additionally, Hurley, *Billy Mitchell: Crusader for Air Power* and Davis, *The Billy Mitchell Story*.
23. All three of these books—by Cooke, Waller, and Jeffers—are referenced above.
24. Cooke, *Billy Mitchell*, p. 6.
25. Sarris, *The American Cinema*, pp. 176–7.
26. Boyer, "Delmer Daves."
27. Case in point: the United States produced 2,141 aircraft in 1939, 6,068 aircraft in 1940, and 19,433 aircraft in 1941, suggesting that FDR's government and the Armed Forces knew avoiding the conflict would be difficult and that air power would be crucial should they join the fight ("By the Numbers.")
28. Waller, *A Question of Loyalty*, pp. 362.
29. Ibid.
30. Franklin, *War Stars*, pp. 87–8.

CHAPTER 10

"This Is Where He Brought Me: 10,000 Acres of Nothing!": The Femme Fatale and other Film Noir Tropes in Delmer Daves' *Jubal*

Matthew Carter

Jubal (1956) is one of three Westerns that Delmer Daves made in successive years with actor Glenn Ford, the two others being *3:10 to Yuma* (1957) and *Cowboy* (1958). As with most of Daves' cinematic output, there has thus far been little academic writing on *Jubal*. This is a point well made by Kent Jones who, in one of his two introductory essays accompanying the 2013 Criterion Blu-Ray releases of *3:10* and *Jubal*, writes: "Many of Delmer Daves' films are beloved, but to say that he remains a misunderstood and insufficiently appreciated figure in the history of American movies is a rank understatement."[1] Despite his having directed two of the most celebrated Westerns of the so-called "classical" era—in addition to *3:10*, there is *Broken Arrow* (1950)—and despite his work across multiple genres, the film theorists who championed the talents of his contemporaries have somehow not awarded Daves the status of auteur. Whilst the likes of Anthony Mann, John Ford, and Howard Hawks are often among those most-praised, particularly as directors of Westerns, auteur theory seems to have passed Delmer Daves by.[2] As Jones puts it, Daves "could be counted as one of its casualties."[3] Frankly, Daves' reputation as one of the great directors of Hollywood Westerns could be cemented by *Broken Arrow* alone. However, what strikes one upon several viewings of his lesser-regarded *Jubal* are not its Western credentials (although these are clearly in evidence) but its relation to other classical-era Hollywood genres and styles.[4] In particular, it is notable how far *Jubal*'s narrative is affected by film noir.

It is often said that through its most notorious trope, the femme fatale, the style of film noir presented a challenge to the dominant ideological values expressed by Hollywood: the male protagonist as hero, the heterosexual, monogamous couple, the family unit as social ideal, and, in particular, to the typically passive roles assigned female characters. On the other hand, it is thought that Westerns (along with other established Hollywood genres) are generally supportive of these values. Beyond celebrating frontier mythology through the "domestication of the wilderness," the Western is understood to have championed male agency whilst reducing the role of the female in the narrative to that of a virtual cipher. Thus, the Western (and Hollywood as a whole) is said to have been inherently patriarchal in character, providing clearly defined gender roles based on active males and passive females. This broad interpretation of Hollywood is open to scrutiny and, indeed, has been scrutinized by many, especially those seeking to account for a "revised" Hollywood Western theme. What has been scrutinized far less in film studies is the belief that the distinctions between film noir and the Western are best articulated by the radical divergence of the respective ways in which they "image" the woman.

What I shall seek to do in this essay is contextualize *Jubal* within both the Western genre and Hollywood more generally, and argue that both formally and thematically, it and other prominent Westerns of the time are more closely aligned with film noir than is generally acknowledged to be the case. To which end, I shall not be concerned with the merits or shortcomings of auteur theory—nor with Daves' other films, for that matter. I shall apply a psychoanalytically-informed feminist analysis that considers the ideological intent of *Jubal*'s use of the femme fatale and, in so doing, evaluate its critical-, or, counter-ideological capacity. First, it will be important to justify such an analysis by providing a cultural–historical and an ideological context for film noir and the Western, two types of Hollywood cinema that do seem, on the surface at least, to be curious bedfellows.

In her Introduction to *Women in Film Noir* (1978), the editor E. Ann Kaplan writes, "film noir is particularly notable for its specific treatment of women."[5] Whereas "in the films of another genre, the western—for example, Ford's *My Darling Clementine* or *The Searchers*—women, in their fixed roles as wives, mothers, daughters, lovers, mistresses, whores, simply provide the background for the ideological work of the film which is carried out through men."[6] Kaplan's passing comments on the Western match with commonly held views on the genre's treatment of women. In *West of Everything* (1992), Jane Tompkins observes that no matter the wide and shifting range of sociopolitical and cultural ideologies to be found in the genre as a whole, one thing remains constant: "[Westerns] either push women out of the picture completely or assign them roles in which they exist only to serve the needs of men."[7] Tompkins reasons that while women "may seem strong and resilient, fiery and resourceful at first . . . when push comes to shove, as it always does, they shatter into words."[8] For her, the Western is essentially an exercise in repression through "the destruction of female authority."[9] This repression is typified by the hero's "flight from women" and the enactment of the homoerotic bond between men. To this, she adds the championing of the "rugged man" of the outdoors and the privileging of the phallic gunfight as the climax of all narrative climaxes. The gunfight confirms the Western's masculine bias: "Performed in the name of keeping the woman safe, [it is, in actuality] the antithesis of everything she stands for."[10] Conversely, what makes film noir so "particularly notable" for Kaplan is that the roles of women defy such easy, secondary categorization. In stark contrast to the Western, she argues, they are not "placed safely" in the background but are instead foregrounded, becoming "central to the intrigue of" the narratives. As opposed to being defined by (and thereby relegated to) their background roles, noir women are defined by their "sexuality, which is presented as desirable but dangerous to men [with] the hero's success or not depend[ing] on the degree to which he can extricate himself from the woman's manipulations."[11]

Kaplan's essays make clear the cultural role played by the femme fatale, and situate the trope historically. They suggest that this trope expresses fears related to the challenge to the patriarchal order effected by the change in the role of women during the Second World War: where men went to war, women went to work. Kaplan et al. understand that the films characterized as noir are driven by a paranoid misogyny and re-enact at a specific historical moment what Christine Gledhill describes as the "perennial myth of woman as threat to male control of the world and destroyer of male aspiration."[12] Janey Place argues that the "attitudes toward women evidenced in film noir—i.e., fear of loss of stability, identity and security—are reflective of the dominant feelings of the time."[13] For Kaplan, "film noir *expresses* alienation, locates its cause squarely in the excesses of female sexuality ('natural' consequences of women's independence), and punishes that excess in order to re-place it within the patriarchal order."[14] These views on Hollywood's gender politics can (perhaps) be best explained by the fact that patriarchal societies invest agency in the male, whose superior strength as warrior and hunter enables him to maintain his power. Within the terms defined by this ideology, the only potent threat to male power is the sexuality of the female, something that the Western is said to avoid through its repression of her agency and, therefore, her "threat." Place argues that film noir's "'liberated' woman is guilty of . . . refusing to be defined" in terms of patriarchy, and that "this refusal can be perversely seen (in art, or in life) as an attack on men's very existence."[15] Through its foregrounding of the dangerous woman, film noir expresses the perceived consequences that will follow the abandonment of male predominance.

It is important to stress that film noir is not progressive in this sense, as the empowered woman is reconstructed according to patriarchal fears as the femme fatale. However, it must also be stressed that this figure is not wholly negative either. As Place concedes, film noir "does give us one of the few periods of film in which women are active, not static symbols, are intelligent and powerful, if destructively so, and draw power, not weakness, from their sexuality."[16] Whilst the emergence of this "empowerment" is generally contained by the end of a given film's narrative through the enactment of closure (usually by way of the destruction of the femme fatale), Place and others argue that the act of female empowerment and emancipation *is* signaled and remains in the mind of the viewer long after the film has finished. Annette Kuhn has identified occasions in which Hollywood's "attempts to recuperate women to a 'proper place' . . . are not always . . . completely successful . . . particularly in cases where the narrative sets up questions that cannot be contained by any form of closure."[17] Kuhn refers to instances where an "excess of narrative disruption" effected by female characters "signal[s] Hollywood's intermittent failure to contain women within the confines of the classic narrative structure."[18] In accordance with Kaplan, she forwards film noir as the exemplar of a "persistent narrative excess in Hollywood cinema," arguing that whilst film noir is, "historically speaking, very much a part of dominant cinema . . . it contains the potential, within its own narrative structure, to subvert the textual organization of dominant cinema."[19] Sylvia Harvey suggests that the result of this is that, in many film noirs, the femme fatale has an impact and meaning that can transcend the category to which she is assigned. Thus does Harvey write: "Despite the ritual punishments of acts of transgression, the vitality with which these acts are endowed produces an excess of meaning which cannot be finally contained. Narrative resolutions cannot recuperate their subversive significance."[20] Echoing this, Place argues that this is what we most vividly remember from film noir: not a memory of the femme fatale's "destruction," but a memory of her "strength and power."[21]

This foregrounding of female agency opens up interesting and important avenues for critical discussion. As Kaplan points out, despite the noir narrative's typical attempt to restore the ideological status quo through "the exposure and then destruction of the sexual, manipulating woman," the male protagonist often fails to resist the allure of the femme fatale.[22] Typically, he is destroyed along with her. Kaplan therefore reasons, as does Place, that since the reduction of female agency is necessary to the functionality of patriarchy, "it follows that the displacement of women" to the foreground "would disturb the patriarchal system, and provide a challenge to that world view."[23] In short, foregrounding the "sexual, manipulating woman" necessarily exposes patriarchal ideology at work. Because of this, and even if in spite of itself, film noir is said to enact a more overt questioning of patriarchy's socio-symbolic authority than is the case with established genres like the Western. Thus, the peculiar intrigues of the film noir style for feminist film scholarship: "the theoretical project of identifying a mode of dominant ideological representation goes along with the impulse to find inconsistencies in a film through which ideological contradiction and tension may be seen to be manifested."[24]

Given the arguments of Kaplan et al. as I have outlined them above, my choice of a Western—particularly one produced in the 1950s—might seem at first to be an unusual or even inappropriate case study for such an analysis. Westerns of this period are most directly associated with traditional Hollywood narrative structures, and are thus perceived to be generally supportive of the ideological status quo. In this regard, it is worth mentioning a 2010 paper by Paul M. Monticone. In "The Noir Western: Genre Theory and the Problem of the Anomalous Hybrid," Monticone confirms the popular orthodoxy that Westerns and film noir are "generally thought to have little to do with one another."[25] He confirms it only to deconstruct it, however, for, as he rightfully informs us, there have been numerous instances, particularly in the late-1940s (the high-water mark for film noir) of what have been termed noir-Westerns. One of his primary concerns is with identifying noir traits in director André de Toth's not insignificantly named B-Western, *Ramrod* (1947), but he provides a great many other examples besides.[26] Furthermore, Monticone insists that dismissing "instances of genre hybridity in order to streamline our narratives or genre models [runs] the risk of deforming our object of study."[27] This is not to suggest that there have been no acknowledgements of hybrid noir-Westerns before this; it is just that, as Monticone rightly reminds us, the "mixing of *noir* and the Western has not yet received adequate scholarly attention."[28]

However one chooses to classify or read *Jubal*, it should be pointed out that genre classification alone is not enough to make an analysis of a Western within terms of film noir entirely inappropriate. Paul Schrader has argued that as film noir depends to a very great extent on the "look" of a given film (and on the mood that this look generates), it should be "defined by tone rather than genre."[29] As such, "it is almost impossible to argue one critic's descriptive definition against another's."[30] Place has suggested that the very mutability of film noir renders generic classifications less important for a study of its tropes and characteristics (though not, of course, completely irrelevant). She argues, above all else, that film noir be "characterized by the remarkably homogeneous visual style with which it *cuts across genres*," and that this "can be seen in the film noir influence" on established genres—including, significantly, "certain westerns."[31] Furthermore, Place suggests that when the themes of a particular genre, such as the Western, "are not conducive to the noir mood, an interesting and confused mix results."[32] Curiously, Place also chose *Ramrod* as her given example of a noir-Western:

> Veronica Lake plays the typically aggressive, sexual "dark lady" of film noir who causes the murders; Arleen Whelan is her opposite, the nurturing stay-at-home good woman. The usual stable moral environment of the typical western is lacking, and the noir influence is evident in the murky moral confusion of the male characters and their inability to

control the direction of the narrative. *Ramrod* has the open, extreme long shots characteristic of the genre, but the clarity they generally signify is undercut by the noir ambiguity.[33]

I too shall oppose the perception that the Western and film noir "have little to do with each other." By offering a close textual analysis of *Jubal*, I identify it, as Place would have it, as just such a "certain western": a noir-Western. I shall support my argument by showing recourse to a number of other prominent Hollywood Westerns, extending the scope of Monticone's paper, and identifying the existence of film noir influences operating within the genre. It is not my intention, therefore, to deconstruct Kaplan's interpretation of film noir. Quite the contrary: I agree with it. What I do disagree with, however, is the assumption—one that Tompkins expounded upon, and that continues broadly to this day—that the Western necessarily stands opposed to film noir by its relegation of female characters to background roles. What I intend to demonstrate through my analysis of *Jubal* is that, like film noir, the Western can, on a significant number of occasions, also be said to be "particularly notable" for its treatment of women. In making my own humble contribution to this underdeveloped area of Western film and film genre studies, I shall also demonstrate *Jubal*'s (and the Western's) critical-ideological capacities by describing how noir influences problematize the patriarchal assumptions of the genre's frontier setting and theme. For in the Western, the woman is *not* always "placed safely" in the background, nor are the woman's discourse and agency necessarily systematically repressed. Even when they are, a psychoanalytically-informed feminist analysis reveals this as a repressed that always returns—as with the femme fatale of film noir—to plague the dominant patriarchal ideology by exposing its internal contradictions and tensions. Such an analysis provides an opportunity to scrutinize the assumption that the Western's formal and thematic engagement with patriarchal ideology is necessarily so distinct from that of film noir. Indeed, it is my contention that it is largely because of *Jubal*'s Western credentials—in particular, the genre's characteristic privileging of male agency—that, when combined with film noir styles and tropes such as the femme fatale, it presents a more effective challenge to patriarchal culture and its dominant ideological values.

It is worth mentioning that the director himself puts the actual classification of *Jubal* as a Western to question. During the film's pre-production stage, Daves, in a letter to his friend and producer Jerry Wald, wrote that *Jubal* "cannot be sold as a western *under any circumstances*."[34] Furthermore, "to do so would be to invite disaster: the western-fans would be dismayed by all the sex and love—the love and sex and decent purpose fans would avoid it because it was advertised with 'western' trimmings."[35] Daves continues: "Since our key is also an emotional story rather than action-western-etc., we must work along that line in regard to the whole pattern of title-exploitation-advertising when it comes time."[36] Beyond displaying an acute appreciation of film marketing and audience expectations (and exploitations), Daves' comments also create their own interesting avenues for critical discussion, especially in terms of *Jubal*'s foregrounding of the "sexual, manipulating woman."

In terms of plot, *Jubal* follows the eponymous hero Jubal Troop (Glenn Ford) as he emerges from the wilderness. He is evidently injured and falls down a hill, lying unconscious on a roadside until found by ranch owner Shep Horgan (Ernest Borgnine). Taken under Shep's fatherly wing, Jubal comes to be favored and trusted by Shep, and starts working for him as a ranch hand. Shep's wife, Mae Horgan (Valerie French), feeling trapped in her marriage, takes a shine to this enigmatic and attractive stranger, and is very forward in declaring her sexual intentions toward him. From the outset, it is clear that the black-haired and red-lipped Mae, like the femme fatale of film noir, is immoral and deceitful (Place's aforementioned "dark lady"), using her beauty and charm to get what she wants. However, Jubal doesn't directly reciprocate Mae's feelings, being seemingly more interested in the timid, innocent and therefore ideologically "safe" Naomi Hoktor (Felicia Farr), who is traveling with a wagon train of Mormons who are temporarily camped on Shep's land—although Jubal does not initially appear very interested in her, either. Most of the ranch workers take to Jubal, but one man in particular, "Pinky" Pinkum (Rod Steiger), who until now was top hand and used to receiving Mae's extra-marital attentions himself, doesn't think much of Jubal, much less Mae's affections toward him. The growing antagonism between the two men inevitably results in violent confrontation for all. Driven by jealousy and frustration, Pinky lies to Shep, telling his boss that Jubal and Mae are having an affair. Shep's initial disbelief of Pinky's claims is destroyed, however, when Mae, though completely unaware of Pinky's Iago-like pouring of poison into her husband's ear, confirms the non-existent affair as a reality in the service of her own efforts to humiliate her husband. Blinded by rage, Shep confronts Jubal in a saloon and, with rifle in hand, threatens to kill him. In self-defense and with the help of his new friend, Reb Haislipp (Charles Bronson), Jubal is forced to kill his employer and fatherly benefactor. The now distraught and fugitive Jubal takes sanctuary with the Mormon train and is comforted by Naomi, who confirms her status as the "nurturing stay-at-home good woman" (as Place would have it) by reassuring in him in his actions, saying that he had no choice. Meanwhile, Pinky seizes upon the opportunity that Shep's death has provided: control over Shep's ranch and, finally, control over Mae. He publicly blames Jubal for murdering Shep, and organizes a posse to hunt him down. He then goes to see Mae privately, telling her that he is the new boss and she should "treat him right." However, after Mae rejects him absolutely ("If I didn't want Shep, what makes you think I'd want you? I'd rather get a dog to spit on me!"), Pinky viciously assaults her, beating her so badly that she eventually dies of her injuries. However, before she dies, Jubal finds her, and Mae reveals what Pinky has done to her and what he plans to do to him. Following these revelations, the posse soon turns on Pinky and, so the film suggests, he will hang for his crimes. The film ends with Jubal, Naomi, and Reb riding off into the mountainous landscape, with the romantic partnership of Jubal and Naomi firmly established, and the brotherly (read homoerotic) bond between Jubal and Reb strongly inferred.

Despite its enactment of closure, the film's foregrounding of Mae's sexual desire ensures that it has a major impact in undermining the ostensible masculinist narrative trajectory on display. Brought about by and fought over sexual jealousy, the gunfight between Jubal and Shep is devoid of any of the "classical" Western's mythic pretense to good triumphing over evil. It would also seem that it is Pinky's brutal killing of Mae (also caused by sexual jealousy and a great deal of sexual frustration), and not the gunfight, that constitutes the narrative climax. Therefore, the film appears to render Mae and her sexual allure as "central to the intrigue" of the narrative in such a way as to be comparable to Kaplan's description of the role, purpose, and fate of the femme fatale in film noir. In so doing, it *exposes* the workings of the patriarchal ideology that informs yet, as Tompkins and others have argued, remains hidden within the Western.

As described by Schrader, film noir's vision of society is "something less than worth fighting for."[37] There is no honesty, with men's sweethearts unfaithful, business partners disloyal, and forces of law and order either irrelevant or as corrupted as the criminals with whom they coexist.[38] As a style, film noir depicts this morally bankrupt environment chiefly through its lighting and shot selection. It typically features chiaroscuro effect: sharply contrasted light and dark, with the accent on the latter. This visual style was strongly influenced by the German expressionism of the 1920s and early 1930s brought over by European émigré directors such as Fritz Lang, Otto Preminger, and Billy Wilder, whose somber vision of the world had been colored by their experiences of European fascism. Place (writing with Lowell Peterson) describes visual style—the "look"—as the leitmotif of film noir. They explain just how the use of *mise-en-scène*, camera angle and movement, camera lens type, composition, and, above all, lighting, are used to create the "anti-traditional" noir style. In order to create moods of "paranoia, delirium and menace . . . the *noir* cinematographers placed their key, fill and backlight in every conceivable variation to produce the most striking and offbeat schemes of light and dark." Place and Peterson also point out how noir filming replaced "day for night" with "night for night," with all the opportunities for lighting effects that this provided.[39]

Despite the Western's usual preference for sunny, exterior frontier landscapes, this expressionist style is not alien to the genre. For example, John Ford's *Stagecoach* (1939): often considered one of the classic examples of the genre, *Stagecoach* makes use of the film noir "look" as outlined by Place and Peterson. Aside from the obvious point of it being shot in black and white, one could briefly reflect upon the climactic shoot-out sequence. This takes place not in broad daylight on Main Street, but at night and in the urban backstreets of the frontier township of Lordsburg. Perhaps more significantly, it takes place off-screen. That is to say, we *hear* the shootout but we do not *see* it. Here one can observe the importance placed upon the interplay between light and dark in creating a noirish atmosphere in which violence is obliquely handled, yet where a deathly atmosphere is all-pervasive.[40]

For its part, *Jubal* opens with what seems like typical Western iconography: bright daylight, and a stunning, Technicolor Bierstadtian spectacle of the Teton Mountains, announce the arrival of the eponymous hero. This descriptive would appear very similar to the opening sequence of George Stevens' *Shane* (1953), where Shane (Alan Ladd) also emerges from the Tetons as the embodiment of the rugged individual frontier hero. However, as mentioned above, *Jubal* initiates with its male hero in danger. Jubal is on foot, not on horseback, and clearly in distress. Also as mentioned above, he collapses down the side of a hill where he lies unconscious, face down on a dirt road. A while later, Shep passes by on a horse and cart, stops to collect the unconscious Jubal, and takes him back to his cattle ranch. This imperiled masculinity—we soon learn of his horse being "lost in the blizzard" and (in curious terminology) "screaming just like a human"—signals a change of tone in the music, and the setting of the sun. In the above-mentioned terms forwarded by Place and Peterson, "day" has now been replaced by "night," and, as it turns out, many of *Jubal*'s significant sequences will take place inside and at night, "night for night."

It has also been widely noted that film noir tended to feature characters trapped by a past from which there was no escape. Of course, it is no secret that many Westerns also tend to feature heroes who are similarly trapped and who are embroiled in existential conflicts. In relation to its eponymous hero, *Jubal* appears to fit this descriptive very well. What makes *Jubal* so intriguing in this regard is the way Daves attempts to depict the male protagonist as atypical if compared with many of his Western contemporaries, particularly in his relation to language. When it comes to communicating, many of the most famous Western heroes are mumbling, almost silent types. As Tompkins writes: "For the really strong man, language is a snare; it blunts his purpose and diminishes his strength."[41] This is to say that, ultimately, the Westerner is a man who *acts*; "the position represented by language [is] always associated with women" and, as Tompkins has already suggested, is presented in the Western as ineffectual ("when push comes to shove, women shatter into words"), eventually to be

Figure 10.1 The "ideologically safe" woman: Jubal opens up to Naomi.

"proven wrong—massively, totally, and unequivocally."[42] She observes, "the Western equates power with 'not language.' And not language it equates with being male."[43]

If the likes of Alan Ladd and John Wayne embodied what Tompkins describes as the genre's "impatience with words as a way of dealing with the world," then Glenn Ford as Jubal embodies something altogether different. Ladd and Wayne may project the "antilanguage" that Tompkins claims comprises the "heart" of the Western, but Jubal himself would appear to embody language.[44] That is to say, he speaks—a lot. One of the most telling scenes in this regard is where he shares a moment with Naomi one sunny afternoon by a lakeside. Visually, the scene embodies the Western's love of open landscapes, but the emotional charge of the film is internalized. Jubal reveals several things about his past to Naomi, a woman he barely knows. He speaks of how his father saved him from drowning as a child, tragically losing his own life in the process. He then speaks of his mother's scorn and resentment of him. "My mom," Jubal tells her, "didn't want me to be born." And of her blaming Jubal for his father's untimely death: "She wanted me to die." This, he explains, is why he leads such a listless, wandering existence. He then reveals something of the surrogate fatherly respect he feels for Shep, and how "I ain't stopped runnin' . . . until Shep give me this job." Naomi says she is glad Jubal opened up to her: "It makes me beholden to you." Naomi, playing the role of the "nurturing stay-at-home good woman" of whom Place speaks, essentially encourages Jubal to accept that it is not a sign of weakness to have to rely on someone else for support, and to share the emotional burden.

This revelation, this emoting through language, is of course in stark contrast to what Tompkins suggests is the silent pain of most Western heroes. Tompkins highlights that, in enacting his typically violent, climactic act of the gunfight, the hero is doomed to exile. Finding support in others, emotional bonding: these become the aspects of himself and his desire that he must sacrifice. "It is . . . the feminine part of himself . . . the part that opens him to other people, the part that 'plays the baby'."[45] She continues:

> . . . he rides away alone . . . because having hardened himself to do murder, he can no longer open his heart to mankind. His love is aborted, cut off. When I think of the hero this way . . . my throat constricts. So much pain sustained internally and denied. So much suffering not allowed to speak its name . . . When I think of how he feels, no words coming out, everything closed inside, the internal bleeding, the sadness of the genre is terrible, and I want to cry.[46]

It is the manner in which Jubal opens up that sets him apart from the type of heroes Tompkins describes: showing his "heart" through words, *language*, not actions, and projecting his neurosis for the sympathetic Naomi—"the innocent, the redeemer"—to hear.[47] The merits of conceding to language, of opening up to others, to *the* "other," in fact, is what ensures that Jubal does *not* "ride away alone" at the close of the narrative.

Maggie Humm describes cinematic images as "not simply mirrors of real life but ideological signifiers."[48] As mentioned above, one of the most important ideological signifiers in American culture is undoubtedly the family. As a cultural institution, the family signifies stability and cements patriarchal values within the socio-symbolic order. It is one that Hollywood is said to have striven hard to reinforce. It is one of America's most cherished myths, functioning, Harvey reminds us, "as one of the cornerstones of Western industrial society."[49] More pointedly, it "legitimates and *conceals* sexuality," serving as a socially sanctioned "point of termination and fulfillment of romance."[50] Harvey argues that the family is "a value-generating nexus," embodying "a range of traditional values: love of family, love of father (father/ruler), love of country" and determining the woman's subordinated place in "the established values of competitive, repressive, and hierarchical relationships."[51] Thus, the family functions in film "as a microcosm containing within itself all of the patterns of dominance and submission that are characteristic of the larger society."[52] As with other Hollywood genres, the family as ideological signifier can be observed in the Western. Again, *Shane* immediately suggests itself. With its family roles delineated into the active, working father/husband Joe (Van Heflin) and the passive, domestic mother/wife Marian (Jean Arthur), *Shane* seems consistent with both Kaplan's and Tompkins' readings of the genre. Also, Shane's (Alan Ladd) killing of the cattle barons Rufus and Morgan Ryker (Emile Myer and John Dierkes), along with their hired gun, Jack Wilson (Jack Palance), ensures that the country will be safe enough for families and for children like little Joey

(Brandon de Wilde) to "look after [his] mother" and to "grow up to be strong and straight."

Harvey argues that one of the most important aspects of film noir—that which would appear to render it distinct from the Western and other established Hollywood genres—is its peculiar engagement with the family as symbolic guarantor of "ideological equilibrium."[53] She describes how film noir goes against this traditional cinematic trope of the family as "stable institution" by demonstrating the erosion of the social values embodied within it. For Harvey, film noir's whole point, in fact, "is that it is structured around the destruction or absence of romantic love and the family."[54] Harvey suggests that it is film noir's "treatment of the family" that provides a vehicle for the return of the "repressed presence of intolerable contradictions"—contradictions which, intentionally or not, form "the beginnings of an attack on the dominant social values normally expressed through the representation of the family."[55]

Whilst broadly supportive of this view, Kuhn suggests that such "erosion of the social values embodied" within the family can be extended to other areas of Hollywood's output, most notably the melodrama. Thus she writes: "by examining ways in which films embody and construct patriarchal ideology, by undercutting these ideological operations and by offering alternative ways of looking at films, [feminist analysis] may be regarded as an intervention within ideology."[56] The result, according to Kuhn (who echoes Kaplan in this respect), is not necessarily the revelation of the existence of a "progressive" narrative but, rather, that the "focusing on a number of contradictions" which, however inadvertently, "challenge ideological hegemony."[57] Indeed, during the course of the detailed textual analysis of any film, Kuhn argues almost for the inevitability of uncovering what Kaplan has termed "ideological contradiction" and "tension." This, she reasons, is because feminist textual analysis is founded on an understanding of texts as constructs, as structured by the work of ideology with the purpose to "lay bare the operations of patriarchal ideology."[58] Furthermore, it "assumes the existence of a body of Hollywood films which already contain an internal criticism of that ideology."[59] She argues that such films "are cracked open internally by the contradictory operations of ideology."[60] Therefore, a feminist approach identifies this "internal tension" and "facilitates the de-naturalization of ideology because it opens films up for 'oppositional' interpretations."[61] Textual analysis thus proceeds "on the premise that all analysis at least starts with deconstruction."[62] Kuhn suggests that, whilst "in dominant cinema the voice of the woman, the woman's discourse, is systematically absent or repressed," there is also the probability that numerous films "may proffer a range of possible meanings, and that . . . the ideological operation of most or all dominant films can be pulled apart, if necessary, by means of textual analysis."[63] She reasons that "feminist (re) readings of classic Hollywood films . . . may be said to actually transform films by advancing ways of looking at and understanding them that 'go against the grain' of their 'preferred' readings."[64]

Harvey and Kuhn's arguments have strong implications for a study of the Western. Although the general perception that the genre and, indeed, Hollywood as a whole are inherently patriarchal contains a great deal of validity—particularly with regards to its privileging of both masculinity and the family—it is an nonetheless an exaggeration to say that it is ideologically monolithic. Despite overwhelmingly formulaic plots, Hollywood has always featured films that are introspective and critical of dominant cultural-ideological values. Feminist film theorists would argue that such contradictions exist because patriarchy has a confused attitude toward its significant "other." As Humm summarizes: "ideological tensions are negotiated mainly through gender [therefore] women's representations are inevitably contradictory."[65] Whilst perhaps not being known as the most subversive of the established genres in this respect, it can be argued that, as often as the Western champions the family, it also demonstrates its opposition through the erosion of family values.

Consider psychoanalytical notions of the internal conflict between the "id" and the "superego," which are suggested in film noir as much as is the associated notion of the double or *doppelganger*. This doubling is associated with the "double" nature of the reality depicted in these films, where the normality of surface appearance serves only to disguise a deeper, more disturbed and corrupt reality underneath. In *The Crowded Prairie* (1997), Michael Coyne suggests something similar for the Western. When discussing *Shane*, he argues that Wilson is "the dark side" of Shane, and that Shane's slaying of Wilson constitutes an act of repression.[66] Referring to the attraction between Shane and Marian, Coyne asserts that it is such an amoral familial disruption that Shane seeks to repress by his fatal actions. After all, Shane "could disrupt the Starrett's marriage; for Shane has the potential to be either Galahad in Camelot or the serpent in Eden."[67]

In *Jubal*, it is clear that familial values are not respected. Mae is married to a man she does not love. She is an adulterous woman who, as we know, unashamedly uses her sexuality to her advantage and refuses to be relegated to a "background" role within the domestic realm. However, neither is the film's depiction of her completely unsympathetic. Her husband Shep is an embodiment of patriarchal values, arrogant in his self-assuredness and blind to Mae's psychological (and sexual) despair. His entry into the domestic realm of the kitchen by slamming the front door "scares the life" out of her. His bold assertion that there are only three things a man needs—"a woman, a full belly, and a roof over your head!"—reduces her status to that of a domestic commodity typical of patriarchal familial structures. As far as Shep is concerned, Mae exists, along with sustenance and shelter, to serve his needs. For, as Harvey informs us, the "woman's place in the home determines her position in society, but also serves as a reflection of oppressive social relationships generally."[68]

At first glance, the characters of Naomi and Mae appear as respective cinematic embodiments of what Place calls the "two poles of female archetypes" of patriarchal culture.[69] Naomi's "marginal female figure" represents what Gledhill describes as "the good woman, worthy of being a wife."[70] Mae, as Place has it, is "the spider woman, the evil seductress who tempts man and brings about his destruction."[71] Mae is presented as fitting many of the contradictory characteristics that Gledhill attributes to the femme fatale of film noir: she is "unstable and fractured," at one and the same time a "sex-bomb," a "hardworking, ambitious woman," a "fearful girl in need of protection" and, ultimately, a "victim of male power" and a "sacrifice to law."[72]

Let us consider some of these characteristics as they are presented in *Jubal*. In a key nighttime scene, Mae, in her dressing gown and with her black hair down, watches Jubal longingly from her bedroom window as he enters the barn outside. She smiles as she spies a chance to get him alone. This brief enactment of an erotic "female gaze" is immediately followed by Mae's display of agency. She pursues Jubal into the barn. This action is accompanied by a noticeable rise in the music on the soundtrack, which reaches a crescendo as Mae reaches the interior of the barn. However, Jubal turns Mae down and, furthermore, tries to make her feel guilty for desiring him. Talking of Shep, Jubal declares, "He loves you, Mae." "Loves me!?" She is quick to retort. "I'm no more than his pet filly, his heifer!" She even confesses to having had thoughts of killing Shep. (We are in recognizable noir territory.) Would Jubal want her then, she wonders? Her language is undoubtedly harsh and her mischievous smiles toward Jubal make her transgressive intentions unambiguous. At the same time, though, this "evil seductress" is also a "victim of male power" and the patriarchal social structures that underpin such power. As suggested above, she is the true tragic figure in *Jubal*. It is she, not the male hero, whose pain must be "sustained internally and denied," she who represents "so much suffering," and she who is ultimately "alone." Her smiles toward Jubal are as often followed by lonely, despairing looks and it is equally clear that her murderous inferences are motivated by jealousy, as she feels that Jubal is more interested in Naomi than he is in her. Mae's choice of words is also illuminating. Fillies and heifers are, of course, young livestock; thus Mae knows that she is seen by Shep as both infantile and inferior.

Jubal's first encounter with Mae is telling in this regard. The scene initiates in daytime with a jovial soundtrack to accompany men at work, chopping wood and breaking in horses: typical manly frontier pursuits. It is when Jubal—now washed and dressed in some of Shep's spare clothes—following an invite from the rancher, looks for coffee in his kitchen and meets Mae,

Figure 10.2 The "female gaze": Mae's display of desire and agency.

that the jovial music "shudders" slightly but noticeably. We first see Mae in this darkened interior environment, emerging from the shadows. A brief aural "strike," connoting danger and perhaps threat, contrasts with the "safe" sounds and the bright exterior of the Wyoming landscape. It is easy to see this sequence as illustrative of the typical Western gendered binary and tie it to feminist notions of Hollywood as a whole. This is to say, in ideological terms, man as positive and woman as negative. However, Mae's resentment of her predicament is foregrounded from the outset. After fairly asking what one would imagine upon finding a stranger in one's home (evidently Shep felt no need to inform his wife of Jubal's arrival)—"Who are you? Where did you get those clothes?"—Mae scornfully remarks, when Jubal explains that Shep lent him the clothes and invited him to enter his home, that "I outta know, I washed them often enough." Her restricted role of domestic expectation is further emphasized by her next, rhetorical question: "I suppose he wants you fed?" However, despite her being placed in a position in the narrative that "serve[s] the needs of men," it soon becomes apparent that Mae exists to serve her own needs. Significantly, she is an active agent rather than a passive object. Her sexual frustration is evidently born out of what we quickly learn is a loveless and passionless marriage with Shep. (The signifier here, perhaps, being an absence of children.) She is clearly attracted to Jubal and, furthermore, her sexual frustration is rendered somewhat sympathetically as we soon see Shep crassly objectify her. Upon entering the kitchen, he condescendingly refers to her as "honey" and "Duchess," makes inappropriate sexual innuendo in front of Jubal, and slaps her behind without a moment's thought for her public dignity. In retrospect, this sequence is rendered more poignant when, in a later scene, Shep asks Jubal for marital advice. Jubal suggests that Shep treat Mae with more respect in public, refraining from objectifying her and advising that she is undoubtedly "fed up with being whacked on the rump." To this, Shep laughs and then tells Jubal to take the next day off work and visit Naomi. "See if you can't cut that little heifer from the herd!" It is clear that Shep has not listened to Jubal at all, and it is difficult for the modern viewer not to cringe at these sorts of exchanges.

With this in mind, it is easier for the viewer to sympathize with Mae's seemingly callous attitude toward her husband, and toward men in general. After Jubal asks Mae the ill-judged question men often ask of abused or neglected wives—why she doesn't just leave her husband—she replies in solid rhetorical fashion, "And go where!?" This is indeed the key, unanswerable question. Despite having received no less than an alleged twenty-three proposals of marriage, she chose Shep. Why? Well, for a woman living in mid-nineteenth-century North America (Canada, to be precise) it was most likely for reasons of economic necessity. He promised her what every young girl is indoctrinated under patriarchy to desire: to become a "queen" and to live in a "castle." Instead, she got a drab, lonely Wyoming cattle ranch. "This is where he brought me," she spits. "10,000 acres of nothing." Jubal counters by declaring it to be a fine ranch. "For men, horses and bulls," she replies. "For a woman, it is 10,000 acres of lonesomeness." Jubal does not respond to this, simply telling Mae (again) that he is not interested in her. "Don't you think you'd better go back to the house, Mae, before your husband misses you?" Implicit in his language—"house" and "husband"—is the suggestion of Mae's "sacrifice to law." If she is not defined by her domestic role as housewife, then she is defined only negatively: a transgressor, a corrupting seducer, a threat to the patriarchal order.

In addition to these things, Shep's employee, Pinky, is a betrayer of his trust. We learn that he was Mae's lover before Jubal arrived on the scene; only now, having had his affections rejected, he has grown dangerously obsessed with her. As the narrative progresses, Pinky becomes increasingly unstable and threatening toward Mae and, as outlined above, it is he who will ultimately destroy her, along with himself. It is also easy to read Pinky as Jubal's *doppelganger*, and it is through him and his misdeeds that our sympathies for Mae find their best expression. As if he is a physical manifestation of Jubal's repressed desires, the black-clad Pinky often appears soon after Jubal has left the scene. Most tellingly, this occurs early on in the narrative following the failed attempt by Mae at seducing Jubal in the livery. Soon after Jubal leaves, Pinky appears. His shadow casts itself across Mae, and the tone of the music on the soundtrack changes dramatically. The door closes and the interior of the livery becomes shrouded in darkness as if at night. Pinky appears almost as an eruption of forces from within—of the "id." He is barely in control of himself, and breathing hoarsely. He seeks only to satisfy his desires. He grabs hold of Mae roughly by the neck and yanks her toward him in an attempt to force himself upon her. Mae can be viewed here unambiguously as a "victim of male power." She is clearly terrified of Pinky and what he might do, flinching when he tries to touch her and demands "some of what he has been missing." Mae's previous marital transgressions are laid bare in this scene, with Pinky regurgitating their shared past of illicit sexual liaisons.

The notion of Pinky as Jubal's *doppelganger* is further supported by what follows this dual encounter for Mae. Whilst Mae is suffering Pinky's aggression in the livery, the oblivious Jubal enters the bunkhouse. He sighs as he slowly sits down, only to be startled by the sound of a violin. One of the ranch hands emerges from the shadows. What he says next is perhaps the film's most telling pronouncement on Jubal's apparent non-attraction to Mae:

> Don't let her bother you, Jube. There wasn't a man in this outfit that didn't pop his eyes when he first saw Mae. Oh, sure gets a fella. Can't sleep nights for a while. Then he starts to get over it. He gets over it coz Shep is such a nice fella that he feels like he's doing him dirt. Ain't that right, Jube?

The ranch hand then proceeds to play a slow, forlorn tune on his violin. As his brief but significant statement is being delivered, the camera fixes on Jubal, slowly zooming in on him until he is held, shrouded in the darkness of the bunkhouse, in a medium close-up. "Yeah," he replies and, after a long pause as if in deep contemplation, "that's right." Finally, it seems that Jubal has admitted his illicit desires, to another *and* to himself. He then lies down on the bunk, ready for what we can safely guess will be a night of broken sleep.

Gledhill makes further observations of the usefulness of a study of the femme fatale trope for an ideological analysis of film noir—observations that, if applied to our reading of *Jubal*, would appear to reveal the film's ideological unconscious. Gledhill writes that while "noir female characterizations . . . superficially confirm popular stereotypes about women, in their stylization and play with the surfaces of the cinematic image they arguably foreground some of the features of that image."[73] Indeed, one has to point out here again that it is Pinky (and therefore patriarchy) who is seen here as the antagonist, as the danger. Mae is powerless to prevent Pinky's assaults and, during the scene in the livery as he grabs her and roughly tries to kiss her, the camera slowly zooms in, focusing on this to the exclusion of all else. The visual rendering of this ideological rupture forces the viewer to watch, to feel disturbed and to feel some of Mae's terror. No erotic gaze this. Mae's only recourse, to tell her husband, would result in her demise as well. When she threatens this, Pinky grabs her again: "You do that. And when I'm saying adios I'll tell him all about your little bag of tricks!" In all, one might say that if it was unrestrained female sexual desire that made the initial transgression here, then it is almost definitely unrestrained *masculinity* and *male* sexual desire that is now seen as

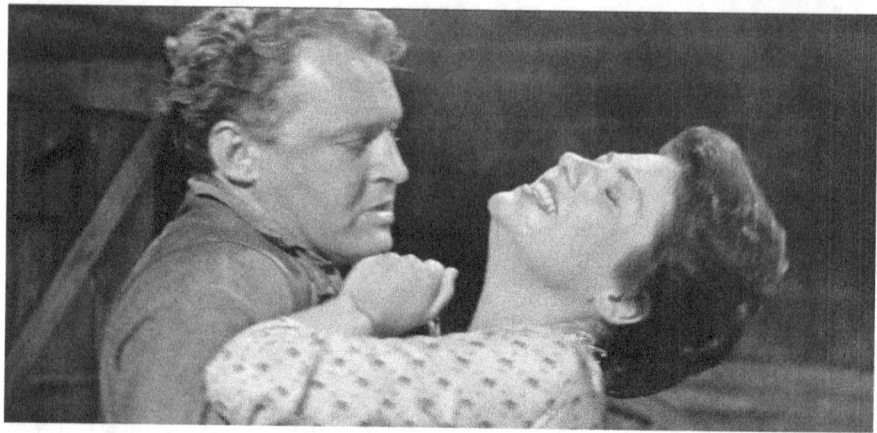

Figure 10.3 Pinky assaults Mae in the livery: woman as "victim of male power".

threatening—both to Mae personally, and the patriarchal order more generally. Indeed, it is in the context of Mae's experiences with Pinky that we can locate *Jubal*'s most pronounced articulation of "ideological contradiction" and "tension": the threat of the return of the repressed violent male sexual desire. No amount of ideological deceit, no narrative closure, of Jubal's assumed coupling with Naomi, or of his homoerotic bond with Reb, can gloss over the film's revelations of what lies at the heart of the ideological unconscious of the patriarchal socio-symbolic order.

By raising the issue of the ideological unconscious, one is compelled to ask the question as to the level of authorial intent operating within *Jubal*. Again, Daves' pre-production comments to Wald suggest themselves. Jubal's repressed desire for Mae, and his culpability for becoming "enmeshed" in the marital dysfunction between her and Shep, are confirmed by the director and described in psychoanalytical terms as a semi- or fully-unconscious "attraction for disaster." Daves continues: "Jubal knows that Mae wants him. Furthermore he knows that Mae likely won't give up until she has got what she wants. He could leave but he does not."[74] According to Daves, Jubal "would try to justify himself for *not* running away when he realizes that to stay near Mae and invite further involvement is to court disaster."[75] Emphasizing Jubal's "unconscious" resentment of Shep, Daves insists that Jubal "would find justification for his seeing [Mae], for wanting her—he would probably justify himself on the many grounds that 'Shep isn't right for her,' that anyway 'he tricked her into this marriage,' and also 'Mae surely has the right to find some happiness in life, like me or anybody else has'."[76] Furthermore, and in line with what I have been arguing above, "that Shep is older than Mae [and] shows off his relations with [her] in front of [Jubal] and the men—and this is gross."[77] Daves' notes certainly muddy the ideological waters somewhat, for the suggestion here is that, simply by staying, Jubal is himself in many ways responsible—at least as much as Mae, Shep or even Pinky—for the disasters that unfold during the course of the narrative.

In conclusion we might reason that, despite the undoubted marginalization of women that the Western typically enacts, Kaplan's reduction of women in the genre in general to the "roles" she lists, is not always so straightforward. As I have argued throughout, in terms of both its narrative drive and generic category, *Jubal* (like a number of other significant Westerns) proves more complex. Mae certainly provides something beyond Kaplan's "fixed roles" for women. Married to Shep, she might indeed be a "wife," a "lover" and, through at least one affair, a "mistress," but she is defined most directly (and dangerously) through her "sexuality." She exhibits enough instability, deception, and sexual allure to be "safely" (word chosen deliberately) classed as a femme fatale. At the same time, the partially sympathetic way in which the film characterizes her and her situation is indicative less of the Western and its privileging of a masculinist narrative than it is of the kinds of "ideological contradiction" that Kaplan attributes to film noir. All this is not to say that I class *Jubal* as a film noir specifically. Rather, and as inferred throughout, I see it as a hybrid of sorts that formally and thematically combines aspects of both the Western genre and the film noir style, producing a profoundly intriguing narrative that exposes ("foregrounds") the dangers inherent in the patriarchal order. Place reminds us that "the characteristics of film noir style . . . are not rules to be enforced . . . and no attempt to fix and categorise films will be very illuminating if it prescribes strict boundaries for a category."[78] An attempt to do so would, she writes, lead to "a suppression of those elements which do not 'fit', and to exclusion of films which have strong links but equally strong differences from a particular category."[79] In my reading of *Jubal*, I see little reason to deviate from this principle. Finally, and with Daves' production notes to Wald in mind, I would suggest that it is at least arguable that *Jubal* was a film *made* "against the grain."

BIBLIOGRAPHY

Belton, John, *American Cinema/American Culture* (New York: McGraw-Hill, 2005).
Cook, Pam, and Mieke Bernink (eds.), *The Cinema Book: 2nd Edition* (London: British Film Institute, 1999).
Coyne, Michael, *The Crowded Prairie: American National Identity in the Hollywood Western* (London: I. B. Taurus, 1997).
Gledhill, Christine, "*Klute* I: a Contemporary Film Noir and Feminist Criticism," in E. Ann Kaplan (ed.), *Women in Film Noir* (London: British Film Institute, 1978), pp. 6–22.
Grant, Barry Keith (ed.), *Film Genre Reader* (Austin: University of Texas Press, 1995).
Harvey, Sylvia, "Woman's Place: the Absent Family of Film Noir," in E. Ann Kaplan (ed.), *Women in Film Noir* (London: British Film Institute, 1978), pp. 22–34.

Humm, Maggie, *Feminism and Film* (Edinburgh: Edinburgh University Press, 1997).
Jones, Kent, "*3:10 to Yuma*: Curious Distances," The Criterion Collection (2013b), <http://www.criterion.com/current/posts/2766-3-10-to-yuma-curious-distances> (last accessed 11 November 2015).
Kaplan, E. Ann, "Introduction," in E. Ann Kaplan (ed.), *Women in Film Noir* (London: British Film Institute, 1978), pp. 1–6.
Kaplan, E. Ann (ed.), *Women in Film Noir* (London: British Film Institute, 1978).
Kitses, Jim, *Horizons West—Anthony Mann, Bud Boetticher, Sam Peckinpah: Studies of Authorship within the Western* (London: Thames and Hudson, 1969).
Kitses, Jim, *Horizons West: Directing the Western from John Ford to Clint Eastwood* (London: British Film Institute, 2004).
Kuhn, Annette, *Women's Pictures* (London: Verso, 1982).
Mitchell, Lee Clark, *Westerns: Making the Man in Fiction and Film* (Chicago and London: The University of Chicago Press, 1996).
Monticone, Paul M., "The Noir Western: Genre Theory and the Problem of the Anomalous Hybrid," Film Studies Association of Canada Conference at the Congress of the Humanities and Social Sciences, Concordia University, Montreal, 3 June 2010.
Mulvey, Laura, "Visual Pleasure and Narrative Cinema," *Screen*, 16:3 (1975): 6–19.
Nichols, Bill (ed.), *Movies and Methods—Vol. I* (Berkeley: University of California Press, 1985).
Place, Janey, "Women in Film Noir," in E. Ann Kaplan (ed.), *Women in Film Noir* (London: British Film Institute, 1978), pp. 35–68.
Place, Janey, and Lowell Peterson, "Some Visual Motifs of Film Noir," in Bill Nichols (ed.), *Movies and Methods—Vol. I* (Berkeley: University of California Press, 1985), pp. 325–38.
Schrader, Paul, "Notes on Film Noir," in Barry Keith Grant (ed.), *Film Genre Reader* (Austin: University of Texas Press, 1995), pp. 213–26.
Staiger, Janet, "*Hybrid or Inbred: The Purity Hypothesis and Hollywood Genre History*," in Barry Keith Grant (ed.), *Film Genre Reader III* (Austin: University of Texas Press, 1995), pp. 185–99.
Tompkins, Jane, *West of Everything: The Inner Life of Westerns* (New York: Oxford University Press, 1992).

FILMOGRAPHY

Blood on the Moon, director Robert Wise, featuring Robert Mitchum, Barbara Bel Geddes, Robert Preston, Walter Brennen (RKO Pictures, 1948).
Broken Arrow, director Delmer Daves, featuring Jimmy Stewart, Jeff Chandler, Debra Paget, Basil Ruysdael (20th Century Fox, 1950).
Colorado Territory, director Raoul Walsh, featuring Joel McCrea, Virginia Mayo, Dorothy Malone, Henry Hull (Warner Bros., 1949).
Cowboy, director Delmer Daves, featuring Glenn Ford, Jack Lemmon, Anna Kashfi, Dick York (Columbia Pictures, 1958).
Jubal, director Delmer Daves, featuring Glenn Ford, Valerie French, Rod Steiger, Ernest Borgnine (Columbia Pictures, 1956).
Man from Colorado, The, director Henry Levin, featuring Glenn Ford, William Holden, Ellen Drew, Ray Collins (Columbia Pictures, 1948).

My Darling Clementine, director John Ford, featuring Henry Fonda, Victor Mature, Linda Darnell, Cathy Downs (20th Century Fox, 1946).
Postman Always Rings Twice, The, director Tay Garnett, featuring Lana Turner, John Garfield, Cecil Kellaway, Hume Cronyn (Metro-Goldwyn-Mayer, 1946).
Pursued, director Raoul Walsh, featuring Teresa Wright, Robert Mitchum, Judith Anderson, Dean Jagger (Warner Bros., 1947).
Ramrod, director André de Toth, featuring Joel McCrea, Veronica Lake, Don DeFore, Donald Crisp (United Artists, 1947).
Searchers, The, director John Ford, featuring John Wayne, Natalie Wood, Jeffrey Hunter, Vera Miles (Warner Bros., 1956).
Shane, director George Stevens, featuring Alan Ladd, Jack Palance, Van Heflin, Jean Arthur (Paramount Pictures, 1953).
Stagecoach, director John Ford, featuring John Wayne, Claire Trevor, Andy Devine, John Carradine (United Artists, 1939).
3:10 to Yuma, director Delmer Daves, featuring Glenn Ford, Van Heflin, Felicia Farr, Leora Dana (Columbia Pictures, 1957).
Yellow Sky, director William A. Wellman, featuring Gregory Peck, Anne Baxter, Richard Widmark, Robert Arthur (20th Century Fox, 1948).

NOTES

1. Jones, "*3:10 to Yuma*: Curious Distances."
2. Even Jim Kitses' 2004 "new edition" of *Horizons West*, his 1969 canonical auteur study of Western filmmakers—expanded to include chapters on the films of John Ford, Sergio Leone, and Clint Eastwood—neglects discussion of Daves. His one mention comes early on in the book's introductory chapter, and even this comment is a negative. Kitses reasons that his decision to omit consideration of Daves in the enhanced 2004 edition of *Horizons West* "reflects the belief" that the director's body of work, despite being "prolific," was not consistently "distinctive" or sufficiently "distinguished" enough for inclusion (p. 16).
3. Jones, "*3:10 to Yuma*: Curious Distances."
4. The term "classic-era Hollywood" is generally assumed to be the three decades or so from 1930. Throughout this essay, the reader can assume that the usage of the word "Hollywood" be considered within this timeframe.
5. Kaplan, *Women in Film Noir*, p. 2.
6. Ibid.
7. Tompkins, *West of Everything*, pp. 39–40.
8. Ibid. p. 61.
9. Ibid. p. 39.
10. Ibid. p. 9, p. 142, p. 143. Others have forwarded similar views. Adapting Tompkins' central thesis, Lee Clarke Mitchell argues that "cultural meaning" in the Western "emerges through binary oppositions patterned on the cultural distinction of simple sexual difference." This "sexual difference" is predicated upon an active, dominant masculinity over a passive, submissive femininity. See Mitchell, *Westerns*, p. 138. For how this gender binary has been appropriated and articulated in Hollywood narrative cinema see Mulvey, "Visual Pleasure and Narrative Cinema." Mulvey's essay is generally considered to be the ur-text from which most contemporary psychoanalytical feminist film theories derive. Jim Kitses reaffirms Tompkins' and Mitchell's views in his 2004 reworked edition of *Horizons*

West, stating that "the feminine in the genre exists only to validate masculinity as the dominant norm." See Kitses, *Horizons West* (2004), p. 21.
11. Kaplan, "Introduction," pp. 2–3.
12. Gledhill, "*Klute* I," p. 19.
13. Place, "Women in Film Noir," p. 37.
14. Kaplan, "Introduction," p. 3. Emphasis in original.
15. Place, "Women in Film Noir," p. 35.
16. Ibid.
17. Kuhn, *Women's Pictures*, p. 35.
18. Ibid.
19. Ibid.
20. Harvey, "Woman's Place," p. 33.
21. Place, "Women in Film Noir," p. 54. More recently, John Belton has reinforced this counter-ideological reading of film noir. In, *American Cinema/American Culture* (2005), Belton argues that, whilst such "acts of transgression" tended to be controlled by a film's male protagonist, or dealt with in the narrative via the downfall of the femme fatale, "that sexuality nevertheless emerged as revolutionary, empowering (albeit briefly) the women who possessed it." See Belton, *American Cinema/American Culture*, p. 115.
22. Kaplan, "Introduction," pp. 2–3.
23. Ibid. p. 2.
24. Ibid. pp. 2–3. See also the section on "Women in Film Noir," in Cook and Bernink, *The Cinema Book*, pp. 186–7.
25. Monticone, "The Noir Western," p. 1.
26. In addition to *Ramrod*, the films suggested range from the well-known to the obscure, including *Pursued* (Raoul Walsh, 1947), *The Man from Colorado* (Henry Levin, 1948), *Yellow Sky* (William A. Wellman, 1948), *Blood on the Moon* (Robert Wise, 1948), and *Colorado Territory* (Raoul Walsh, 1949).
27. Monticone, "The Noir Western," p. 3.
28. Ibid. p. 5. Monticone is himself influenced by earlier hypothesizing on the porous nature of genre categorizations. See, for instance, Staiger, "Hybrid or Inbred."
29. Schrader, "Notes on Film Noir," p. 214.
30. Ibid.
31. Place, "Women in Film Noir," p. 39 (emphasis added).
32. Ibid. p. 41.
33. Ibid.
34. Delmer Daves Papers, Department of Special Collections, Stanford University Libraries, box 41, folder 7 (emphasis in original).
35. Ibid.
36. Ibid.
37. Schrader, "Notes on Film Noir," p. 214.
38. Ibid.
39. Place and Peterson, "Some Visual Motifs of Film Noir," pp. 325–6.
40. Equally, Ford's *My Darling Clementine* (1946) could be understood as an example of a noir-Western with its reliance on interior night scenes illustrated by chiaroscuro, both of which emphasize the film's psychological focus on death.
41. Tompkins, *West of Everything*, p. 51.
42. Ibid. p. 55.
43. Ibid.
44. Ibid. p. 52.

45. Ibid. p. 220.
46. Ibid.
47. Place, "Women in Film Noir," p. 35.
48. Humm, *Feminism and Film*, p. 13.
49. Harvey, "Woman's Place," p. 24.
50. Ibid. pp. 24–5 (emphasis in original).
51. Ibid.
52. Ibid. pp. 23–4.
53. Ibid. p. 23.
54. Ibid. p. 25.
55. Ibid. p. 23.
56. Kuhn, *Women's Pictures*, p. 95.
57. Ibid.
58. Ibid.
59. Ibid. p. 88.
60. Ibid.
61. Ibid.
62. Ibid. p. 95.
63. Ibid. p. 88 and p. 94.
64. Ibid. p. 95.
65. Humm, *Feminism and Film*, p. 13.
66. Coyne, *The Crowded Prairie*, p. 75.
67. Ibid.
68. Harvey, "Woman's Place," p. 23.
69. Place, "Women in Film Noir," p. 35.
70. Gledhill, "*Klute* I," p. 18.
71. Place, "Women in Film Noir," p. 35.
72. Gledhill, "*Klute* I," p. 18. NB Gledhill's list of characteristics are in specific relation to the role of Cora (Lana Turner) in *The Postman Always Rings Twice* (Tay Garnett, 1946) and are drawn from the essay by Richard Dyer: "Four Films of Lana Turner," *Movie*, 25 (1977/8); see Gledhill, "*Klute* I," p. 21, fn. 18.
73. Gledhill, "*Klute* I," p. 18.
74. Delmer Daves Papers, box 41, folder 3.
75. Ibid.
76. Ibid.
77. Ibid.
78. Place, "Women in Film Noir," p. 39.
79. Ibid.

Index

Air Force see Hawks, Howard
Aleiss, Angela, 69, 82, 87, 99n
Alexie, Sherman, 99n
All that Heaven Allows see Sirk, Douglas
American Indians, 48–50, 53–5, 56, 69, 80, 81–3, 85, 87, 88–9, 90, 93, 96, 104, 128, 158, 161
   "Bad Indian" archetype, 55, 88, 94, 95
   "Indian princess" archetype, 83, 90, 93–5, 99n
   "Pro-Indian" Western, 36–7, 48–50, 82, 86, 92, 93, 96, 104, 120
Anger, Kenneth, 7
Antonioni, Michelangelo, 12
Apache, 48
Argentieri, Simona, 169
Arnold, Henry "Hap," 188, 193
Astruc, Alexandre, 10, 11–12, 15, 42n
auteur theory, 2, 8, 13, 200
   criticisms of, 8–9, 13, 14–16, 21, 22, 23–5, 28
   and genre, 12–13, 17–18, 22, 25, 28
   Politiques des auteurs, 11–12, 13, 15, 40–1n, 42n
   and post-structuralism, 22, 25, 27, 28, 45n
   and structuralism, 16–17, 19–21, 22, 28, 51–2
   and the Western, 25–7, 33–4, 50–1, 52, 53, 54, 62n, 219n

Bader, Douglas, 195
Bagni, Gwen, 68
Barthes, Roland, 22–5, 27, 28, 45n
Bauer, Ralph, 124
Bazin, André, 10–11, 12, 13, 14–15, 40–1n, 42n
Belton, John, 220n
Bergman, Ingmar, 12
Bierstadt, Albert, 131
Big Heat, The, 110
Big Sleep, The see Hawks, Howard
Bigger than Life see Ray, Nicholas
Billington, James, 149
Bird of Paradise (1932 film) *see* Daves, Delmer
Bisplinghoff, Gretchen, 124, 125
Boetticher, Bud, 26, 33, 51, 53, 54, 56, 58, 75, 106
   Man from the Alamo, The, 106
   Seven Men from Now, 53
   Tall T, The, 75
   Time for Dying, A, 53
Borzage, Frank, 5
Bourget, Jean-Loup, 66
Boyer, Jay, 191
Brady, Mathew, 153
Broken Lance, 48
Brown, Helen Gurley, 142
Burlingame, Roger, 189
Buscombe, Ed, 13, 14–15, 21–2, 24, 42–3n, 48, 50, 81, 90, 99n

Canby, Vincent, 150
Capra, Frank, 103
Chabrol, Claude, 10, 12

INDEX   223

Chapman Report, The, 142
Cheyenne Autumn see Ford, John
Church, Frederic, 131
Churchill, Ward, 88
Citizen Kane see Welles, Orson
civil rights movement, 50, 64, 66, 68, 82, 90, 96, 178
Clarke, Graham, 131
Cobweb, The see Minnelli, Vincente
Cocteau, Jean, 11
Cole, Thomas, 131
Collier, John, 81
Command Decision, 195
Cook, Pam, 11, 24, 40n
Cooke, James J., 187, 190
Cooper, Gary, 32, 185, 195–6, 198n
Cooper, James Fenimore, 19, 49, 85
Corkin, Stanley, 80, 83, 99n
Cortez, Stanley, 9
Costner, Kevin, 101n
Coursodon, Jean-Pierre, 1, 3–4, 53, 55, 103, 113
Court Martial of Billy Mitchell, The see Preminger, Otto
Coyne, Michael, 211
Crist, Judith, 144
Crowther, Bosley, 7, 49, 118–19

Daly, Maureen, 4
Daves, Delmer
  authorship, 9, 53, 56–9, 60
  career, 3
  education, 2–3
  personal politics, 64, 81, 99n
  reputation, 1–4, 7–8, 29, 53, 136, 190, 199
  working methods, 5, 6, 35–6, 37, 54
Daves, Delmer (films)
  Affair to Remember, An (screenplay), 5
  Badlanders, The, 52–3, 54, 62n, 63, 69, 71–3, 103, 137
  Battle of the Villa Fiorita, The, 3, 37
  Bird of Paradise, 59–60
  Broken Arrow, 1–2, 29, 30, 34, 36–7, 38, 48–60, 62n, 63, 64, 65, 66–9, 78n, 80–96, 99n, 100n, 103–4, 119, 120, 132, 150, 161, 166, 190, 198n, 199
  Cowboy, 29, 30, 31, 52, 63, 69, 73–4, 102–5, 106, 107–9, 111, 112, 113–15, 118–33, 137, 164n, 199
  critical responses to, 5, 7, 37, 49, 118–19, 144, 149–50

Dark Passage, 5, 7, 34–6, 190, 191
Destination Tokyo, 2, 3, 7, 60, 77n, 105
Drum Beat, 30, 34, 52, 55–7, 63, 80–96, 103, 104, 120, 157, 166
films noir, 7, 34, 151, 156–7, 159, 161, 199–200
Hanging Tree, The, 32, 53, 54, 57, 62n, 63, 64, 103, 104, 106, 111, 120, 137, 145, 166, 171–6, 177, 180
Jubal, 29, 30, 32, 52, 54, 63, 64, 69–71, 103, 105, 106–7, 108, 109, 111–14, 136, 142, 147n, 199–200, 203–8, 211–17
Kings Go Forth, 166
Last Wagon, The, 66–8
masculinity in, 60, 85, 104, 121, 135, 152, 156, 158, 215–16
melodramas, 3–5, 7, 37–8, 60, 135–9, 142, 143, 145, 166
Never Let Me Go, 166
Parrish, 2, 3, 4, 7, 60, 137
Pride of the Marines, 7, 60
Red House, The, 5, 7, 32, 166, 167–71, 180, 190
Return of the Texan, 63
Spencer's Mountain, 2, 7, 31, 32, 56, 104, 120, 135–46, 166, 176–80
Summer Place, A, 3, 4, 5, 8, 37–8, 60, 137, 166, 190
Susan Slade, 2, 5, 7, 137
Task Force, 32, 184–96
3:10 to Yuma, 1–2, 6, 29, 30, 31, 52, 53, 54, 57–8, 63, 69–70, 74–5, 103, 104, 105–6, 107–10, 112–13, 114, 115, 120, 149–62, 164n, 190, 198n, 199
war films, 3, 7, 37, 53, 60
Westerns, 52–60, 63–4, 103–4, 113
Youngblood Hawke, 7
de Saussure, Ferdinand, 23–4
DeGeorge, Richard and Fernande, 16
Delacroix, Eugene, 72
Deloria, Philip, 84
DeMille, Cecil B., 78n, 99n
Derrida, Jacques, 25
Destry Rides Again, 55
Devlin, Rachel, 168–9
Dietrich, Marlene, 7
Django Unchained, 68
Dodge City, 55
Donohue, Troy, 4, 5
Douhet, Giulio, 196

Earhart, Amelia, 195
Eisenstein, Sergei, 72, 142
Elsaesser, Thomas, 138–9

Falconer, Peter, 161
Fehrle, Johannes, 155, 158, 161
   film noir, 34, 199–203, 206, 210
   and the Western, 203–4
femme fatale, 34, 201–2, 212, 215, 220n
Fixico, Donald, 87
Flaming Star, 48
Fojas, Camilla, 100n
Fonda, Henry, 142, 146
Ford, Glenn, 30, 57, 69, 70, 73, 75, 103–15, 136, 150, 151, 199, 205, 208
Ford, John, 2, 11, 14, 17, 18–19, 21, 22, 26, 27, 28, 29, 30, 31, 33, 37, 38, 42n, 45–6n, 46–7n, 50, 54, 58, 71, 73, 105, 128, 129, 131, 132, 135, 142–3, 199, 219n
   Cheyenne Autumn, 48
   Fort Apache, 48, 80
   Man Who Shot Liberty Valance, The, 190
   My Darling Clementine, 200
   Searchers, The, 50, 74, 190, 200
   She Wore a Yellow Ribbon, 48
   Stagecoach, 31, 50, 128, 131, 207
   Wings of Eagles, The, 195
   Young Mr. Lincoln, 45n
Fort Apache see Ford, John
Foucault, Michel, 25, 27, 28
Franklin, Bruce, 196
French, Philip, 150–1

Gallagher, Tag, 131
Gauvreau, Emile and Lester Cohen, 188–9
Gilbert, Lewis
   Reach for the Sky, 195
Gledhill, Christine, 135–6, 201, 212, 215
Godard, Jean-Luc, 10, 12, 36
Godfrey, Arthur, 7–8
Gold Diggers of 1933 see LeRoy, Mervyn
Grant, James Edward, 68, 79n
Grant, Ulysses S., 83, 87

Hamner, Jr., Earl, 135, 136, 137, 143, 145
Harless, Richard, 78n
Harvey, Sylvia, 202, 209–10, 211, 212
Hawks, Howard, 11, 14, 19, 20, 28, 29, 31, 33, 37, 38, 41n, 42n, 47n, 113, 130, 132, 143, 150, 199
   Air Force, 195
   Big Sleep, The, 34
   Red River, 31, 119, 121, 130
   Rio Bravo, 37, 57
Hayward, Susan, 11
Hearne, Joanna, 99n
Heath, Stephen, 24–5

Heflin, Van, 150
Hemingway, Ernest, 194
Henderson, Brian, 20–1, 50
Hitchcock, Alfred, 11, 14, 20, 21, 28, 32, 38, 40–1n, 42n, 190, 194–5
   Lifeboat, 190
   Rear Window, 190
   Rope, 190
Homecoming, The (novel) *see* Hamner Jr., Earl
Hoveyda, Fereydoun, 40n
Howard, Oliver Otis, 65–6
Humm, Maggie, 209, 210, 211
Hunter, Evan, 4
Hurley, Alfred F., 190
Huston, John, 14

Jackson, William Henry, 131
Jeffers, H. Paul, 187
Jesse James, 55
Jones, Kent, 64, 70, 88, 107, 111, 114, 139, 199
Jubal Troop (novel) *see* Wellman, Paul I.

Kachru, Braj B., 94, 95
Kaplan, E. Ann, 200–1, 202–3, 204, 206, 209, 210, 217
Kehr, Dave, 37–8
Kilpatrick, Jacquelyn, 83, 99n
Kitses, Jim, 25–7, 28, 33–4, 51–2, 54, 62n, 120, 219–20n
Kristeva, Julia, 92–3
Kuhn, Annette, 202, 210–11

Ladd, Alan, 82, 106, 110, 208
Lady in the Lake see Montgomery, Robert
Lang, Fritz, 11, 42n
Lange, Dorothea, 74
Langlois, Henri, 10, 11
Lapsley, Robert and Michael Westlake, 12–13, 15, 16, 17, 18, 22, 24, 42n, 45–6n
Lawrence, Mary, 2
Lawton, Charles, 150, 151
Lee, Robert E., 190
Lefebvre, Martin, 142
Lemmon, Jack, 102, 108, 111, 119
Leonard, Elmore, 74, 149
LeRoy, Mervyn
   Gold Diggers of 1933, 7
   Thirty Seconds over Tokyo, 195
Lenihan, John H., 56, 100n
Lévi-Strauss, Claude, 16, 17, 18, 20–1, 23, 43n, 51
Lindbergh, Charles, 195

Lifeboat see Hitchcock, Alfred
Lourcelles, Jacques, 131–2
Love Affair (novel) *see* McCarey, Leo

MacArthur, Douglas, 188
McCarey, Leo, 5
McCarthy, Cormac, 44n
McCarthy, Joseph, 55, 82, 99n
MacCurdy, Carol, 151
Magnificent Ambersons, The, see Welles, Orson
Magnificent Seven, The, 57
Man Who Shot Liberty Valance, The see Ford, John
Maltby, Richard, 27, 28, 49
Maltz, Albert, 65, 68, 69, 75, 77n, 78n
Man from the Alamo, The see Boetticher, Bud
Mankiewicz, Herman J., 8
Mankiewicz, Joseph, 99n
Mann, Anthony, 2, 26, 30, 33, 37, 50–1, 53, 54, 56, 58, 105, 113, 199
  Cimarron, 53
  Last Frontier, The, 53
Martin, James V., 189
Marubbio, M. Elise, 90, 93, 99n
Meyer, William, R., 53, 60
Minnelli, Vincente, 37, 42n, 142
Mitchell, Billy, 32, 184–5, 187–96
Mitchell, Lee Clark, 85, 219n
Mitchell, Ruth, 189–90
Modoc Ambush (screenplay), 54
Momaday, N. Scott, 99n
Monaco, James, 11–12
Montgomery, Robert, 36
Mothers and Daughters (novel) *see* Hunter, Evan
Moviegoer, The (novel) *see* Percy, Walker
Murdoch, David, 152
My Darling Clementine see Ford, John

Neale, Steve, 34, 81, 82
North, Edmond H., 73

O'Sullivan, Timothy, 131

Percy, Walker, 137
Petch, Simon, 157
Peyton Place, 145
Pippin, Robert, 47n
Place, Janey, 201–2, 203, 212, 217
Pleshette, Suzanne, 4
Pocketful of Miracles see Capra, Frank
Powers, James, 149
Prats, Armando José, 91–2

Preminger, Otto
  Court Martial of Billy Mitchell, The, 185, 190, 195
Professionals, The, 57
Propp, Vladimir, 17
Pye, Douglas, 158

Ray, Nicholas, 32, 143, 194
Reach for the Sky see Gilbert, Lewis
Rear Window see Hitchcock, Alfred
Red River see Hawks, Howard
Remington, Frederic, 73, 129
Renoir, Jean, 11
Rio Bravo see Hawks, Howard
Rivette, Jacques, 10, 12, 42
Robinson, Edward G., 167
Rohmer, Eric, 10, 12, 41n, 42n
Roosevelt, Franklin D., 81
Rope see Hitchcock, Alfred
Run of the Arrow, 48
Russell, Charles Marion, 73

Said, Edward, 83, 92
Sarris, Andrew, 1, 7–8, 13–15, 27, 28, 42–3n, 190–1
Schaefer, George, 9
Schatz, Thomas, 139
Schreyvogel, Charles, 131
Scorpio Rising see Anger, Kenneth
Scorsese, Martin, 63
Searchers, The see Ford, John
Seven Men from Now see Boetticher, Bud
Seventeenth Summer (novel) *see* Daly, Maureen
Sex and the Single Girl, 142
Shane (novel) *see* Schaefer, George
Shane see Stevens, George
Shanley, Kathryn, 85
She Wore a Yellow Ribbon see Ford, John
Shipman, David, 103
Silko, Leslie Marmon, 99n
Singer, Ben, 137
Sirk, Douglas, 37–8, 142
  All That Heaven Allows, 37, 139
  Written on the Wind, 143, 147
Sleep see Warhol, Andy
Slotkin, Richard, 25, 47n, 49, 99n, 100n, 101n
Sontag, Susan, 7
Spaatz, Carl "Tooey," 193
Spencer's Mountain (novel) *see* Hamner Jr., Earl
Spivak, Gayatri Chakravorty, 92–3
Stagecoach see Ford, John

Stanwyck, Barbara, 7
Steiner, Max, 5, 138
Stevens, Connie, 4, 5
Stevens, George, 52
   Shane, 52, 110, 161, 207
Stewart, James, 48, 49, 53, 58, 64, 66, 86, 88, 91
Stoddart, Helen, 15–16, 18, 19, 21, 22, 42n
Strike, 72
structuralism *see* Lévi-Strauss, Claude
Sturges, John, 54

Tall T, The see Boetticher, Bud
Tavernier, Bertrand, 3, 38, 58, 64, 77n, 113, 114, 126–7, 128, 143, 149, 150, 152–3, 158, 159–60, 161
Thirty Seconds over Tokyo see LeRoy, Mervyn
Thompson, David, 107
3:10 to Yuma (2007), 149, 150–1, 191
Time for Dying, A see Boetticher, Bud
Todd, Derek, 154, 156
Toland, Gregg, 8
Tompkins, Jane, 200–1, 204, 206, 207–9, 219n
Townsend, Leo, 68–9, 75
Trenchard, Hugh, 196
Truffaut, François, 10–11, 38, 41n
Truman, Harry S., 30, 81, 84, 86, 100n
Trumbo, Dalton, 73, 74, 79n
Twelve O'Clock High, 195

Union Pacific, 55

Vizenor, Gerald, 90, 94–5

Wald, Jerry, 70, 204, 216, 217
Walker, Michael, 53–4, 55, 56, 106, 152, 154
Waller, Douglas, 190, 195
Wallington, Mike, 152, 156, 157, 161
Walsh, Raoul, 135

Waltons, The (TV series), 136, 137, 145
Warhol, Andy, 7
Warner, Jack, 2, 3, 4–5, 7, 36, 136, 141–2
Warner Brothers *see* Warner, Jack
Washington, George, 65
Watkins, Carleton E., 131
Wayne, John, 30, 58, 68, 79n 105, 208
Welles, Halsted, 62n, 74
Welles, Orson, 8–9, 12, 14, 38, 40n
   Citizen Kane, 8–9
   Magnificent Ambersons, The, 8–9, 39n
Wellman, Paul I., 70
Westerns
   and authorship studies, 25–7, 33–4, 50–1, 52, 53, 54, 62n, 219n
   and the Cold War, 55–6, 82, 83
   opposition of civilization and wilderness in, 17–18, 25–6, 33–4, 49, 51, 58, 120, 128–9, 152
   "Pro-Indian" cycle, 36–7, 48–50, 82, 86, 92, 93, 96, 104, 120
   women in, 200–1
White Feather, 48, 68
Whitehall, Richard, 73–4, 150, 161–2
Wicking, Christopher, 38, 104, 119–20, 127, 131, 156–7, 159
Wings of Eagles, The see Ford, John
Wise, Robert, 9
Wollen, Peter, 17–22, 25–6, 27, 28, 51
Wood, Robin, 42n
Written on the Wind see Sirk, Douglas
Wyler, William, 14

Yamamoto, Isoroku, 189, 192
Yank in the RAF, A, 195
Young, Diana, 157
Young Mr. Lincoln see Ford, John

Zinn, Howard, 84
Zinnemann, Fred, 52

EU representative:
Easy Access System Europe
Mustamäe tee 50, 10621 Tallinn, Estonia
Gpsr.requests@easproject.com

www.ingramcontent.com/pod-product-compliance
Lightning Source LLC
Chambersburg PA
CBHW061712300426
44115CB00014B/2652